THE EVOLUTION OF
THE ENGLISH HOUSE

Photo : Lafayette

SIDNEY OLDALL ADDY

THE EVOLUTION OF
THE ENGLISH HOUSE

By
SIDNEY OLDALL ADDY, M.A.

Revised and Enlarged from the Author's Notes by
JOHN SUMMERSON
B.A.(Arch.), A.R.I.B.A.

With a Foreword by
CLOUGH WILLIAMS-ELLIS

ILLUSTRATED

EP Publishing Limited
British Book Centre, Inc
1975

Republished 1975 by EP Publishing Limited
East Ardsley, Wakefield
West Yorkshire, England

and

British Book Centre, Inc
996 Lexington Avenue
New York, NY, USA

by kind permission of the copyright holders

This is a reprint of the 2nd edition, 1933, originally
published by George Allen & Unwin Limited

ISBN 0 7158 1111 8 (UK)
0 8277 4083 2 (USA)

Library of Congress Cataloguing in Publication Data

Addy, Sidney Oldall, 1848-1933.
The evolution of the English house.

Reprint of the 1933 ed. published by G. Allen & Unwin,
London.
Bibliography: p.
1. Architecture, Domestic—England. I. Summerson,
Sir John Newenham, ed. II. Title.
NA7328.A25   1975   728'.0942   74-28143
ISBN 0-8277-4083-2

Please address all enquiries to
EP Publishing Limited (address as above)

Printed in Great Britain by
The Scolar Press Limited
Ilkley, Yorkshire

FOREWORD

TO witness the performance of some feat of skill and endurance impossible to ourselves, is, I suspect, absorbing to all of us, provided that the thing to be done seems worth the doing and the technique displayed sufficiently accomplished.

I think it must have been the staggering erudition and relentless thoroughness of Mr. Addy in his tracking down of the remote ancestry of the English Home that first attracted me to his remarkable work. I recall consulting it when engaged some eight years ago in writing my book, *The Pleasures of Architecture*, wherein it is well commended. But, as a workaday general-practitioner architect of a flip-flap generation (that must surely shock the venerable author by its neglect of research and lack of scholarship), it may well seem strange to him and impertinent to others, that I, being sadly typical of my superficial age, should presume to add a foreword to this book which is so manifestly beyond my normal range. And I will at once confess that it is rarely indeed that books of architectural history and research seduce me into more than an ungrateful skipping with a pause. here and there for plans or pictures.

Yet somehow Mr. Addy, having once caught my roving attention, contrived to hold me under his spell until he had unfolded the whole length of his entrancing story.

For one thing, I delight in the origins of names and phrases, in " unlikely " information of any kind and in knowing just what Modern Conveniences cheered the domestic life of my hardy twelfth-century ancestress and how her rude man came to contrive his new-fangled refinements, chimneys, windows, staircases, and suchlike.

It throws some light on the amenities of the early home to learn that " window " was originally " wind-hole " or " wind-eye " and that when the great innovation of " glazing " first came in, it was the caul of a new-born calf that was stretched across the opening.

5

Even down to the sixteenth century, it appears, window glazing was regarded as a non-essential, a rather luxurious and fanciful extra—a " tenant's fixture " and no part of the freehold.

Now I am myself sufficiently venerable to recall disputes over another innovation—" fixed baths "—on precisely the same grounds, so that I can easily believe this otherwise surprising statement.

But it is extraordinary—or perhaps it is not—how quickly one passes under the Addy spell and becomes ready to believe anything that he says—even if it is some new proposition or theory as to the truth of which he is frankly in doubt himself.

That is his secret, I think, he is so modest in his claims, so scrupulous in his argument, and in the just use of the available evidence, *whether it supports his case or not.*

For my part, I am humbly aware that had *I* made his discoveries, nothing could have kept my sense of drama— my showmanship, if you like—within the strait scientific limits set himself by Mr. Addy who, with the utmost detachment, proclaims and proves that, through the yoke of oxen and the corresponding " bay," our architecture, our land surveying, certain of our laws and social usages and even, so it seems, our coinage, all have their root in and derive from the average girth of a bullock's belly.

And this fundamental eduction, if you please, is announced with no more fuss or flourish than if the author had found out how colourwash was mixed in the Middle Ages, which incidentally, of course, he has.

Probably it is due to this characteristic humility, this pedantic matter-of-factness of the author that his book, though out of print since before the war, has not been clamorously demanded in a new edition long ere this.

Yet there are enough odd sidelights on the ways of our forbears scattered through the book to make it of absorbing interest not merely to historians, architects and archæologists, but to all who find pleasure in looking back in time for explanations of the perplexing present and perhaps for some clue to the even less manageable future. It is good actually to read (what I had long suspected)—that holy solitaries and hermits were often a nuisance to their neighbours and a thorn in the side of local government bodies who had sometimes to dislodge them by legal processes or by force from their chosen pitches, often unauthorized squattings encroaching on the highway or other public property. One learns too how new a thing is the desire for home privacy and quietness, and how the goodman of the medieval homestead carefully planned his home so that he might as far as possible both see and hear all that went on about the place from his very bed.

I am intrigued too by such glimpses of my own primitive Welsh ancestors of the twelfth century as are quoted from Giraldus Cambrensis, more particularly as I still hold the lands that were theirs when he actually observed them :

" But at last, the hour of sleep approaching, they lie down all together on a place thinly strewn with rushes and covered with hard rough cloth which the country produces and which in common parlance is called *brachan*. And they are clad by night as by day : for they keep off the cold at all times with only a thin and transparent cloak ; they are, however, much comforted by a fire at their feet and likewise by the near heat of their sleeping companions. But when their underside begins to weary of the hardness of the mattress or their upper side to get cold from exposure, they instantly jump up to the fire, from whose benefit they seek the promptest relief for their discomforts ; and thus going back to lie down and constantly turning over when discomfort prompts them, they expose, alternately, one side to the cold and the other to the hardness."

As a somewhat tepid ecclesiologist I find my interest in churches vastly stimulated by the discovery that they were formerly far less frigidly religious than I had in my ignorance supposed.

To see such as " The Lord's House " understood in another than the accepted sense, to see it as the local temporal lord's justice court, as the Local Government Offices,

as the watch-tower and citadel against raiders, and as the
general assembly rooms (they danced in the Yorkshire
churches as late as the seventeenth century), as school and
hospital—all this warm and intimate contact with the civil
life of the people, gives me, I say, a new interest in and a
new eye for what many of us have too innocently accepted
as purely " sacred " buildings. If, somehow, the churches
could once again resume their old importance in the daily
lives of the people, if literally they could be " profaned "
and become again the basilicas that once they were and
more besides—as valiantly attempted for instance at
Thaxted—why then they would surely attract to themselves,
as buildings, the admiring attention they still deserve
instead of being increasingly neglected by the architecturally
minded young.

Yet in the old days discipline seems to have been enforced
where discipline was needed, for Mr. Addy quotes an order
in council of 1307 wherein rectors were summarily enjoined
" Not to presume to cut down trees in the churchyard
except when the chancel required repair."

I shall have the keenest pleasure in drawing the attention
of certain beneficed clergy of my acquaintance to that
most laudable and explicit instruction.

I shall henceforth too take a livelier pleasure in my foot-
rule, for instead of my measurements having their former
pedestrian reference to the " British Standard Foot—one-
third of the distance between the centres of two gold studs
set in a bronze bar at a temperature of (what was it ?)
deposited at the offices of the Board of Trade "—or some
such joyless abstraction as memorized (probably wrongly)
in my school days—I can now envisage something altogether
more festive and engaging—the pretty Sunday morning
ceremony of " Refreshing the Surveyor " as quoted from
Jacob Koebel's *Geometrei*, a German text-book of 1556.

" To find the length of a rood in the right and lawful
way, and according to scientific usage, you shall do as
follows : Stand at the door of a church on a Sunday and
bid sixteen men to stop, tall ones and small ones, as they
happen to pass out when the service is finished ; then make

them put their left feet one behind the other, and the
length thus obtained shall be a right and lawful rood to
measure and survey the land with, and the sixteenth part
of it shall be a right and lawful foot.

" In the measurement of English land the perch was also
the unit. For, says an old writer on surveying, ' when ye
measure any parcell of land, ye should painfullye multiply
the breadth of the perches thereof with the length of the
perches of the same.' "

Such a technique must surely have greatly humanized
the science of geometry, and I certainly missed in any
text-book of mine the sympathy shown by that under-
standing " painfullye."

Which word appropriately brings me to Mr. Summerson's part as resurrectionist-in-chief of this most valuable
book.

The author's age and health entirely forbade any action
on his part to rescue his work from the obscurity imposed
by its being out of print, and my own erudition and assiduity
were both quite inadequate to the task of editing, expanding
and re-illustrating proposed to me by the publishers. But
in the event I claim to have served them, the author, and
the public, most excellently well, for, by finding the precisely right man for the job, I have done far better by proxy
than ever I could in my own proper person.

The arrangement had the further great advantage of
putting all the work on to Mr. Summerson's shoulders,
shoulders I would add upon which the mantle of Mr. Addy
seems to fall most becomingly.

What the work has actually been, I would rather guess
than know, but for many months I was distantly aware of
visits undertaken to remote parts of the country to verify
or photograph this or that, of long researches at the British
Museum, and of the meticulous tracking down of out-
landish references.

'Thanks to the great mass of most illuminating additional
material diligently collected by Mr. Addy over a long
period and preserved in his notes now skilfully infused
into the body of the book by Mr. Summerson, I think it

---

might be fairly claimed that *The Evolution of the English House* has undergone a highly successful " rejuvenation " operation, a claim that will, I feel sure, be generously endorsed by the author, whose original thesis it has been thus sought to amplify.

CLOUGH WILLIAMS-ELLIS.

REVISER'S PREFACE

IN this new edition of Mr. Addy's book, the original
text has not been substantially altered. The work of
revision has consisted simply in incorporating a
quantity of additional material, based on notes made by
Mr. Addy over a number of years. Where I have included something not based on one of these notes, the
passage concerned is enclosed in square brackets. The
illustrations have been almost entirely redrawn, partly for
the sake of clarity and partly in order to embody additional
facts and corrections. Wherever possible, the examples
illustrated in the former edition have been visited and
information obtained as to their condition or their fate.
Many illustrations have been added.

Among those who have helped me with information,
illustrations or suggestions, I should like to thank Mr.
F. H. Cheetham, F.S.A. (who prepared some valuable
notes on the Meols houses), Mr. F. H. Crossley, F.S.A.,
Mr. S. A. Cutlack, Mr. H. Dan, L.R.I.B.A., Mr. Geoffrey
Grigson, Messrs. F. B. and S. B. Kenworthy, the Rev. W. F.
Kerr, of Treeton, Mr. W. L. Mellersh, Mr. Bernard A.
Porter, F.R.I.B.A.; the Rev. W. J. Sumner; of Mappleton,
Mr. Basil Sutton, F.R.I.B.A., Mr. W. J. Carpenter Turner,
A.R.I.B.A., and Mr. F. Williamson, of the Derby Museum.
I am also indebted to Dr. A. Bulleid and Mr. H. St. G.
Gray, joint authors of *The Glastonbury Lake Village*, and
to the Glastonbury Antiquarian Society for permission to
use two illustrations from their book ; also to the editors
of *Archæologia Cambrensis* for the loan of three blocks and
to the several publishers whose names appear beside the
respective illustrations which they have allowed me to use.
The Birmingham Architectural Association has kindly
allowed the reproduction of the two drawings of Handsworth " Old Town Hall," prepared for their survey.

March, 1933.   JOHN SUMMERSON.

NOTE OF ACKNOWLEDGMENT IN THE FIRST EDITION

THE author offers his best thanks to Mr. Joseph Kenworthy for the interest which he has taken in the present work. With him he has spent happy days in the country examining and measuring old buildings. His thanks are also offered to Mr. Edmund Winder, architect, and to Mr. Barton Wells for their survey and plans of the keep at Castleton ; to Professor Meitzen, of Berlin, for leave to make use of illustrations in his books ; to Professor Theodor Siebs, of Greifeswald, for a similar kindness ; to Mr. E. Sidney Hartland and to Sir George Reresby Sitwell, Bart., for their advice and assistance ; to Mr. Thomas Winder, architect, of the Duke of Norfolk's office in Sheffield, for drawings, plans, and other valuable help ; to Mr. E. C. Skill, of the same office, for photographs and plans ; and to Mr. Charles Macro Wilson for the use of a manuscript in his possession.

SHEFFIELD,
October, 1898.

CONTENTS

LIST OF ILLUSTRATIONS

IN THE TEXT

14

PLATES

AUTHOR'S PREFACE

IN discussing the evolution of the English house we are more concerned with the popular and native art of building than with forms or styles borrowed from other countries.

English writers on domestic architecture have been content for the most part with describing the remains of great villas, or the picturesque timber houses which adorn some of our old cities. Such buildings are more attractive to the casual eye than wattled huts or combinations of dwelling-house and cattle-stall.

And yet, if we would learn how the masses of the English people lived in past times, we must not omit these plainer, but assuredly not less interesting dwellings.

Professor Meitzen, Professor Theodor Siebs, and other German scholars have described still-existing houses in northern Germany which are built, like basilicas or churches, in the form of nave and aisles, with dwelling-rooms, usually three in number, at one end ; and Dr. Konrad Lange has shown that these remarkable survivals resemble the peasants' houses described by Galen as existing in Asia Minor in the second century of the Christian era.

At the present day there are no houses in England which resemble the old Greek peasants' houses, or the typical basilica, so nearly as do these German survivals. Our menservants and maidservants no longer sleep in galleries above the aisles of a great farmhouse ; and yet we are by no means without traces of the former existence here of similar habitations. We still have examples of barns or " shippons " built in the form of nave and aisles, in which the oxen faced inwardly to the main floor, as they did in the German peasant's house, and at the end of which there is either a small dwelling-house, or, in place of that dwelling-house, a stable, separated from the " shippon " by a threshing-floor.

Taking an ordinary parish church as an illustration of our subject, the main entrance to the German peasant's house was through a pair of large folding-doors at the west end. In the English peasant's house, as now seen in numerous survivals, the main entrance was not in the west end, but in the transept, a position recalling the arrangement of the Anglo-Danish house.[1] In one of the outer walls of the transept (or " floor," as it was sometimes called) was a pair of folding-doors, commonly called barn-doors. In the outer wall on the opposite side of the transept was a smaller door, called the winnowing-door. The transept was the " threshold," or threshing-floor. It must not, however, be supposed that these houses were oriented, as the ordinary church is. They may, or may not, have anciently been so, and no assertion on that point is made here.

Although we cannot point to the existence in England of such complete survivals of the ancient " three-naved " house as are found in Germany, we still possess abundant remains of an architectural feature which lies at the root of Gothic architecture.

An example will show best what is meant. The roof of a barn at Upper Midhope, near Penistone, is supported by six thick " forks " of oak, locally known as " crucks," or " crutches." The " forks " stand on little stone pillars, or plinths, embedded in the walls, their bases projecting outside. The " forks " and the little pillars are older than the walls : the pillars are not of the same kind of stone as that which forms the walls. In such a building as this the whole construction from floor to roof is apparent to view. The weight of the foot rests on the stone pillars, which rise a foot or more above the ground. There is no " thrust " on the walls; "the arch which never sleeps" thrusts only on the soil.

" Forks " like these are still abundant in old dwelling-houses. Sometimes they are concealed in the walls, and are all but invisible in the lower storey. In barns and rooms where cattle are housed they are either curved or straight. In dwelling-houses they are usually curved or lancet-shaped. The object of the curve was to gain head-room, trees having been chosen which were naturally bent.

[1] HENNING, *Das deutsche Haus in seiner historischen Entwickelung*, p. 55.

You have only to erect a pair of such bent trees on pedestals, however short, of wood or stone, and the Gothic arch of a church or ancient hall, with its subjacent pillars, stands before you in its nascent form.

No living man can now remember the time when " forks " like these were set up, and there are reasons for believing that they have not been used by builders during the last two centuries. But building with " forks " can be traced up the stream of time for at least two thousand years. Such " forks " supported the roofs of Roman cottages in the days of Ovid, and they were regarded by Vitruvius as evidence of the oldest kind of building. In this case, then, we need not look for the past in the present, for traces of this method of construction appear in a long and all but unbroken record.

Anciently buildings supported by " forks " had no vertical side walls ; only the two gable ends were upright. Horizontal beams were laid across the " forks," and the slope of the roof extended down to the ground. Hence, when the " forks " were curved or bent, these buildings, more especially when their length was considerable, resembled ships or boats turned upside down.

Complete examples of ship-shaped houses are extremely rare at the present day. But they were once extremely numerous, and if we examine some of the " forks " which support old buildings we shall find that they bear on their outer faces " housings," or cavities, to receive the horizontal beams which were once laid across them.

The addition of projecting tie-beams to the " forks," and of the upright side walls on which the two ends of the tie-beams rested, was an invention of later times.

It was easy to extend a building supported by " forks " by adding to its length ; it was not so easy to extend its breadth. Lateral extensions, however, were made, when the occasion required it, by means of an elaborate wooden framework. The building then had wings, or aisles, sometimes called " little bays," on one or both sides. The central room only had the form of an inverted ship, or rather of the skeleton or main timbers of an inverted ship.

Any addition to the ends of such a building, or any

extension, whether at the ends or the sides, which did not form an integral part of the great wooden framework, or was shut off from the rest of the building, was called an "outshot" or "outshut." In Old English such an addition was called *gescot*, or "shot." For example, the chancel at the east end of a church is a "shot" or "outshot." The *culacia* at the ends of great barns mentioned in mediæval documents were probably "outshots."

It must not, however, be supposed that houses supported by "forks" comprehended or included every kind of building in England. Such houses were probably more frequent than any other on account of their cheapness. But wooden houses containing upright columns supporting a middle room or nave, with aisles on both sides, were also common. Extant examples of this basilical type of house are now hardly to be found ; their forms have rather to be inferred from records and from similar buildings which now exist in some parts of Germany, and which are known to have existed in Wales and Ireland. The former kind of building was more suitable for the poorest cottages ; the latter could be developed, either in wood or stone, into buildings of great splendour.

Nothing is known as to the relative antiquity of these two kinds of buildings. All that can be said is that buildings supported by "forks" are, on account of their simpler construction, probably of an older type than buildings supported by upright columns.

Both these two kinds of buildings were divided into "bays," and again into "half bays," the normal length of the "bay" being sixteen, and the breadth fifteen, feet. The "bay" became the unit of measurement, and the area of such buildings was estimated by the number of "bays," including "half bays," which they contained.

When, therefore, we read in an ancient survey, or other old document, that such a building was forty feet in length, we know that it must have contained two "bays" and a half. If the building was eighty feet in length it must have contained five "bays."

Consequently the length of such a building, when measured in feet, will be found to be a multiple either of eight

or sixteen. If it was a multiple of eight and not a multiple
of sixteen—for example, if the building were forty feet in
length—it contained a " half bay."

In old Norse buildings, according to Vigfusson, the distance between two posts, or pillars, was known as a *staf-
gólf*, or stave-space, and was about two yards, the length
of a building being " denoted by its number of *staf-gólf*."
Here we are not told what the exact measurement was, but
the *staf-gólf* seems to be identical with the English "half
bay."

In English ox-houses the " bays " or spaces between the
great " forks," or, as the case might be, between the upright
pillars, were divided into two equal parts by partitions
known as " skell-boosts," the word " skell " being derived
from the Old Norse *skilja*, to divide or separate.

The " bay " was just of sufficient length to accommodate
a " long yoke " of oxen, or four oxen abreast. The " half
bay " was sufficient for a " short yoke," or a pair of oxen.
As oxen ploughed the land, and were the labouring cattle of
our forefathers, it was considered necessary that they should
stand together in the house as they stood together in the
field. By standing in pairs or fours in the house they grew
more familiar with the accustomed yoke. Moreover, it was
necessary that buildings should be so constructed as to hold
the greatest number of objects with the least possible waste
of timber-work or of space.

The length of the " bay " was identical with the length
of the perch or rod in land measurement. Accordingly the
normal length of a " bay " of building is equivalent to the
breadth of a rod or rood of land.

The necessities or requirements of oxen had more to do
with the sizes and forms of our ancient houses than any
other factor, for this length of " bay," fixed as it was by
the " long yoke " of oxen, became the rule in every kind
of domestic building, except mere huts or booths supported
by a single pair of " forks."

We learn, then, that the origin of our common architectural forms is not to be sought in arbitrary designs. We
must look for it in the simple hut whose roof was held up

by a pair of wooden " forks," as well as in the more elaborate wooden house, of which the cathedral is the highest development. The pyramidal outline of the great farm-house, or peasant's house, which still rises above the plains of northern Germany, and which still, in a less perfect form, may be seen in English villages, is the most striking feature of Gothic architecture. Church and dwelling-house had this feature in common, and Henning[1] remarks that East Frisian houses look from afar like great German village churches.

[1] *Ut supra*, p. 42.

THE EVOLUTION OF
THE ENGLISH HOUSE

CHAPTER I

THE ROUND HOUSE—UNDERGROUND HOUSES

The round hut the earliest form of European house—The modern charcoal burner's hut a type of the earliest form—The marsh village near Glastonbury—Round or roundish houses there built of wood and mud-clay—Circular hearths—The village near Glastonbury fortified by palisades, and of pre-Roman date—The arts practised by its inhabitants—Resemblance of the village to prehistoric villages in North Italy—Roofs of these houses—Oval forms very difficult to build—Stone " beehive " houses —Tendency of such houses to assume a rectangular form —Underground houses—Late survivals from them— —Traditions about underground passages—Underground dwellings of the ancient Germans—Related etymology of houses and garments.

IN Great Britain, as elsewhere in Europe, the evidence leads us to the conclusion that the earliest form of dwelling, fit to bear the name of house, was round. Round huts are still used in Africa, and such huts seem to have been common to many different races at an early stage of their development.[1] In Italy the type of the round form of house lasted down to historical times in the temples of Vesta.[2] In England it may have been preserved in the round temple found at Silchester and one or two round churches, like that of Little Maplestead in Essex.

" In Ireland," says Professor Sullivan, " round houses were made by making two basket-like cylinders, one within the

[1] LANGE, *Haus und Halle*, p. 51 ; SMITH's *Dictionary of Greek and Roman Antiquities*, 3rd ed., i. 654.
[2] See the whole subject discussed in HELBIG, *Die Italiker in der Poebene*, p. 51 *et seq.*

other, and separated by an annular space of about a foot, by inserting upright posts in the ground and interweaving hazel wattles between, the annular space being filled with clay. Upon this cylinder was placed a conical cap, thatched with reeds or straw. The kreel houses of many Highland gentlemen in the last century were made in this way, except that they were not round.

The early Irish houses had no chimney. The fire was made in the centre of the house, and the smoke made its exit through the door or through a hole in the roof, as in the corresponding Gaulish and German houses."[1] The walls of this kind of round house did not slope inwardly, so as to meet in a point at the summit. But the sloping jambs of doors, so often found in the oldest examples of Scotch and Irish buildings, may afford evidence that in some forms of round houses the walls were not upright but took the shape of a cone. The sloping jambs of Pelasgic buildings may also point to the same conclusion.

An account of the building of a round wicker house is given in the Gaedhelic Life of Saint Colman Ela. It was completed by the weaving in of a single rod at a time. The writer says :

> " Of drops a pond is filled ;
> Of rods a round-house is built ;
> The house which is favoured of God."[2]

In England charcoal burners, whose occupation is ancient, build round huts to this day. They are composed " of a number of thin poles laid together in the form of a cone. The feet are placed about nine inches apart, and they are interlaced with brushwood. A doorway is formed by laying a lintel from fork to fork, and the whole is covered with sods laid with the grass towards the inside, so that the soil may not fall from them into the hut. A lair of grass and bushwood is formed upon one side, and a fire, often of charcoal, is lighted upon the hearth in the threshold."[3] The

---

[1] In *Encyclopædia Britannica*, 9th ed., xiii. 256.

[2] O'Curry's *Manners and Customs of the Ancient Irish*, iii. 32. It is popularly said of a London minister of religion that he built his church round to keep the devil out of the corners.

[3] T. Winder in *The Builders' Journal*, vol. iii. p. 25.

Photo: S. O. Addy

Charcoal burner's hut in Old Park Wood, near Sheffield.

mention of a "lair of grass and bushwood" recalls the passage in the *Odyssey* where Telemachus returns and is greeted by Eumaeus. "And the swineherd strewed for Telemachus green brushwood below and a fleece thereupon and there presently the dear son of Odysseus sat him down."[1]

The hut shown in the illustration stood in Old Park Wood, near Sheffield. We have here a curious survival of the way in which some prehistoric dwellings seem to have been built. The sloping jambs of the door should be particularly noticed, and compared with those found in ancient Irish and Scotch stone buildings.

The Gaulish huts shown on the Antonine column have both a round and a rectangular shape, and the forms there given show a higher stage of development than that exhibited in the modern charcoal burner's hut, for the walls had already become straight and the roof domical. The charcoal burner's hut, shaped like a cone, and having neither window nor chimney, is a type of the very earliest forms of human dwellings, though it is better than the miserable huts of the ancient Fenni. This savage German tribe, according to Tacitus, slept on the ground, and had no other protection for its children against wild beasts and the weather than a few boughs twisted together. These people lived a nomadic life, and thought that better than groaning over agriculture or toiling at building houses.[2]

In Great Britain the foundations of circular houses, with much else of great historical value, have been found in marsh villages or lake villages. The most interesting of these is the village discovered about forty years ago near Glastonbury.[3] Here between sixty and seventy huts or houses stood upon an artificial island raised above the surrounding marsh. The village covered nearly three and a half acres. It was surrounded by a palisade formed of poles from five to fourteen feet in height and three to nine inches in diameter.

[1] BUTCHER AND LANG'S *The Odyssey of Homer.*
[2] TACITUS, *Germ.* 46.
[3] Fully described in A. BULLEID AND H. ST. G. GRAY, *The Glastonbury Lake Village*, 2 vols., 1911–19, on which work the following account is based.

The upper portions of the palisades were bound together with coarse wattle-work. The dwelling-floors were circular areas of clay ranging from fourteen to forty feet in diameter and from three to nine inches in thickness. " Distinct traces of split-wood flooring-boards were observed in eight mounds, and in two of these there were signs of joists supporting the

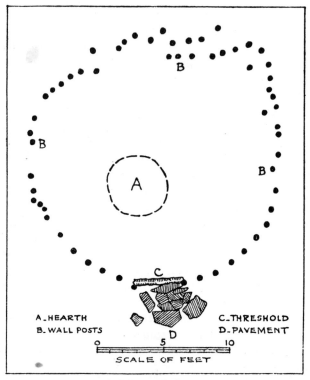

A. HEARTH
B. WALL POSTS
C. THRESHOLD
D. PAVEMENT

SCALE OF FEET

PLAN OF A HOUSE IN THE BRITISH VILLAGE, GLASTONBURY

boards. The flooring-boards were from six to eight inches wide and arranged either in concentric circles parallel with the margin of the dwelling or across the floor." In the centre was a hearth formed either of baked clay, slabs of lias, gravel, sandstone, or marl. One of the clay hearths was ornamented with small impressed circles.

As regards the foundations of the dwelling-mounds, " the

method commonly adopted was to place lengths of timber on the surface of the soft peat at from six to fifteen inches apart ; then a second layer of timber at right angles to the first layer ; followed by six to nine inches of brushwood. Sometimes a third layer of timber was added and placed parallel with the first."

The dwellings themselves were circular and " formed by driving a line of posts vertically through the clay into the underlying substructure, the spaces between the posts being filled in with wattle and daub." The posts were from three to nine inches in diameter and placed at from six to fifteen inches apart, the diameters of the huts themselves varying from eighteen to twenty-eight feet.

The roofs were supported by a central pole placed near the margin of the hearth. Bases of these poles were found in several cases, as well as charred fragments of thatch in huts which appeared to have been destroyed by fire. The entrance was marked by an arrangement of eight or nine slabs of lias roughly fitted together to cover a space 4 ft. wide, bordered on the inner side by pieces of timber or door-sills, placed in line with the terminal door-posts.

Among the most remarkable discoveries were fragments of oak beams which had evidently formed portions of the " wall-plates " of rectangular cottages. None of these fragments was found *in situ*, and they appeared to have been thrown upon the timber foundation as a reinforcement. The supposition is either that they were brought from a neighbouring settlement where square huts were known and made, or that the square hut was at one time known at Glastonbury and was superseded by a reversion to the round or oval shape. These beams or planks were half notched at the ends to enable them to be fixed at right angles to other beams similarly notched. They were pierced with mortise holes, which, in one case, corresponded with the uprights of three hurdles lying alongside. These hurdles were six feet three inches to six feet six inches in height, thus allowing for an effective wall height of about six feet. Perforating the overlapping ends of the planks was a square mortise-hole presumably intended to hold a corner-post.   None of the planks was complete.   The longest measured 9 ft. 3 ins.

Six feet, the probable height of the rectangular hut walls, corresponds to the measurement, from ground to eaves, of a very large number of old English cottages which still exist, and such is still the usual height of the rooms in the smaller kinds of old houses.   The timber walls of these existing houses, as we shall see further on, are constructed in the

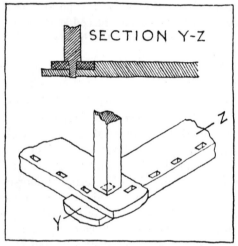

Diagram showing the construction of oak " wall-plates," fragments of which were found in the British village, Glastonbury.

same way as the walls of this rectangular house at Glastonbury.   It is not apparent how the roofs of the Glastonbury rectangles were supported, but we shall see hereafter in what way the sloping roofs of still-existing timbered houses are supported, viz. by pairs of " crucks."   The beam of oak containing mortise holes, found at Glastonbury, corresponds to the beam which, as will be seen on a subsequent page, is called the " pan " or " pon."   In modern English it is known as the wall-plate.

The position of the village near Glastonbury and its palisades seems to show that its inhabitants lived in constant danger of attack by foes.   Nevertheless the village must have lasted for a long period, as the various hearths in the dwellings, superimposed one upon another, show. In one hut these superimposed hearths amounted to seven in number, the two uppermost being of stone. It appears from the shapes of the skulls discovered on the site that the inhabitants were of an Iberic type.[1] The skulls were long, like those found in the long barrows. No coin was discovered, nor a single fragment of Samian or other Roman pottery, though there are numerous villas and extensive Roman potteries in the neighbourhood. The village is said to belong to a period dating from somewhere between 200 and 300 B.C. down to the Roman occupation. It is wonderful that a people living under such unfavourable conditions could have practised so many arts. The vast number of remains which have been unearthed show that they were spinners and weavers, their weaving combs being both abundant and perfect. They used iron instruments, including the knife, the awl, the spade, the bill-hook, and the gouge. They also used the lathe. They made pottery ; they practised metal-working. " They used rings of jet, amber, and glass, and bracelets of bronze and Kimmeridge shale, and beads of glass, and fastened their clothes together with safety-pins and split-ring brooches of bronze."[2] They practised agriculture, and ground their corn in querns. They used decorated and highly-finished pottery, large quantities of which have been found. Amongst the remains are a well-preserved bowl of bronze, a complete ladder 7 ft. long, and a small door of solid oak.[3] Their skill in the arts is perhaps best shown in the specimens of gracefully-carved woodwork which have come to light. If these men had not the civilization of their contemporaries in Greece and Italy, at least they were far removed from barbarism.

In many respects the village near Glastonbury resembles the prehistoric villages discovered in North Italy. These

---

[1] BOYD DAWKINS at meeting of British Association. (*Times*, 19th Sept., 1895.)

[2] BOYD DAWKINS, in *The British Lake Village*, Taunton, 1895. (*Somersetshire Arch. etc. Proceedings*.)

[3] MUNRO, at meeting of British Association. (*Times*, 19th Sept., 1895.)

villages were for the most part "oriented oblongs," and usually had an area of from seven to ten acres, though some of the larger villages had an area of nearly twenty-five acres, whilst in others the area was less than three acres.[1] They were surrounded by a ditch and an earth-wall, the latter being in some cases strengthened by wooden palisades. As at Glastonbury, the huts within the area stood upon an elaborate framework of wooden balks, the walls being composed of brushwood, straw and clay. These pile-dwellings were erected on dry land, as well as in the water, and there seems to be no doubt that the former kind of settlement was copied or evolved from the latter.[2] We do not know for certain how the huts in the marsh village at Glastonbury were thatched. But the thatched Gaulish huts shown on the Antonine column, and the thatch, held in place by branches or logs slung over it, which appears on Albanian hut urns, make it probable that the Glastonbury huts, so similar in other respects, were thatched in like manner. It appears from the Albanian hut urns that the doorway served both to admit light and to let smoke out, and we have seen that such is the case in the modern charcoal burner's hut. But besides the doorway the hut urns sometimes show a small triangular dormer window or louvre, either on the front or back slope of the roof.[3] It is most likely that the smoke in the Glastonbury huts escaped by holes in the roof.

Dr. Lange thinks that the round hut gradually assumed an oval form.[4] Although oval forms have been noticed amongst Etruscan and Albanian hut urns, we must bear in mind that a house in that form would be very difficult to build, and we shall see further on that in Great Britain the rectangular house arose in quite another way. Only in stone "beehive houses" can we find any trace of a gradual transition from a round to a rectangular form. On the island of Skellig Michael, in the county of Kerry, there are six

[1] HELBIG, *Die Italiker in der Poebene*, p. 11. Orientation is very distinct in the sites of some prehistoric villages in England popularly known as "camps."

[2] HELBIG, *ut supra*, p. 58.

[3] HELBIG, *ut supra*, p. 50.

[4] *Haus und Halle*, p. 51.

" beehive houses " built entirely of dry rubble masonry.
" The cells are rectangular in plan inside, and round or oval
outside ; except in one case where the outside is rectangular
at the bottom. The roofs are domed, and formed with
horizontal overlapping courses, as in the pagan ' Cloch-
hauns.' The only openings are the door, which has inclined
jambs and a flat head, and a small rectangular hole to allow
the smoke to escape."[1] With this exception, there is nothing

A MONASTIC CELL AT SKELLIG MICHAEL

to show that the rectangular house was gradually evolved
from the round house. And we must remember that whilst
the " beehive house " was built of stone, nearly all other
ancient houses, whether round or rectangular, were built of
wood.

Each of these " beehive " cells was a separate house.
There are, however, double cells of the beehive type, both
in Ireland and Scotland. On Eilean na Naoimh, one of the
Garveloch Islands, between Scarba and Mull, is a cell with

[1] *Arch. Cambrensis*, 5th Ser., ix. p. 157. See also LORD DUN-
RAVEN's *Notes on Irish Arch.*, ed. by Miss Stokes, vol. i. p. 31, and
ANDERSON, *Scotland in Early Christian Times*, 1881, p. 80.

a diameter of 14 ft. Contiguous to it " is another of the same form, 13 ft. in diameter, and communicating with the first by a square-edged opening through the point of contact."[1] These double cells seem to suggest the twofold arrangement of " hall and bower," which we shall have occasion to discuss further on.

Besides the round huts built on artificial platforms in marshes, the early inhabitants of Great Britain made use of round dwellings sunk below the ground. Pit-dwellings, as they have been called, have been found at Fisherton, near Salisbury, and elsewhere. They " are proved to be of neolithic age by the absence of metal, and by the spindle-whorls of baked clay and fragments of rude pottery. The pits are carried down through the chalk to a depth of from seven to ten feet, and the roofs are made of interlaced boughs coated with clay. They were entered by tunnels excavated through the chalk, sloping downwards to the floor."[2] The depth to which such dwellings were sunk in the ground grows less as we approach historical times. In the neighbourhood of Bologna a great number of round huts sunk in the ground to a depth of rather less that three feet have been found. The walls were made of a mixture of clay and brushwood, and were supported by a circle of wooden posts. The diameter of the huts was usually from three to four metres, but never exceeded six. In Bologna this kind of building extended down to the fifth century B.C., about which time fragments of Greek vases began to appear in the larger huts. Then, too, the walls of that part of a hut which was sunk below the ground began to be strengthened by a sort of " footing,"—the " basing " as we shall see that it was called in England—made of rough sun-dried bricks laid together without mortar.[3] To this day there is a great abundance of old English houses built a foot or more below the surface of the soil, and into which you descend by one or two steps.

[1] ANDERSON, *ut supra*, p. 97, and the authorities cited by him.

[2] TAYLOR, *The Origin of the Aryans*, 174 ; TACITUS, *Germ.* 16 ; CLODD, *The Story of " Primitive " Man*, p. 106.

[3] HELBIG, *ut supra*, p. 47 *et seq.*

On the subject of these underground houses we may get some help from tradition. The very numerous tales, current in every part of England, about passages communicating between one old house and another must have had some reasonable justification in fact.[1] That fact is not far to seek. Many of the huts at Bologna, to which we have just referred, were united to each other by passages dug in the earth, and similar passages between houses have been noticed in other parts of Italy. According to a statement of Ephoros, reported by Strabo, the Kimmerians dwelling on the Lake of Averna inhabited underground houses, which they called *argillæ*, and which communicated with each other by underground passages.[2] We read in the Landnáma that " Leif harried in Ireland and found there a great underground house. He went in, and it was dark till there shone out a light from a sword that a man was holding. Leif then killed the man, and took the sword, and much money besides."[3] In Ireland, according to Professor Sullivan, " every *Dun* and *Rath* had small chambers excavated under the *Airlis* or ground within the enclosing mound or rampart. These chambers vary in size, but are usually nine or ten feet long, three or four feet broad, and three or four feet high. The entrance is a very narrow passage, barely sufficient to allow a man to creep in on his belly ; and similar narrow passages connect the several chambers with each other."[4] The huts built within the enclosing mounds were almost invariably round. Is not the English " worth," which occurs in so many place-names, and means an enclosure adjoining a house, identical with the Irish " rath " ?

In England we find underground dwellings in Cornwall ; such, for instance, as the " fogou " (Cornish, meaning " cave "), near Bolleit, a subterranean gallery with two small

[1] In castles, abbeys and old cities, the traditions may relate to the large sewers often found. Thirteenth-century sewers in London are mentioned in the *Rotuli Hundredorum*, i. 432 b.

[2] HELBIG, *ut supra*, p. 49 ; STRABO, v. 244 ; ADDY, *Household Tales, etc.*, p. 57.

[3] *Landnáma* in VIGFUSSON and POWELL'S *Icelandic Reader*, p. 5.

[4] Introduction to O'CURRY'S *Manners and Customs of the Ancient Irish*, p. ccxcvii. *et seq.*

c

chambers.[1]   The principal passage is 36 ft. long and 4 ft.
7 in. wide.   Its greatest height is 6 ft. 2 in., but the entrance
is much lower.   The sides are rudely walled with unhewn
stones and the roof is formed of slabs of granite, thrown

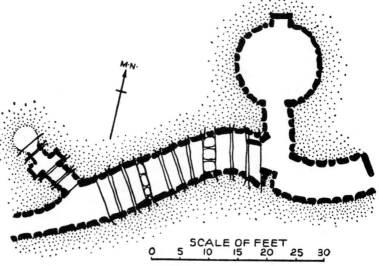

SCALE OF FEET
0   5   10   15   20   25   30

*Reproduced from " The Archæology of Cornwall and Scilly," by
H. O'Neill Hencken, by permission of Messrs. Methuen & Co. Ltd.*

Plan of a " fogou " at Carn Euny (Chapel Uny), near Sancreed,
Cornwall

across.   As in many similar examples, this " fogou " is surrounded by a fort.

At Chapel Uny, near Sancreed,[2] also in Cornwall, a
narrow passage leads into a circular beehive chamber,
15 feet in diameter, and then runs on again till it ends in
ruins after a total distance of 65 feet.

There are several caves or " weems " of a similar kind
near Aberdeen and others in Midlothian.   One, at Middleton,
now destroyed, was described by Pennant.   Another, at

[1] See J. T. BLIGHT, *Churches of West Cornwall*, pp. 131, 132,
and 203.
[2] BLIGHT, *ut supra*, p. 137. [For a recent and admirable account
of the Cornish fogous see H. O'NEILL HENCKEN, *The Archæology
of Cornwall and Scilly*, 1932.]

Crichton, was discovered as recently as 1869.[1] It has a long curving passage widening out from the entrance, with another passage branching to the left for a short distance. We learn from Tacitus that, in the first century of the Christian era, some of the wilder and remoter tribes of Germany occupied subterranean dwellings. " They are accustomed," he says, " to make artificial caves in the ground. They cover these with great heaps of dung, so as to form a shelter during the winter, and a storehouse for the produce of the fields. For in such dwellings they moderate excessive cold, and if at any time an enemy should come he ravages the parts that he can see, but either discovers not such places as are invisible and subterraneous, or else the delay which search would cause is a protection to the inmates."[2]

Pliny[3] likewise mentions the underground dwellings of the Germans, while Seneca says that they " have no shelter from the rigour of the elements except subterranean caves."

Judging from extant remains, Professor Sullivan has expressed the opinion that " they had two stories, the upper for living in, the lower to serve as a store-room for corn and other food. This custom seems to have been common to the inhabitants of Switzerland, Gaul, and Britain, as well as to the Germans. The women especially lived in such earth holes, where they wove the fabrics used for clothing ; for this purpose they continued in use after the knowledge of lime would have enabled them to build better houses. The German name for such holes appears to have been *tunc* or " dung " ; among the Frisians and Franks the name was *screuna*. . . . In England such underground dwellings are called pennpits."[4] Modern architects say that the object

[1] See *The Reliquary*, new series, v. 174.
[2] *Germ.* 16.   [3] *Hist. Nat.*, 19, 1.
[4] Sullivan's Introduction to O'Curry, *ut supra*, p. ccxcvi. We are reminded of our own cellar kitchens, and of the " taverns," to be discussed on a subsequent page. The M. H. German *tunc* seems to be unknown in English unless it occurs in place-names like Dungworth. It seems more probable that the caves described by Tacitus were separate rooms, and resembled the chambers under the Irish " duns " and " raths."

of building old English houses somewhat below the ground was to obtain warmth. The old German *tunc* or *dung* had also the meaning of a winter-house or winter-room, and was used either as a weaving-room or as a store-room for preserving the fruits of the earth. We may compare it with the Icelandic *dyngja*, a lady's bower and the *dings*, or small shops, of mediæval York, Beverley, and Hull.[1]

A curious comment on the psychology of primitive house-building is to be found in the relations between words for dwellings and words for articles of clothing. Thus the Anglo-Saxon word *ceosol*, a cottage, is doubtless connected with the Latin *casula*, diminutive of *casa*, a house, and this word *casula* is used in mediæval Latin to mean both cottage and chasuble. In a curious pictorial vocabulary of the fifteenth century,[2] the word *casula* is given, under the heading " Nomina Domorum," as meaning a cote (i.e. cottage), and again under " Nomina Ecclesie Necessaria," as meaning a chesypyl, or, as we should say, a chasuble. The chasuble was not always an ecclesiastical vestment. Augustine mentions it as an ordinary outer garment, a large, round, sleeve-less cloak with a hood, while Isidore of Seville mentions the " vestis cucullata, dicta per diminutionem a casa, quod totum hominem tegat, quasi minor casa."[3]

Another instance of extended meaning is the word *capella*, which meant originally a little cloak. Similar again is the use of *mantellum* in mediæval times to designate a flue (see *mantellum camini* in Chapter VII, p. 127.

The English *cot* with its more common derivatives *cottage* and *cote* (in the sense of sheep-cote, dove-cote, etc.) seems to be cognate with *coat*, but the connection is remote. The French word *cotte* is given in Littré as a peasant's skirt. *Coit*, a word common in Yorkshire (see p. 89), possibly springs from the same root.

A still more remarkable group of related words is de-scended from the Indo-Germanic root, which gave the Latin

[1] *Notes and Queries*, 9th series, iv. pp. 181, 270.
[2] WRIGHT-WÜLCKER, *Vocabularies*.
[3] *New Oxford Dictionary*.

tego, the Greek τέγος, the modern German *dach*, and our own *thatch* (compare the Cornish dial. *datch*). Parallel derivation in the Latin gave *tugurium*, a hut, and *toga*, a cloak.

CHAPTER II

WE have already said that an oval house would be
difficult to build. It is of course possible that
an oval may have been occasionally evolved from
a round shape, the sides of the building may have been
flattened, and the ends left round as in the remains of some
Romano-British houses, and in the chancels of old churches
where apses exist. Although it must be granted that such
a course of evolution is possible, and although oval forms
are said to have been noticed in the Glastonbury marsh
village, there is abundant evidence that in England the
rectangular form of house had quite another origin.

In whatever part of England we look for examples of the
smaller or humbler domestic house or cottage we shall find
that an old method of construction prevails. These buildings were erected in " bays," the house of one " bay " being
the simplest form. The principle of construction of the
house of one " bay " was simple. Two pairs of bent trees,
in form resembling the lancet-shaped arches of a Gothic
church, were set up on the ground, and united at their

apexes by a ridge-tree. The framework so set up was strengthened by two tie-beams and four wind-braces, and was fastened together by wooden pegs. The bent trees or arches were placed at a distance of about sixteen feet apart, and the space included between them was known as a " bay." Thus the " bay " formed a sort of architectural unit, for the building of one " bay " might be increased indefinitely in length by adding other " bays."

The use of the word " bay " in this connection does not seem to be of great antiquity. The Anglo-Saxon word for the space between two forks was probably *cleofa*, a cell.[1] The modern German word is *fach*, derived, according to Kluge, from *fügen*, to join. More illuminating, perhaps, is the fact that the German *gebäude*, a building, is a plural word, implying a number of huts or booths (*baude*, = a shepherd's hut). " Booth " seems often to have been used in mediæval England to mean " bay," and in the *Feodarium Prioratus Dunelmensis*[2] we read that a house in Hartlepool " dividitur in iij bothas." But elsewhere in the same document occurs the more usual designation of " bays " as *partes*.

The couples, or pairs of bent trees, which formed the structural basis of a house were anciently known as " forks," or, in Latin, *furcae*. They were also known as " gavels,"[3] or " gavelforks," but this term can only be strictly applied to the " forks " at the two ends of the building, which thus acquired the name of " the gable end."

The " forks " were also known by other names. They are now popularly called " croks," " crucks," and " crutches," and a building erected in this way is now said to be " built on crucks." In some old surveys these " crutches," which were intended to support the building, are described as " couples," or " couples of syles," or " siles."[4] The dis-

---

[1] Compare A.S. *cleöfun*, to split.
[2] Ed. SURTEES SOCIETY, p. 25.
[3] A.S. *gaflas*, forks.
[4] In 1772 William Borlase, vicar of Zennor, wrote of " sills," meaning the principals of a roof. See BLIGHT, *Churches of West Cornwall*, p. 99. In the *Durham Halmote Rolls* (ed. SURTEES SOC., p. 34) we read of " vj paribus de scilles " to build a house with.

tinction which in old documents is made between " couples of syles " and " gavelforks " arose from the fact that the " syles " were straight, and were two straight pillars inclined towards each other, whilst the " gavelforks " intersected each other at the top. Usually all the " forks " were curved, and this is the form usually met with at the present day. So when a building is described as containing " one couple of syles and two gavelforks," we know that it would have two " bays " and be 32 ft. in length ; if it contained " three couples of syles and two gavelforks " it would be four " bays " in length, and so on.[1]

A fifteenth-century document relating to property in Halifax[2] directs that a house shall be built " de octo laquearibus contiguis—anglice viij crukkes." A similar expression, " ad laquearium juncturae," occurs in the *Nova Legenda Angliae*.[3] The original Latin *laquear* meant a coffered ceiling, but in mediæval usage the meaning seems often to be simply the space adjoining a " cruck," i.e. a " bay."

The oldest of these buildings had no upper storey, and the walls were made of wattle-work plastered over with clay or mud. Sometimes they were covered by planking resting on the " crucks " and laid parallel to the ridge. Bede tells us that Bishop Eadberht removed the wattles from a church built in this way, and covered the whole with lead, both the roof and the walls themselves. Again, according to Malmsbury, an old church at Glastonbury was covered with lead from the summit to the very ground (*usque deorsum in terram*).[4] In Iceland the shieling was built with one main beam as a ridge-pole, and this rested on the two gable ends.[5]

---

[1] " Precium hyemalis domus est viginti denarii de unaquaque furca que sustinet laquear."—*Leges Wallice*, ii. 802. In 1365 : " Et edificabit unam domum sufficientem, infra duos annos, de ij copul de siles, quas cum firstis et ribis habebit de meremio Domini." —*Durham Halmote Rolls* (Surtees Soc.), i. 48. In 1371 : " Unam grangiam de uno pare de siles, et duobus gauilforks."—*Ibid.*, p. 111.

[2] See ROTH, *Yorkshire Coiners*, p. 155.

[3] Vol. i. p. 41.

[4] See the subject discussed and authorities quoted in GUEST'S *Origines Celticae*, ii. 73.

[5] *Laxdæla Saga* in VIGFUSSON and POWELL'S *Icelandic Reader*, p. 53.

The door of these buildings was in one of the gable
ends.

A house at Scrivelsby, near Horncastle, popularly known
as " Teapot Hall," is an excellent example of a building of
this kind. It is built of two pairs of straight " crucks,"
which extend from the four corners of the house to the
ridge-tree, and which support the ridge-tree, the framework
being further strengthened by the addition of wind-braces.
The length, breadth, and height of the building is 19 ft.
respectively. The doorway is in the south gable end, and
a small " outshot " building, whose roof is considerably
below that of the main building, projects from the opposite
gable end. This " outshot," built of wood, and coeval with
the house, contains the buttery and scullery, the buttery
being, as is usually the case, in the north-west. From the
floor of the " outshot " a ladder goes up to the bedroom above.

The walls, which are about six inches thick, are composed
of wooden studs, with twigs or branches of trees interwoven,
the whole being overlaid with mud and plaster. The sides
are thatched with straw down to a point a little below the
bedroom floor. From this point grey slates extend to the
ground. The roof of the " outshot " is rounded, and
thatched with straw. The fireplace, which may be in its
original position, is of brick, and it, as well as the chimney,
is of more recent date than the rest of the house. An additional room on the ground floor has lately been annexed to
the building, and for that purpose a doorway has been cut
through into the old structure. The greatest care, however,
of this interesting house is taken by its owner.[1] It will be
seen that if the fireplace is in its original position, the chimney, if used at all, must have been of the simplest kind. A
house of this kind was formerly known as a booth, and it
is interesting to notice that the size of the booth in the
fourteenth century was about the same as that of the house
which we are now examining.[2] In the fifteenth century

[1] For a survey of this house the author is indebted to Mr. E. C.
Skill of Sheffield.

[2] c. 1350. " Iohannes Flesshewer ten. j botham de novo edifi-
catam super vastum, longitudinis xx pedum et latitudinis xviij

the gable of such a house was regarded as the "front view."[1]

Owing to the perishable nature of wood and plaster-work, as well as to the inconvenient form of these buildings,

"TEAPOT HALL," SCRIVELSBY, LINCS

existing specimens are extremely rare.   But if we compare the house near Horncastle with a similar building near Dingle in the west of Ireland, known as the "oratory" of Gallerus,[2] we shall see that this form of building is very

pedum."—*Bishop Hatfield's Survey* (Surtees Soc.), p. 32.   Another booth, as well as the village forge, is described as being of the same size.
   [1] "A gavelle of a howse, *frontispicium*."—*Cath. Angl.*   The O.H.G. *Gibil* had the same meaning.
   [2] Galley house, ship house, from the shape (?).   COTGRAVE, 1632, has "*gallere*, a galley."

ancient. For the " oratory " of Gallerus is merely a " booth "
copied in stone. If wood had been plentiful in the neighbourhood it would have been built of that material. The
" oratory " is composed of dry rubble masonry, and consists
of a single rectangular chamber 15 ft. 3 in. long by 10 ft.
wide inside.

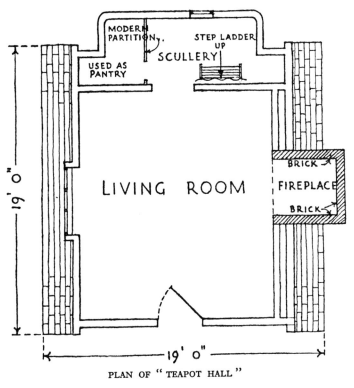

PLAN OF " TEAPOT HALL "

" It has a flat-headed western doorway with inclining
jambs, 5 ft. 10 in. high by 1 ft. 11 in. wide at the top, and
2 ft. 5 in. wide at the bottom inside. . . . The only other
opening is a round-headed window in the east wall, deeply
splayed on the inside. The outside aperture is 1 ft. 3 in.
high by 9½ in. wide at the top, and 10 in. at the bottom.
The window measures on the inside 3 ft. 3 in. high by
1 ft. 6 in. wide at the top, and 1 ft. 9 in. wide at the bottom.

On the inside of the doorway, at a height of 8 in. above the bottom of the lintel, is a projecting stone on each side, with a hole 3 in. square through it to receive the door-frame. Above the east window are three projecting stone pegs, at different levels near the roof. . . . The roof is constructed

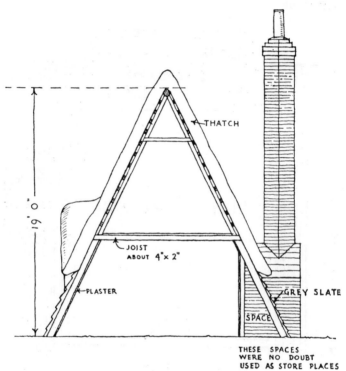

SECTION THROUGH " TEAPOT HALL "
The chimney is of comparatively recent date.

entirely of stone laid in flat courses, without cement. Up to the level of the lintel of the doorway the batter of the side walls is nearly straight, but above this it curves round grace-fully, giving an outline like that of a pointed Gothic arch. The end walls have much less batter than the side walls, and are slightly curved outwards, so as to be convex at the middle of the height. . . . The present ridge-stones are restorations by the Board of Works. The flags below

these are 1 ft. 4 in. wide."[1] The door faces the small
window.

A few small stone buildings of exactly the same type
remain in the west of Ireland and also in the west of Scotland.   Here it is unnecessary to consider the question
whether they were intended for religious uses or not.   In
any case they are copies in stone of the boat-shaped type of
house, which, in places where wood was abundant, were

THE ORATORY OF GALLERUS, NEAR DINGLE

built of that material.   A most interesting example of this
type, built of stone, remains on Eilean Mor, the largest of
the Flannan Isles, which lie to the west of Lewis.   It is
known as Teampull Beannachadh.   It is " composed of rough
stones joggled compactly together without mortar, built in
the form of a squared oblong, but irregular on the ground-
plan, the lengths of the side walls externally being respectively 11 ft. 11 in. and 12 ft. 2 in., and the lengths of the end
walls 10 ft. 3 in. and 9 ft. 2 in.   The walls vary in thickness
from 2 ft. 5 in. to 2 ft. 11 in.   The roof, which is formed
internally by transverse slabs laid across from wall to wall,

[1] *Arch. Cambr.*, vol. ix. (5th S.), 148.

takes externally the form of the bottom of a boat. The
chamber measures about 7 ft. long by 5 ft. wide, and 5 ft. 9 in.
high. The doorway in the west end is but 3 ft. high, and
there is no window or other opening of any kind in the
building. Its exceptionally small size, irregular construction,
and the want of the usual east window, are quite uncommon
features, and wholly inconsistent with any attribution of an
ecclesiastical purpose."[1] One cannot fail to be struck with
its resemblance to the booth " built on crucks." It appears
from the Brehon Laws that an Irish oratory (*duirtheach*) of
15 ft. in length and 10 ft. in breadth cost, when built of
wood, ten cows, or a cow for every foot in breadth. We
have just seen that the inside measurement of the stone
" oratory " of Gallerus is 15 ft. 3 in. by 10 ft.[2]

This simple form of house, built of wood, is mentioned
in the old Welsh laws, and is there described as a " summer
house." It consisted of two *nenfyrch* or " forks " supporting a *nenbren* or ridge-tree, and *bangor* or wattles. These
" forks " are identical with the " crucks " which we have
just mentioned.[3] In other words, the form of the Welsh
" summer house " was exactly like that of the one near
Horncastle, and like that of the " oratory " of Gallerus.
Thus we have seen how this simple form of house extended
from the east coast of England to the west coast of Ireland.
" Crucks " are mentioned, under the name of *sudes binales*,
in Adamnan's *Life of St. Columba*.[4] They are still to be
seen in Gloucestershire. They are common throughout
Yorkshire and Lancashire, and are to be found in many
English counties.[5]

[1] ANDERSON, *Scotland in Early Christian Times*, 1882, p. 121,
from MUIR'S *Characteristics*.
[2] O'CURRY'S *Manners and Customs of the Ancient Irish*, iii. 49, 55.
[3] " Omnis camposus edificator a siluano herede tria edificii ligna
debet habere, uelit, nolit ; scilicet nenbren [tecti trabem] et dwe
nenforch [duas tecti furcas]."—*Welsh Laws*, ii. 777.
[4] REEVES' ed., p. 114. *Cf.* also VIRGIL, *Georg.* ii. 359. " Fraxin-
casque aptare sudes, furcasque bicornes."
[5] See the diagrams of various local types in H. S. COWPER,
Hawkshead, p. 146 *et seq.* [For a map showing the districts in
which cruck-building is found, see C. F. INNOCENT, *Development
of English Building Construction*, 1916. It is almost non-existent

This form of house can be traced into a higher antiquity and into distant lands.[1] It was noticed by Sallust in the century preceding the Christian era. According to him the Numidian peasants had a kind of house which they called *mapale*. It was of oblong shape, with curved sides, and resembled the keel of a ship.[2] In other words, it was like the house we have just been considering. That this form of house was unfamiliar to the Romans is evident from the surprise of Sallust, as well as of Procopius, that Roman civilization had not effaced these singularities. Sulpicius Severus speaks of such houses as being very liable to be blown over by the wind. From him it appears that they were small huts, contiguous to the ground, and covered by boards of sufficient strength.[3]

But although houses having an external resemblance to inverted boats or ships seem to have been unfamiliar to the Romans, they were not wholly unacquainted with the use of forks or " crucks." Ovid in his *Metamorphoses* relates how a small thatched cottage was magically changed into a temple. In the process of change, he says, " columns succeeded forks."[4] But it is evident from a remark of Vitruvius that building in this way was regarded as obsolete

in the southern counties and East Anglia, though the reviser was recently informed of an example as far south as Tufton, Hants. In Staffordshire the word " cruck " is used to denote a temporary shelter of curved branches, usually thatched with bracken, for farm-stock, roughly erected in fields, far away from the farm buildings.]

[1] The " barracas " of Spain frequently bear a remarkable superficial resemblance to Tea-pot Hall. The type is of some antiquity in Valencia and a barraca is depicted in a 15th-century panel in the Museo de San Carlos.—*Reviser's note.*

[2] " Ceterum adhuc aedificia Numidarum agrestium, quae mapalia illi vocant, oblonga incurvis lateribus tecta quasi navium carinae sunt."—*B.I.* 18. " Mapalia," with one exception, is only found in the plural. According to passages in Facciolati, *mapalia* seem to have been round.

[3] See the passages cited in Capes's *Sallust*, 1889, p. 252.

[4] " Dumque ea mirantur, dum deflent fata suorum ;
Illa vetus, dominis etiam casa parva duobus,
Vertitur in templum ; furcas subiere columnae ;
Stramina flavescunt ; adopertaque marmore tellus,
Caelataeque fores, aurataque tecta videntur."
                                        Ovid, *M.*, viii. 700.

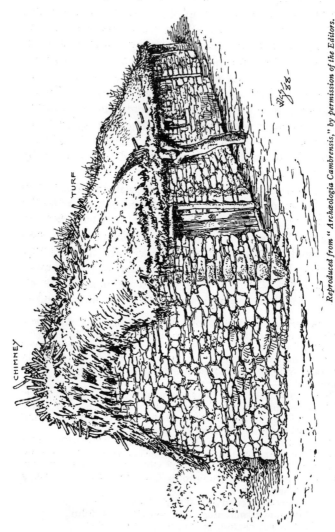

CHIMNEY

TURF

Reproduced from "Archæologia Cambrensis," by permission of the Editors.

FARM-HOUSE NEAR STRATA FLORIDA (NOW DESTROYED)

The roof is supported partly on rough unhewn crucks, partly on internal pillars, and partly on the walls. The foot of one cruck is raised on a post stuck in the ground.

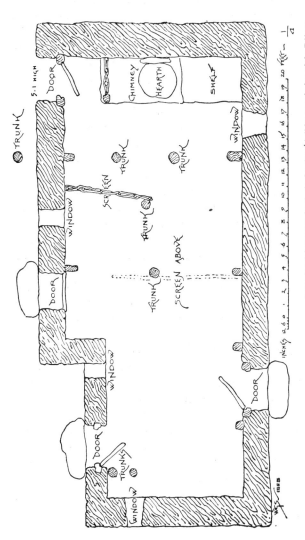

Reproduced from "*Archæologia Cambrensis,*" by permission of the Editors.

PLAN OF THE FARM-HOUSE NEAR STRATA FLORIDA

The cow and pig occupied one portion of the house, screened only by a lattice-work partition plastered with mud. The roof consisted of plaited twigs and turf. (For interior see opp. p. 128.)

D

or barbarous in his time. He speaks of it as the oldest kind of building. " First," he says, " men erected forks, and weaving bushes between them, covered the walls with mud."[1]

Seneca[2] has an interesting passage in which he describes a primitive dwelling. " Forks set up at one end and the other supported the cottage : with brushwood laid on thickly and with leaves heaped up and slanting downwards, the greatest showers ran off. Beneath these roofs they dwelt in safety. The thatched roof covers the free ; slavery dwells between marble and gold." Columella,[3] a contemporary of Seneca, describes the methods used to protect figs in the process of drying. " On each side they place, flat upon the ground, shepherds' hurdles, woven either with haulm or sedge or fern, so that, when the sun is near setting, they may be erected, and, being placed leaning towards each other, may, with their roofs arched in the manner of huts, protect the figs." Another passage worth quoting in this connection is from Priscus of Byzantium, who describes a structure in which " the crutches, beginning from the foundation, go up to the top in due measure."[4] Priscus here refers to the crutches as κύκλοι, though the actual Greek word for crutch seems to have been δοκος, which occurs in Priscus and which Kluge connects with the German *zacke*, a twig, prong, or fork.

The use of forks for building seems to have been general in early times, but by no means universal. Olaus Magnus says that " there are many forms of house in the northern parts, viz. pyramidal, wedge-shaped (*cuneatae*), curved in arches (*arcuales*), round, and quadrangular."[5]

We have said that the house near Horncastle and the " oratory " of Gallerus, like the Numidian hut, resemble a boat or ship turned bottom upwards. It is from this source that we get our word " nave," which is the Latin *navis*, a

---

[1] " Primumque furcis erectis, et virgultis interpositis, luto parietes texerunt."—VITRUV. ii. 1.

[2] *Ep.* 90, ante med.

[3] Lib. 12, cap. 15, " *Of dry figs.*"

[4] Quoted by HENNING, *ut supra*, p. 123.

[5] *Hist. de gent. septentr.* (1555), quoted in V. GUDMUNDSSON, *Privat boligen.*

ship, and perhaps also the pointed Gothic arch.[1] The German word, too, for the nave of a church is *schiff*, ship.[2] It is interesting to find that in England a house in the tenth century was sometimes called a " hulk "[3] for that word also meant " ship." In old Norse poetry, too, the house was called the " hearth ship,"[4] while in Iceland the chief door of a house was often surmounted by ship's beaks, called *brandr*.[5] Icelandic sagas are full of passages which refer to houses in terms borrowed from ship-building. Here is one such passage from the Ynglinga-Tal.[6] " The fever of the cliff-weeds (forest fire) rushed upon the king in the fire-ship (hall), when the timber-fast craft of the croft (hall) burnt, full of men, about the king's ears." Clearly the Icelander thought of his house as a ship built to stay on land and, as Henning[7] says, " in their long-accustomed ship-building the Scandinavians found a fit school of architecture."[8] Our modern phrase " on board " (the Swedish *ombord* means the same) preserves the Anglo-Saxon *bord*, meaning framework or side of a ship. *Bord* in its diminutive forms, *bordel*, *brothel*, meant originally a little house.

The next evolutionary step was to make the walls of the buildings straight, whilst still retaining the original construction. For, obviously, when the walls were straight there was more space in the house, and it became a more convenient place to live in. The change was accomplished in the following way. The ends of the tie-beams which braced the " crucks " together were lengthened outwardly,

[1] The nave of a church is sometimes called the galilee, Low Lat. *galilea*. Is this connected with " galley," a long ship ?
[2] *Schiff* is applied to the aisles as well as to the central division. On the other hand English writers sometimes speak of the central division as an " aisle."
[3] *Liburna*, hulc ; *tugurium*, hulc—*Wright-Wülcker Vocab.*, 181, 28 ; 185, 12. The word is said to be derived from the Greek ὀλκάς, a ship of burden, a merchantman.
[4] *Corpus Poeticum Boreale*, i. 245.
[5] CLEASBY-VIGFUSSON, *Icelandic Dictionary*.
[6] *Corpus Poeticum Boreale*, Ynglinga-Tal, l. 115.
[7] *Ut supra*, p. 154.
[8] *Carina*, a street in Rome, was so called from the houses being built in the form of inverted ships. The Greek Βᾶγις, an Egyptian boat, afterwards meant a large house.

so that the tie-beam became equal in length to the base of
the arch formed by the " crucks." Upon the tops, or at the
ends, of these extended tie-beams, long beams known as
" pans " or " pons " were laid,[1] and then the rafters were
laid between the " pans " and the ridge-tree. Finally a side
wall was built from the ground as far upwards as the " pan,"
so that the " pan " rested on the top of this wall.[2] The
annexed illustration of a partly demolished house, in which
a pair of " crucks " and their tie-beam are laid open to view,
shows how this was done. The walls were built in after the
wooden framework had been set up. It is obvious that this
must have been so when they were composed of upright
posts and interlacing twigs. But we should hardly expect
to find that such was the case when the walls were of stone.
Numerous extant examples, however, prove that it was so,
and the annexed section of a barn at Treeton,[3] near Sheffield,
will show one way in which stone walls were added to a
building of this kind. In this case there was no complete
tie-beam. Very often the feet of the " crucks," or the large
stones or pillars on which the " crucks " stand, project a little
from the outsides of the walls, forming, as it were, the bases
of buttresses. Sometimes they form small internal pillars,
suggesting a Gothic arch in a church standing on pillars of
stone. The walls were built of whatever material could most
conveniently be had. The material first in use was wood and
clay, or, as it is variously called, " stud and mud," " clam
staff and daub," or " wattle and daub." After this came stone
and bricks. It often happened that after the wattle and daub
had perished, new walls, either of stone or brick, were inserted. On the west coast of Lancashire, and in Gloucestershire, such substitutions are still made. Hence the wooden
framework of a house is often far older than the outer walls,
so that the plainest exterior may be accompanied by an
ancient and picturesque interior.

The change from the ancient method of supporting the

---

[1] They are " pans " in Yorkshire, " pons " in Lancashire. The
modern name is wall-plate.

[2] Compare the provincial verb *pan*=to unite, to fit.

[3] Copied from a drawing by Mr. T. WINDER.

Photo : S. O. Addy

Crucks of a demolished house.

Photo : S. A. Cutlack

A cottage at Haughton, Staffs., showing a pair of crucks in the gable.
The brick filling is comparatively modern.

roof by pairs of arches springing from the ground to the modern way of supporting it by " pairs of principals " was made very slowly. To us, in these days, the modern roof resting on upright walls of stone or brick seems too plain and simple a thing to be regarded as a triumph of human

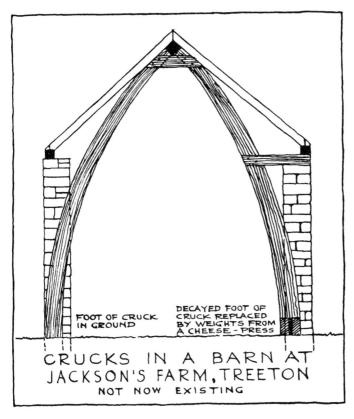

FOOT OF CRUCK
IN GROUND

DECAYED FOOT OF
CRUCK REPLACED
BY WEIGHTS FROM
A CHEESE - PRESS

CRUCKS IN A BARN AT
JACKSON'S FARM, TREETON
NOT NOW EXISTING

skill. And yet it is of comparatively modern date in the English popular art of building. Nowhere is the spirit of conservatism more conspicuous than in architecture. As the Romans usually framed their roofs with tie-beam and king-post,[1] it is strange that the English people should have been so long in adopting this method of construction.

[1] SMITH'S *Dictionary of Greek and Roman Antiquities*, i. 685.

The subdivision of the cruck-built house was the next stage in its evolution. The natural method of subdivision was, of course, into bays, or spaces between the pairs of crucks. It is impossible to say whether the Greek shepherd's κλισια was divided equally in this way, but the primitive

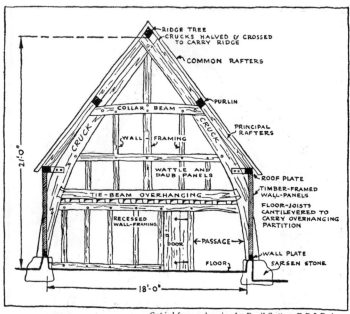

Copied from a drawing by Basil Sutton, F.R.I.B.A.

SECTION OF A HOUSE AT LAMBOURN, BERKS

An example of well-finished mediæval cruck construction. The method of supporting the ridge is noteworthy, and may be compared with the cruder methods employed at Treeton (p. 53) and Handsworth (p. 57).

Greenlander's hut, divided into stalls, " like the stalls in a stable,"[1] seems to have been something like it. One family lived in each stall and there was a separate stall for the unmarried women.

In England we find houses being shared by separate families. Thus, among the Saxon wills preserved in

[1] NILLSON, *Primitive Inhabitants of Scandinavia*, trans. by Lubbock, 3rd ed., 1868, pp. 133, 134.

Photo: J. Bradbury

Reproduced from " The Lure of Midhope-cum-Langsett," by
Joseph Kenworthy.

Interior of a barn, built on crucks, at Watson House Farm,
near Deepcar.

Thorpe's *Diplomatarium*[1] is one of the time of Æthelred in which Wulfwaru leaves sundry lands to his son and daughter, " . . . and let them divide the chief dwelling between them, as they most justly can, so that each of them may have equally much of it." At a later date, we read, in the *Feodarium Prioratus Dunelmensis*,[2] of an indenture in which the Prior and Convent of Durham cede to Thomas Robynson and his wife two bays (*partes*) of a cottage at Billingham, together with the dovecot over the third bay ; the third bay being tenanted by Thomas Tydd.

The old surveyors regarded the bay as a standard of measurement. Thus John Harrison, who about the year 1637 made a survey of the estates of the Earl of Arundel, in South Yorkshire, speaks of " a dwelling-house of 4 bayes, a stable being an outshut and other out houses are 7 little bayes, besides a barn of 4 bayes."[3] Just as buildings were measured by the number of bays which they contained, so they were sold or let by the bay, as cloth is sold by the yard. In deeds and wills of the sixteenth and seventeenth centuries houses are very often estimated or described by the number of bays which they contain. Often too we meet with deeds of this period in which bays of houses or other buildings are separately conveyed.[4] In Derbyshire hay is sometimes sold by the " bay," and in the sixteenth century a " gulf of corn " was as much as would lie between any two pairs of " crucks."[5] Holinshed in 1577 speaks of " two and fortie baies of houses."[6] In *Measure for Measure* Pompey the servant says, " If this law hold in Vienna ten year, I'll rent the fairest house in it after three-pence a bay."[7]

[1] *Diplomatarium Anglicum aevi Saxonici.* Section ii. p. 529.
[2] Ed. SURTEES SOC., p. 44 (note).
[3] *Sheffield Glossary* (Dialect Soc.), 81.
[4] *E.g.* a conveyance dated 1679, " of one bay of a barne or lath abuting on the lath of Alexander Fenton in the possession of John Wood of Gleadless," county Derby.—Deed in the author's possession. Surrenders of " bays " are frequent in old Court Rolls.
[5] " Goulfe of corne, so moche as may lye bytwene two postes, otherwyse a baye."—PALSGRAVE. Compare the Icelandic *staf-gólf*, and *gólf*, an apartment.
[6] *Chronicles*, iii, 1198.
[7] Act ii. Scene i. 255.

As the length of the bay was 16 ft., or a little more or less, measurement and valuation by this quantity was reasonable,

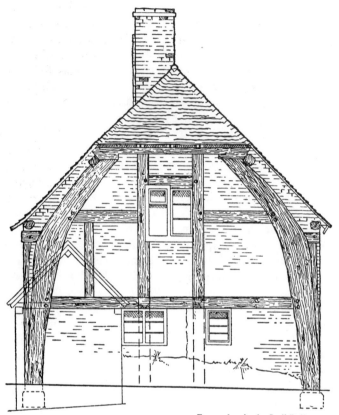

From a drawing by Cyril P. Farmer.

" OLD TOWN HALL," HANDSWORTH, NEAR BIRMINGHAM

This drawing and the one on the opposite page show two ends of the same building and two common methods of using crucks. The natural bend in the timber is clearly illustrated in each case. The original filling, between the timbers, appears to have been of twisted willow twigs, plastered both sides with a composition of mortar and cow-dung.

and this length seems to have been everywhere maintained, except in the case of some cottages which consisted of a single bay. In 1352 we read that William de Strattone " appropriated to himself a piece of land 16 ft. in breadth

on the property of the community without the gate of Ludgate, in London, and built thereon a room (*camera*) 16 ft.
in length and 12¾ ft. in breadth."[1] This was a single bay.

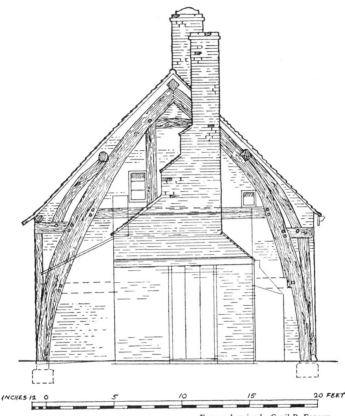

INCHES 12 0   5   10   15   20 FEET

From a drawing by Cyril P. Farmer.

"OLD TOWN HALL," HANDSWORTH, NEAR BIRMINGHAM

he oldest part of the building (including the pair of crucks
shown on the opposite page) is said to date from before 1500.
There are four pairs of crucks, dividing the building into bays
of 15 ft. 3 in., 24 ft. 6 in., and 17 ft., the latter being the
oldest bay. The house has been much altered, the chimney-
stack and brick filling dating from about 1625.[2]

[1] RILEY, *Munimenta Guild. Lond.*, vol. ii. pt. ii. p. 454.
[2] The reviser is indebted to Mr. Bernard A. Porter, F.R.I.B.A.,
foreman-supervisor of the Birmingham Architectural Association
Survey, for information regarding this building.

The hall of Oakham Castle, Rutlandshire, of the twelfth century, consists of a nave and aisles, and is built of stone. It is in four bays of 16 ft. each in length.[1] We shall see further on how this length of 16 ft. came to be fixed. In breadth and height the bays varied considerably, though not enough to prevent the cubic contents of a bay serving as a rough and ready measurement. For instance, in the inquisition of the manors of Glastonbury Abbey,[2] in the year 1189, we read of the contents of a barn at Wrington. " Ibi est una grangia, in aquilonali parte cujus debet esse unum tas durans usque ad proximum hostium aquiloni. et debet esse plenum usque ad festum. . . . In australi parte est unum tas ayene durans ad furcas in longum. in altitudine durans ad trabem furcarum."

In the " Farming and account books of Henry Best " (1641),[3] under " shorte remembrances of thatchinge," we find mentioned what were apparently usual heights for crucks in Best's day, as well as some interesting terminology. " If the forkes bee fifteene or sixteene foote high, then they (i.e. the thatchers) will sewe in three severall places ; if nineteene or twenty foote high then they will sowe downe theire thatch in fower places, viz ; first close to the very wall-plates, then two foote belowe the side wivers, then two foote above the side wivers, and then, lastly, aboute a yard or more belowe the rigge-tree ; . . ."

We have already seen that the Welsh " summer house " consisted of a pair of " crucks " and a ridge-tree, and was completed by wattles. Such a house was originally a sort of portable tent[4] which might be carried up to the elevated pastures where the cattle grazed in summer.[5] It is well known that pastoral people " divide the year into two seasons —the one when the cattle are fed in the open, the other when

[1] See the plan in TURNER's *Domestic Arch. of the Middle Ages*, p. 28.
[2] Ed. ROXBURGH CLUB, p. 94.
[3] Ed. SURTEES SOC., p. 148.
[4] " Schepherdes house—*bourde portable*."—PALSGRAVE, 1530.
[5] " But what shall be said of him who has been ejected from a wooden house ? He is entitled to an assise if it stands on his own ground whether it is attached to the ground or not."—BRACTON, *De Legibus Angliae* (Rolls Series), iii. 65.

they are housed in the stall."[1] Like many other nations, the
inhabitants of Great Britain once divided the year between
their winter houses and their summer houses, the winter
house being larger and more substantial than the summer
house. We shall deal with the winter house further on. In
England many place-names speak plainly of the old summer
house and temporary abode on the hills and moors. Thus
we have Summerscales near Skipton, Summerlodge near
Askrigg in Yorkshire, Somergraines, Somerguage, Somerby
(summer dwellings), le Somergranges, Somerasse, Somersall,
Somerset, Summerley. There are two parishes in Lincolnshire known as Somercoates. In Norway these temporary
summer settlements still exist, and are known as *sæters*. They
lie " generally on a small piece of table-land some way up a
mountain, whither the Norwegians bring their cattle during
the summer months to feed upon the moist rich pastures of
those high lands where they themselves live as in a sort of
encampment."[2] In England these summer abodes or folds
were known as " sets " or " seats," as in Somerset, Moor-
seats, Outseats, Woodseats, Thornsett, Runsett, Lord's Seat,
and in hundreds of other examples. The pastures themselves
were known as " summer gangs," and when sheep were
brought into the valleys after the harvest they were called
" winterers."

Besides the summer house and the winter house the Welsh
laws mention the autumn house. Of this there were two
kinds. The cheaper and inferior kind was " without augur
holes."[3] The better kind had augur holes ; in other words
the woodwork was more carefully put together.[4] The inferior
kind of autumn house was even cheaper than the summer
house, and was, of course, a step nearer to the primeval tent.
In later times the " summer house " began to be occupied
in winter as well as in summer.

A Roman writer on husbandry mentions summer houses

---

[1] CLODD, *Story of " Primitive " Man*, 1895, p. 161.
[2] KEARY, *Norway and the Norwegians*, p. 41. The A.S. *set*
usually means a fold or stall for cattle.
[3] The timbers seem occasionally to have been fastened by ropes.
See HENNING, *ut supra*, p. 164.
[4] *Leges Wallice (Ancient Laws, etc.)*, ii. 803.

as existing amongst his own countrymen in the century preceding the Christian era. When the flocks fed in woodland pastures in the summer-time, and were far away from their winter homes, the shepherds took hurdles or nets with them (by means of which they made cattle-yards in desert places) as well as other utensils. For their custom was to feed their flocks up and down the country a long way from home, so that their winter pastures were often many miles distant from their summer pastures.[1]

This annual migration of the whole or part of the family to " desert places " in summer was due in part to nomadic habits. Even when the village had been formed down in the valley very little land was cultivated. Flocks of sheep and other cattle could not be fed in summer in the town fields near the hamlet, for these for the most part were then covered by the " acres " of sown corn uninclosed or unbounded save by a turf balk, a few stones, or a temporary fence. By the old laws of Norway summer huts were to be built on the *almenning* or common pasture.[2] They were not to be built in the town fields, but on the uncultivated lands outside those fields. In later years the shepherds found out, as in Spain, that the annual visits of their sheep " to these upland pastures were essential to the beauty of their fleeces."[3] But in earlier times nomadic habits and a primitive form of agriculture can alone explain this annual migration to the hills. In Europe this custom of having both winter and summer houses is as widespread as it is ancient, and we find it in Israel : " I will smite the winter house with the summer house ; and the houses of ivory shall perish, and the great houses shall have an end, saith the Lord."[4]

---

[1] " Contra illae in saltibus quae pascuntur, et a tectis absunt longe, portant secum crates, aut retia, quibus cohortes in solitudine faciant, caeteraque utensilia. Longe enim et late in diversis locis pasci solent, et multa millia absint saepe hibernae pastiones ab aestivis."—VARRO, *De R. R.* ii. 2, 9.

[2] " Sel skal hverr göra sér í almenningi er vill ok sitja í sumarsetri ef hann vill."—*Norges Gamle Love*, i. 251. A man could build his shed where he liked on the common, and live in his summer abode the year round if it pleased him.

[3] *Quarterly Review*, vol. clxxxii. p. 488.

[4] Amos iii. 15.

Besides the temporary summer houses built on the hills, there were in England certain houses known as " grass-houses."[1] These appear to have been occupied by a class of men called grassmen, to distinguish them from husband-men,[2] or men engaged in sowing and tilling the land. The two classes are often referred to as husbandmen and cotmen,[3] though in one document we read of three classes—husband-men, cotmen, and grassmen.[4] The grassman was engaged in tending cattle on the uninclosed lands or wastes,[5] and, unlike the husbandman, grew no corn and had no oxen for the plough. As affecting the old social life the distinction is an important one. The word " grasshouse " implies some corre-sponding term which would describe the house of the man who grew corn. Such a term may perhaps be found in " berewick," meaning " barley-dwelling," or in " barton," meaning " barley-court."

The cot or booth was frequently built of mud, and with-out the support of " crucks." A good example of a mud house, not now occupied, may be seen at Great Hatfield, Mappleton, in East Yorkshire. The outside length is 28 ft., and the inside breadth 15 ft. 2 in. The height to the eaves, which project 10 in., is 6 ft. 2 in. The mud walls are 1 ft. 7 in. thick. The house has one door, 3 ft. 3 in. wide, facing south, and the orginal hearth is at the east end. The " speer," or screen, which stands opposite the door, is composed of mixed mud and straw. It forms one of the two sides of the open hearth, round which the family could sit, the other side being the north wall of the house. The length of the

[1] 1504. " Quadraginta domibus pauperum, vocatis gresse-howses, in parochiis meis de Lowthorpe et Catton, singulis vj[d]."—*Test. Ebor.* (Surtees Soc.), iv. 233. In 1557 a bequest was made of a bushel of rye " to every grisse house within the parish which hath no corne growing."—*Richmond Wills* (Surtees Soc.), p. 102.

[2] 1461. " Item lego cuilibet husbandman de Nid, xij[d]. Item cuilibet gresman de eadem, vj[d]."—Will in *Ripon Chapter Acts* (Surtees Soc.), p. 100.

[3] Fourteenth century. *Durham Halmote Rolls* (Surtees Soc.), pp. 67, 83, 84, 81.

[4] *Circa* 1304. " Bondos, cottarios, gresmannos."—*Whitby Chartulary* (Surtees Soc.), i. p. 28.

[5] See the Grassmen's Accounts in *Memorials of St. Giles's, Durham* (Surtees Soc.). Compare the *bordarii* in Domesday.

" speer " is 4 ft., so that it just covers the door. Its height is 6 ft. 2 in. Across the top of the wooden post at the west end of the " speer " one of the beams of the roof is laid, thus serving the twofold purpose of beam and mantel-tree. Above the mantel-tree, its three sides sloping upwards to the roof, is the chimney, built of studs and laths, plastered with mud. The fireplace next to the east wall, as well as that next to the west wall, is of modern brick ; the original hearth in the east was open. Level with the beam which forms the mantel-tree the hearth is covered by a flat inner roof of lath and

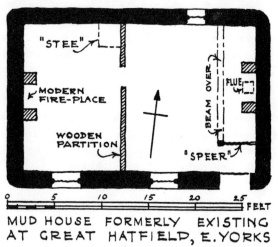

MUD HOUSE FORMERLY EXISTING AT GREAT HATFIELD, E. YORKS

plaster, with a square hole left in it over the jambs of the modern brick fireplace for the smoke to escape. Thus the smoke found its way into a little smoke chamber with a hole in the top next the roof. There is also an opening in the western slope of the chimney, not in the centre, but in the southern half. This opening is 2 ft. 6 in. in height. At its base it is 1 ft. 9 in., and at its top 1 ft. 5 in. in breadth. The aperture is neatly formed, and may have been originally there. Its base is the beam which forms the mantel-tree, and its sides are two of the studs which support the chimney. What it was used for can only be guessed. The roof is of tie-beam and king-post.

The house is divided into two lower rooms of unequal

size by an old wooden partition which does not extend above the beams which support the chamber floor. In the ceiling of the inner room, next to the partition, was a " throp hetch," or " trap hetch,"[1] i.e., a trap door which swung on hinges, and was lifted by an iron ring. Against the opening of the trap door a broad " stee " or ladder was placed to give access to the single room in the roof. The " stee " is still there, but the " throp hetch " has gone. The " chaamer " in the roof is not five feet high, and one wonders how human beings could have slept in such a place. The author was told by the tenant that the house was originally open to the roof, and that the " chaamer floor " was put in by her husband's father, who died a year or two ago, aged 93. If this was so, the lath and plaster roof in the chimney may have been put in at the same time.

The mud walls of this house are very interesting. They are perforated by countless holes made by a kind of bees, locally known as " mud bees " or " sink bees," which make a great noise when they are at work in hot weather. The walls are built of layers of mud and straw which vary from five to seven inches in thickness, no vertical joints being visible. On the top of each layer is a thin covering of straw, with the ends of the straws pointing outwards, as in a corn stack. The way in which mud walls were built is remembered in the neighbourhood. A quantity of mud was mixed with straw, and the foundation laid with this mixture. Straw was then laid across the top, whilst the mud was wet, and the whole was left to dry and harden in the sun. As soon as the first layer was dry another layer was put on, so that the process was rather a slow one. Finally the roof was thatched, and the projecting ends of straws trimmed off the walls. Such mud walls are very hard and durable, and their composition resembles that of sun-burnt bricks. This method of construction reminds us of the house-martin, which in making her nest of loam and bits of broken straws " gives it sufficient time to dry and harden. About half an inch seems to be a sufficient layer for a day. Thus careful workmen, when they build mud-walls (informed at first

[1] Connected, perhaps, with German *treppe*, Swedish *trappa*, a stair.

perhaps by this little bird), raise but a moderate layer at a time, and then desist."[1]

Close to the door of this mud house is a well, as is every-where usual when the well is not in the house itself.[2] The

J.N.S. FROM PHOTO

Mud cottages at Mappleton in process of demolition, showing straight crucks and rubble plinth.

original windows, and also the door, were of " harden "— a kind of coarse sack-cloth.[3] The door could be lifted up like a curtain, and there was no inner door.[4] Robbers were not feared.

[1] WHITE'S *Selborne*, letter lv.
[2] According to HENNING (*ut supra*, p. 18) the well is found opposite the entrance in houses in the Black Forest. The same author quotes (p. 130) a passage in PLINY, *Hist. Nat.*, xvi. i., where a German tribe is described as drinking rain-water, collected " in vestibulo domus." HENNING also mentions (p. 156) an old Norse hall through which a small stream ran.
[3] Compare this method with that employed in the Saxon church at Avebury, where a row of holes, some still containing stumps of willow twigs, in the stonework of the windows showed that they had once been filled in with a wattle screen.
[4] Information by Mrs. W. DUNN, derived from her father-in-law, who lived all his life in this house, and died there aged 93. The house was said to have been " in the family over 300 years." No date can be given. Compare an article on " Cob Walls " in *Quarterly Review*, lviii. 529.

Photo: F. H. Crossley
Reproduced from " Old English Household Life," by Gertrude Jekyll, by permission of B. T. Batsford, Ltd.

A cottage at Steventon, Berks., showing a wooden "outshut."

[The house described above has disappeared. The local joiner recently informed the Vicar of Mappleton that he had pulled down several of these mud houses and that within the last thirty years there were at least five of them in the parish. One of them was taken by the sea owing to coast erosion. Two that were pulled down are illustrated in the accompanying sketch, made from a photograph taken during demolition. It will be seen that they are supported on crucks, the ends of which are buried in sloping plinths of rough stone-work. One of these cottages is said to have been about twelve feet square and divided in the middle by a wooden partition, the space on the far side of which being called the " back rent." The fireplace was open, with a curved beam over it. There were two windows, one of which was next to the door. The walls were about five feet high.

A mud house still exists in the parish of Sigglesthorne, which adjoins Mappleton, but the outer walls have been covered with cement.[1]]

[1] For the above information concerning the demolition of the mud houses in the Mappleton district, and also for the loan of a photograph, the reviser is indebted to the Rev. W. J. SUMNER, Vicar of Mappleton.

E

CHAPTER III

THE RECTANGULAR HOUSE WITH " OUTSHUTS "

A house of one " bay " inconvenient—Such a house increased in size either by adding fresh " bays " or by " outshuts "—" Outshuts " are additional buildings outside the " nave " or main structure—Examples of this kind of house—The " house part " or " house "—The " speer "—The " aitch "—The " chamber "—Clay floors —" Clam-staff and daub "—The " house-place " is the *megaron* of the Greeks and the *atrium* of the Romans— A house near Penistone described—Long table made in, and forming part of, this house—Evolution of the staircase—How the long table was used—The " house " or " fire-house "—Combined dwelling-houses and barns— Position of the various rooms—The " entry " or " floor " —The " threshold "—The typical old Norse house— Sizes of Irish dwellings.

IT is obvious that a house consisting of one " bay " would be a poor place for a family to live in. It could, however, be increased in size by adding other " bays " to the ends, or by building additional rooms at the ends or the sides. When the latter course was adopted, the additional rooms were known as " outshots "[1] or " outshuts," the name being still preserved in the " outshot " kitchens often built at the back of workmen's dwelling-houses. Though " outshuts " adjoined and formed part of the house itself, they were not " built on crucks," and could not strictly be described as " bays." They were outside the " bays " or nave, as we may call the central or ship-like part of the building.

In a small " outshut," measuring 10 ft. by 4 ft., at an old house at North Meols in Lancashire,[2] boards covered the

[1] Compare O.E. *gescot*, O.N. *skot*, part of a building shut off from the rest ; the chancel or apse of a church. The modern German is *anbau* or *nebengebäude* or *seitenausbau*. Compare the Icelandic *af-hus*, a side apartment, also the Norwegian *skut* or *utskut*, and the illustration in MEITZEN's *Das nordische und das altgriechische Haus*, p. 480.

[2] North Meols is the name of the ancient parish in which the town of Southport grew up. Nearly the whole of North Meols is

outer walls of the " outshut " which were framed with posts. The posts or studs stood close together, and the walls were plastered by clay mixed with straw to the depth of an inch, the plaster being covered by several coats of white lime. This kind of building is known in Lancashire as " clam-staff and daub."

In the larger buildings the " aisles " at the sides usually extended along the whole length of the structure, like the aisles of a church. We shall deal with these larger buildings further on, and shall now examine the cottage built of one bay only, with upright walls and with additions at the ends as well as the sides in the nature of " outshuts." Our first example is a thatched cottage at a place called Westward, near North Meols.[1] The cottage is plain, square, and white-washed, with eaves 5 ft. 8 in. from the ground. There are no upper rooms, and there is no ceiling beneath the roof. In other words, it is not " underdrawn." The room in which the family live is here known as the " house-part." In Derbyshire it is called the " house-place " or " house," and in Halifax the " house-body."[2] In London such a room was called " the house " (domus) early in the thirteenth century to distinguish it from the bower or chamber (thalamus).[3] " The house itself " (ipsa domus) was the name given to the largest room in the gardener's house in the original lay-out of the monastery of St. Gall.[4]

The " house-part " in our Lancashire example contains the only fire-place, and consists of a single bay of sixteen feet

now included in the county borough of Southport. All the cottages mentioned in this chapter appear to have been destroyed, though examples of the same type are still to be found in the district.—*Reviser's note.*

[1] This cottage was situated at the corner of Cambridge Road and Hesketh Road, Southport. It was pulled down in August 1932, together with two other cottages of similar type. One cottage still (November 1932) remains, tucked away between the back gardens of modern houses. " Westward " consisted formerly of a group of cottages standing isolated on the edge of the sand-hills about half a mile west of Churchtown (N. Meols).—*Reviser's note.*

[2] ROTH, *Yorkshire Coiners, etc.*, p. 154.
[3] TURNER, *Domestic Architecture of the Middle Ages*, pp. 23, 282.
[4] HENNING, *ut supra*, p. 143.

long and about fourteen feet broad, the "crucks" being in the usual positions. Within the doorway is a covered inner porch, with a screen which keeps the wind out, and protects the "house-part" from the gaze of the stranger and from the

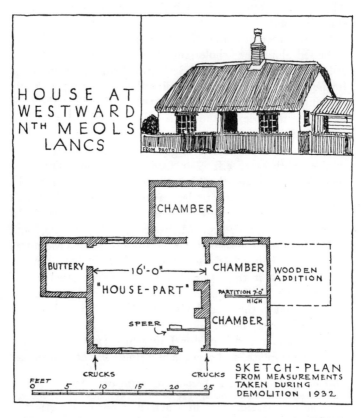

HOUSE AT
WESTWARD
N^{TH} MEOLS
LANCS

FROM PHOTO

CHAMBER

BUTTERY

←———16'-0"———→

"HOUSE-PART"

CHAMBER   WOODEN
           ADDITION

PARTITION 7'.0"
HIGH

SPEER

CHAMBER

↑   ↑
CRUCKS   CRUCKS

FEET
0   5   10   15   20   25

SKETCH-PLAN
FROM MEASUREMENTS
TAKEN DURING
DEMOLITION 1932

wind when the outer door is opened. This screen is known as "the speer."[1] In Scotland and in the north of England, it was known as a "hallan" or "halland." The screen across the lower end of large halls, such as those in the colleges of Oxford and Cambridge, was known as the "speer,"

[1] "Spere or scuw. *Scrineum, ventifuga.*" *Prompt. Parv.* "In vj bordis empt. pro j spure pro camera Domini." Bailiff's Roll, dated 1337, in *Bishop Hatfield's Survey* (Surtees Soc.), p. 203. In the same roll, "In factura j spere infra hostium coquine, 3*d.*"

and was intended as a protection against the wind. In the smaller houses of Cumberland the screen was known as a " sconce." In 1530 Palsgrave gives *buffet* as the French for " speer " in a hall. In the house we are describing a wooden bench is fixed against the inner side of the " speer," so as to form a seat. The top of the " speer " forms a large shelf for holding dishes, pots, and other things. These " speers " and benches are found in nearly all the oldest cottages on the west coast of Lancashire. Sometimes the door of a house is protected by wooden posts in front of it.[1] The mantelpiece, known in the West Riding of Yorkshire as " the aitch," extends across the whole width of the room. Upon it are displayed the pair of pot dogs so common in houses of this kind, and a number of small earthenware figures and statues. The chimney in such houses is rarely straight ; it usually leans considerably to one side, and this is often the case when the chimney-stack is outside the wall. From the " house-part " a door opens into a small " outshut " room known as the " buttery," where food and pots are kept, this room having originally had no windows. Another door opens into two small bedrooms on the ground floor, known as " chambers,"[2] the inner " chamber " being divided from the outer " chamber " by a brattice or wooden screen— anciently known as a parclose or enterclose—which extends about half-way up to the roof, and is not unlike the partition which divides cow-stalls from each other. Opposite the " speer " is another small " chamber." The floor of these " chambers " is made of clay,[3] as that of the " house-part " formerly was. The whole cottage was originally built of " clam staff and daub," there being no stone in the neighbourhood. Brick has, however, of late years been inserted in the place of the woodwork and clay, so that only a part of the original outer walls can now be seen. The present occupant can remember when this was done, and she also informed the author that she had seen men tread the clay

[1] " Stoulpe before a doore—*souche*."—PALSGRAVE, 1530.
[2] 1538. " One copborde next the chamber dore in the halle." —*Bury Wills* (Camden Soc.), p. 136.
[3] The floor of the old Norse hall was of clay. HENNING, *ut supra*, p. 156.

used for similar walls with their feet,[1] and mix it with the star grass which grows upon the sandhills in the neighbourhood. The cottage is thatched with rye straw, as is usual in the neighbourhood. It is whitewashed within as well as without, and is exquisitely neat and clean.

[During its recent demolition (August 1932) this cottage was examined by Mr. F. H. Cheetham, F.S.A., of Southport.[2] The outer walls of the greater part of the house had been entirely rebuilt in brick (9 in. thick) since 1900, though the roof had not been moved. *All* the brickwork appeared quite modern and the floors were tiled. The " clam-staff and daub " was examined and found to consist, not of clay with straw, but of " sea-slutch " or mud with straw. There is no clay in the immediate vicinity. The roof timbers appeared to have been wreckage picked up on the shore ; two of the longest were clearly a ship's mast split in two. The builder who demolished two other cottages at Westward informed Mr. Cheetham that most of the roof-timbers of these were also wreckage re-used. The wreckage may have been used in the construction of the cottages, or perhaps only for repairs.]

Our next example is at Burscough in Lancashire, about eight miles from North Meols. The illustration shows a very quaint cottage resembling in plan the cottage just described. But it is rather larger at one end, and has one little upper room, with a tiny window which may be seen peeping through the boards at the gable end. The way in which the roof slopes downwards at the gable ends will be noticed, Roofs like the one in the illustration are still common in Lancashire, and they are usually rounded off at the gables. This cottage at Burscough, with its fencing of stakes, may remind us of the cottage of the poor widow in Chaucer's tale :

> " A yerd sche had, enclosed al aboute
> With stikkes."[3]

---

[1] Mud for building (*lateum*) was usually carried by women or girls.—*Durham Household Book* (Surtees Soc.), p. 181.

[2] The reviser is indebted to Mr. Cheetham for much valuable information in connection with this chapter.

[3] *The Nonne Prestes Tale*, l. 27.

The " house-part " consists of a single bay of the usual
size " built on crucks," and without an upper story. Instead
of a " speer " there is a rude outer porch. On one side of
the fire-place is a large brick oven, with a flue leading into

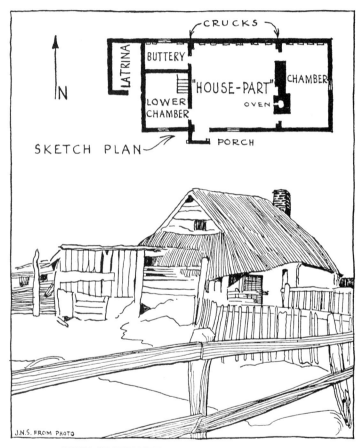

HOUSE AT BURSCOUGH, LANCS, NOW DESTROYED

the chimney of the fire-place. The oven projects about two
feet into the " chamber " behind the " house-part," and
would make that room warm. The chimney is of lath and
plaster. On the side opposite the fire-place are the " buttery " and a small " chamber," about seven feet square and

not quite six feet high. The buttery, as usual, is in the north-west corner. Over the " chamber " and the " buttery " is a small low " chamber."[1] The stairs are modern, and probably access to the upper room was formerly gained by a ladder, as is still the case in some small cottages. The wooden lintels of the inner doors are arched. Adjoining the " buttery," and under the roof which covers the cottage, is the *latrina*. The cottage was built of " clam-staff and daub," which still remains in a perfect state on the north side, but the walls have been strengthened by the addition or insertion of brick-work.

Our third example is a larger cottage or farm-house at North Meols.[2] It contains the usual central " house-part," which is " built on crucks," and the length of the bay, measured from the centre of one " cruck " to another, is 15 ft. 6 in. The " house-part " has no upper story, and is open to the roof. It contains the usual " speer." The top of the " speer " is in the same plane with the top of the mantel-piece, and the shelf of the mantel-piece is continued across the room on both sides. Annexed to the " speer " on the inner side is the usual wooden bench. A crooked beam is fixed to the side-trees in the roof, just over the fire-place. Such a beam seems to have been formerly known as a " perch," and was used to hang clothes on, as in the line :

" Pertica 'diversos pannos retinere solebat."[3]

These beams are found in many of the old cottages of West Lancashire. But often the fixed beam has been replaced by a clothes rail which can be moved up and down by a rope. The fire-place at the east end of the house is modern. This cottage differs chiefly from that at Burscough in having an upper chamber over both the end rooms, and two staircases. Two staircases were necessary because, as the " house-part "

[1] Compare " the ij chambrys with the soler above in the ende of the halle towarde my gardeyn."—Will, dated 1463, in *Bury Wills*.
[2] This cottage was disused in 1898 and has now disappeared.
[3] In WRIGHT's *Vocabularies*, p. 133. The author has never heard people call this beam the " perch."

is open to the roof,[1] there could be no communication on
the upper floor between the two upper chambers. Henning,[2]
quoting Eilert Sundt, says that some Norwegian houses have

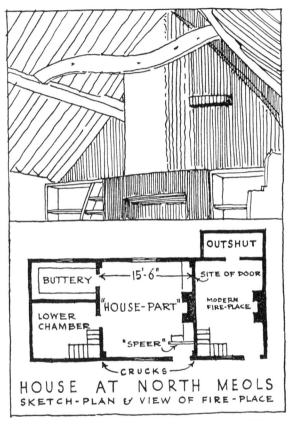

HOUSE AT NORTH MEOLS, LANCS, NOW DESTROYED

a similar arrangement of upper stories at the gable ends.
The smoke in the " house-part " could thus escape directly
through the roof, or the " house-part " could even be lighted
from the roof, as it was in the old Germanic house.

[1] Of the vicarage of Selborne, WHITE says, " According to the
manner of old times, the hall was open to the roof."—*Antiquities
of Selborne*, letter iv.
[2] HENNING, *ut supra*, p. 67.

The stairs are of later date than the rest of the building, and originally ladders may have been used instead. The oak shelves or benches of the " buttery " are of great thickness, as also are the posts on which they rest. The floor is of clay. Only the " house-part " is " built on crucks." Brick-work has taken the place of the original " clam-staff and daub," but a good specimen of the latter material is preserved in the small " outshut " on the north side. The house faces south, and the " buttery " is in the north-west corner.[1]

The oak used in the construction of these Lancashire houses is very roughly hewn. For the most part the wood displays all its natural crookedness, and is merely trimmed by the adze, or split by wedges.[2] In some houses the " lats " or laths are laced to the ribs or rafters by star grass. There is no stone in the neighbourhood of North Meols, the subsoil being sand, which is of a great depth. The walls which surround the fields are made of mud or sods, and timber must have been brought from a considerable distance in early times. In such a place one might expect to find many interesting examples of old houses, but they are rapidly passing away.[3]

Thornber speaks of them in his *History of Blackpool.* He says : " I might point out a few specimens of these houses, supported on crooks, and occasionally dignified with a porch : the interior dark, low, open to the smoky rafters, well stored with bacon, dried beef, etc., having a large open fire-place, over which a low, heavy, oaken beam ran across the room, forming a sort of canopy, beneath which was the family

---

[1] Compare the position of the pantry (*speisekammer*) and the lumber-room (*gerätkammer*) in an Anglo-Danish house in HENNING, p. 57.

[2] For *asseres* or spars of wood obtained by splitting (*laceratio*) see the glossary to the *Durham Household Book* (Surtees Soc.).

[3] It is difficult to determine the date of erection of the cottages at N. Meols. Mr. F. H. CHEETHAM is of the opinion that the system of building on crucks may have persisted in S.W. Lancashire well into, if not till the end of, the 18th century. N. Meols was a very isolated parish (between the mosses and the sea) until that time, and it is likely that archaic forms of building continued to be used there till a late date.—*Reviser's note.*

hearth. Opposite the fire-place were the chamber, pronounced ' chomer,' and the pantry ; so that the good housewife might overlook her store with readiness : nor was the ' speere,' or ' God-speed stoop ' wanting. The old ' kist ' (chest) of oak, dated wardrobe, and the door of the cupboard, opening in the wall, shone brightly, from the diligent care and labour of the polisher's hand."

The " house-part " of these cottages corresponds to the *megaron* of a primitive Greek house, the *megaron* being the kitchen and men's room of the family. It also corresponds to the *atrium*, or " house-place " of the Romans, that word being derived by some authorities from *ater*, black, on account of the blackened roof.[1] In Chaucer's time the " house-part," with its open hearth, must have been black enough, as in the tale told by the " Nonne Prest "—

" Full sooty was hir bour, and eek hir halle."

Although in most cases the " house-part " is in the centre of the old English cottage, it is sometimes found at one end of the building. Such is the case in a well-preserved house at Upper Midhope, near Penistone, which bears over its doorway the date 1671, though that is not necessarily the date when the wooden framework of the house was reared. This house is " built on crucks," in two bays, the fire-place at the end being outside the " crucks." The " crucks " are massive beams of oak whose bases rest on stone slabs, or stylobats. These slabs project about three inches from the outside walls. The original building consists of four rooms, two on the ground floor and two on the upper, and is unequally divided by a massive oak framework or wooden partition wall which extends from the floor to the roof. The " house-place," 7 ft. 2 in. high, is entered by a door adjoining the road. Here a portion of the oak framework is seen. It is highly polished, and against it is placed a heavy carved

---

[1] SMITH's *Dict. of Greek and Roman Antiq.*, i. 668. The suggested etymology is very doubtful. Compare the " inseat " of a Scotch farm-house.

oak table, with heavy carved benches to form seats. The largest bench is fastened to the oak framework which divides the building.[1] The other two benches are movable, and the

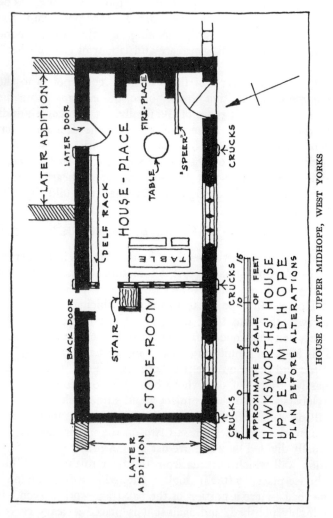

HOUSE AT UPPER MIDHOPE, WEST YORKS

HAWKSWORTHS' HOUSE
UPPER MIDHOPE
PLAN BEFORE ALTERATIONS

APPROXIMATE SCALE OF FEET

[1] Observe the frequent mention of benches on the walls of houses in HENNING, *ut supra*.

In Norway the table by the gable wall is called *langbord* and the bench *pall*, O.N. *pallr*. See HENNING, *ut supra*, p. 66.

Photo: John Summerson

Exterior of Hawksworth's house, Upper Midhope. The door between the windows is a recent insertion.

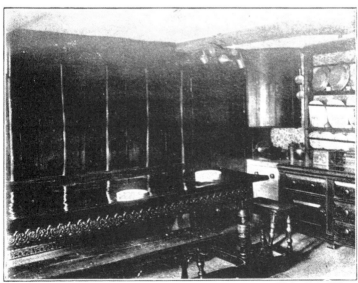

Photo: S. O. Addy

The " house-place " at Upper Midhope.

smaller of them can be put at the head of the table so as to form, when required, a seat in that position. This table and its benches are an original part of the building, for the table could not have been brought in either through the door or the windows. An identical arrangement of bench and table may still be seen in Norway.[1] At one end of the table is a doorway leading into the adjoining room, which is used as a pantry or buttery, and on the north wall next to this doorway is a delf-rack filled with bright pewter plates and dishes, and blue-and-white pottery. A pair of white wooden trenchers, which the family once used as dinner plates, will be noticed on the table shown in the illustration. They are made hollow on both sides, so that meat could be eaten on one side and pudding on the other. The trenchers are very neatly turned, and show no signs of the use of knife or fork, as though people had used their fingers only, as the custom once was.

The " house-place " contains a wide fire-place screened from the street door by a " speer." In one corner of the buttery is the wooden box or case which contains the stair leading into the two upper rooms, the stair being supported by a massive inclining beam. Opening the staircase door we see an almost perpendicular series of steps, arranged like the rungs of a ladder. The lowest step is of stone ; the rest are thick triangular blocks of oak, not fastened together in any way, but with open spaces between them. The first five steps are perpendicular, and the remaining steps incline slightly towards the top. A round oak hand-rail, as old as the stair itself, is fastened to the wooden wall, and by its help we can get into the two bedrooms above.[2] The stair leads straight to the bedroom floor, there being no lobby or

---

[1] See a plan in KEARY's *Norway and the Norwegians*, p. 43. Anciently it was known as a " table dormant," as in the Prologue to the *Canterbury Tales* ;—

> " His table dormant in his halle alway
> Stood redy covered al the longe day."

[2] A rope was often used for this purpose and WITHAL's *Dictionarie* (1616) gives, " The rope of the stare, *funis scansorius*, vel *ductorius*."

outer passage.[1] On one side the opening in the floor is protected by the framework which divides the house, and on the other side it is protected by an immense " ark," or meal chest. Otherwise the landing or stair head is unprotected, and there is nothing which would prevent a somnambulist sleeping in the outer bedroom from falling down to the bottom. In East Yorkshire the opening in the floor was protected by a trap-door known as a " trap hetch," or " throp hetch." In some old cottages the bedroom is still approached by a " stee " or ladder fastened by hooks to a hole in the chamber floor. This stair at Midhope is of no little interest, for it shows us the intermediate stage between the ladder and our modern stair with its " case." In Yorkshire the staircase is often called the " stair hole." In a house at Treeton in South Yorkshire the upper chamber was reached by a ladder which was set in a round well or hole cut in the thickness of the wall.[2]

The walls of this house at Midhope are two feet thick ; they are plastered, but are apparently built of stone. The floor is of stone.

Adjoining the west end is another room of later date, not shown in the plan, with a chamber above it. This does not communicate with the store-room, but is entered by an outside door. Now it is a workshop, but formerly it was the weaving-room. Here spinning and weaving were done for the use of the inmates, the surplus of the woven material being sold.[3] Such a room was formerly known as a " spinning house."[4] A range of buildings of later date is connected with the " house-place " by a door opening into it on the north side. In this neighbourhood houses " built on crucks " which had no upper rooms, but were open to the roof, are still remembered.

----

[1] 1556. " The lytyll chamber at the greisshedde. . . . The utter chamber at the gresse hed."—*Richmond Wills* (Surtees Soc.), p. 91. Old wills often mention the outer and inner chambers at the stairhead.

[2] Information by Mr. T. WINDER.

[3] Tradition among the occupants.

[4] 1463. " The dore that is out of the parlour into the spynning hous."—*Bury Wills* (Camden Soc.), p. 20.

In the plan of the house at Midhope it will be noticed that there is a round table near the fire. The use to which the tables in this house were put may be explained by a communication made to the author by an old Derbyshire farmer from the memories of his youth.

" The master of the house and his servants had dinner in one and the same room—the kitchen—a large apartment. The master and his family sat at a table near the fire, and the servants at a long table on the opposite side of the room. First the master carved for his family and himself, and then the joint was passed on to the servants' table. The head man presided over the servants' table, and always sat at the end of it, and at the opposite end sat a woman. The men sat next to the chair in order of seniority, and were very particular about keeping their proper places."[1]

At Midhope the farm servants still have their meals at the long table, the place of honour being the small round table near the fire.[2] It is remarkable that the Roman *villicus* dined with his farm labourers in the same way.[3]

[The above account of the cottage at Upper Midhope was written before the recent sale and alteration took place. A visit to the cottage in March 1932 disclosed the following facts about the later history of the building. In 1926 the property, which for generations had been in the hands of the Hawksworth family, was sold and the contents of the cottage dispersed. The table, which is said to have fetched £114, went to a Bradford dealer. Subsequently the cottage was considerably altered and re-let. The old staircase was removed and now serves as a hay-rack in a neighbouring out-building. A partition was put in, cutting off the west end of the house and forming an entrance-hall between itself and the old partition, approached through a new door-way

---

[1] In Iceland the seat at table marked a man's degree.—VIG-FUSSON and POWELL'S *Icelandic Reader*, p. 358.

[2] " In a corner or recess stood a round table, with its attendant carpet or cover of plain or raised work."—*Richmond Wills* (Surtees Soc.), p. xi.

[3] " Consuescatque rusticos circa larem domini, focumque familiarem semper epulari, atque ipse in conspectu eorum similiter epuletur."—COLUMELLA, xi. i. 19.

cut in the outside wall. The " speer " was removed and the original door-way, though not blocked up, is now disused.]

We have just seen that the common living-room, corresponding to the Roman *atrium* or the Greek *megaron*, is called " the house-place," " the house-part," and " the house." It was also called " the hall," " the hall-house," and " the fire-house." The best and possibly the oldest of these names was " fire-house "—the *eld-hús* of the Norsemen. The room which usually contained the only fire in the building, and which gave warmth to its inmates by day and night, may well have been called " the house," as an abbreviation of " fire-house." In 1392 the Prioress of Nun Monkton took a lease of property at Nun Stainton and in it covenanted to repair the buildings of the messuage, viz., " a house called the fire-house, containing five couples of syles and two gavelforks, a storehouse for grain containing three couples of syles and two gavelforks, and another storehouse for grain containing one couple of syles and two gavelforks, a little house to the west of the said fire-house containing three couples of syles and two gavelforks."[1]

It is probable that the fire-house and the " little house " were contiguous, so that the fire-house was the hall, and the " little house " the bower[2] or women's side of the house, a division to which we shall have occasion to refer again. The identity of hall and fire-house can be proved from a document of the seventeenth century.[3] In the sixteenth century the word fire-house was also used as a synonym for the better

---

[1] " Omnia ædificia dicti messuagii, videlicet, unam domum, vocatam le Fire-house, continentem quinque coples de syles et duo gavelforkes, unam grangeam continentem tres coples de syles et duo gavelforkes, et unam aliam grangeam, (continentem) unum copille de syles et duo gavelforkes, unam parvam domum ex parte occidentali dicti Fyrehouse, continentem tres coples de syles et duo gavelforkes."—*Feodarium Prioratus Dunelm* (Surtees Soc.), p. 167.

[2] " Bow'r, back room without a fireplace."—Glossary to JOLLIE, *Cumberland Manners*, 1811.

[3] 1632. " The Hall or Fier-house of the nowe mansion house of the said John Parker, etc., with the entry leading into the same." —*Derb. Arch. Journal*, v. p. 45.

Photo: S. O. Addy

Stair at Upper Midhope (now removed).

kind of dwelling-house.[1] In the eleventh century an apartment with a chimney was known as *caminata* or *caminatum*, and an English vocabulary of that period explains the word as " fyrhus," i.e. a room containing a fire. In old German the room was known as *kemenate*. In old Frisian the whole house is called *herthstede*, and this is rendered in the Latin text of old Frisian laws as *laris locus* and even *laris domus*. In larger country houses the fire-house or hall was often in the centre of the building, with the women's apartments consisting of the " chamber " and buttery at one end and a barn or combined barn and ox-house at the other.[2] The main entrance to the building was a passage which divided the " fire-house " from the ox-house or barn, and which was the threshing-floor. This passage was known by various names. Anciently it was called the " floor "[3] or the " threshold," a word which means " threshing-floor," because in ancient times the floor at the entrance was for threshing.[4] It was sometimes called the " entry." Doors opened out of this passage both into the " fire-house " and into the barn or ox-house. Where there was no barn or ox-house the " fire-house " sometimes formed one end of the building ; and where there was no barn or ox-house there was no " entry " or threshold, but the door opened straight into the " fire-house," and, as we have seen, was screened by a " speer."[5]

[1] 1532. " I witto every hows within the parisheing of Acclome whar os fyer is dailly used, xiijd."—*Test. Ebor.* (Surtees Soc.), v. p. 291. 1542. " The fyer-howse that Foxe wyffe off Ulverston dwellithe in."—*Richmond Wills* (Surtees Soc.), p. 32.

[2] WRIGHT in his *Homes of Other Days*, 1871, p. 141, says that in the twelfth century the chamber was at one end, the hall, open to the roof, in the middle, and a *croiche* or stable at the other end. There was a doorway between the hall and *croiche*. His opinion was founded on statements in old French romance writers.

[3] " *Excussorium*, flor on huse."—WRIGHT-WÜLCKER, *Vocabularies*, 126, 5.

[4] VIGFUSSON's *Icelandic Dictionary*, s.v. þreskjöldr. In South Yorkshire the threshold is called the " threskeld," or sometimes " threskill." In Derbyshire it is the " threshel " and the " threskut."

[5] At Fulham in 1428 the widow of a customary tenant was to have for the rest of her life " mansionem suam in una camera ima ad finem orientem domus vocate le Ferehows cum Feer et Flet in

F

There were usually separate doors at the free end of the ox-house for the admission of the oxen. A very large number of English farm-houses still exist in which the dwelling-house, barn, and stables are combined under one and the same roof. But it is now a rare thing to find a communication between the threshing-floor and the dwelling-house. What is generally seen in these days is a long row of old buildings divided transversely by a barn floor, or entry, at one end of which is a small " winnowing door," and at the other a large barn door, or a pair of folding doors. In these buildings the barn floor forms a dividing line between the dwelling-house and the barn, or the combined barn and cow-house.

The arrangement of these houses corresponds to the arrangement of an old Norse house. There are, says an old Norse law book, three apartments in every man's dwelling. The first is the women's apartment or " chamber " (*stofa*), the second is the fire-house, i.e. the house-place or hall, the third is the pantry or buttery (*búr*), where women make the food ready.[1] At a later period the *stofa*, which is the German *stube*, lost its distinctive character as a woman's apartment, and became the " parlour." The simplest form of German house consisted of the *flur* or hearth-room and the separate and smaller *stube*. The *stube* eventually became the more important apartment of the two, but, as Henning remarks, " the further back we go the more significant becomes

eadem."—Court Rolls in Public Record Office, 188/70. It is interesting to compare this " camera ima " or chamber on the ground floor in the east with similar " chambers " *ante*, pp. 71, 73. Compare also " kammer für den ·leibzüchter " in HENNING, *ut supra*, p. 33, and " die stube des Altsitzers," *ibid*. p. 81, and elsewhere. The word *flet* or *fletze* (O.H.G. *flazzi* or *flezzi*) formerly meant the whole living-room of a German ˉhouse, but later the meaning became restricted to a vestibule.

[1] Eitt er stofa, annat eldhus, et iii. bur þat er konor hafa matreiþo i."—*Grágás*, ed. SCHLEGEL, i. 459. In the *Sturlunga Saga* the *stofa* is distinguished from the *skáli*, or men's hall. Compare the threefold division of the gardener's and physician's houses in the plans for the monastery of St. Gall (A.D. 820) in HENNING, *ut supra*, p. 143. In these, and in the three-roomed houses mentioned in the Capitularies of Charles the Great, HENNING recognizes a Carolingian type.

the *flur* and the more subsidiary the *stube*." The fire-house, the chamber or women's apartment, and the buttery are well illustrated in the Lancashire houses described in this chapter. A good example of the entry or " threshold," paved with stone, and dividing the fire-house, chamber and buttery from a small barn, may be seen in a long, ruined farm-house at Fulwood, near Sheffield. Here the barn floor was the " threshold " in the true sense of the word, for it was at once the threshing-floor and the main entrance to the building. At one end of the " threshold " is the large barn door, and at the other the " winnowing door." From the " threshold " a doorway leads into the house-place or " fire-house." The hearth of the " fire-house " adjoins the " threshold " wall.

Some years ago there was a combined house and barn at Hornsea, in East Yorkshire. The barn was built of mud, and had the usual " winnowing door," and a pair of barn doors on the other side. The two doorways had round arches. The only way into the house was across the barn floor. The house consisted of two lower rooms, with two chambers over them. The room next to the barn floor was the " house-place," and the hearth, as in the house at Fulwood, stood against the wall which divided the barn from the house. The barn floor was a little below the level of the house floor, and one or two steps led up into the " house-place." The fire-place was open, and the fire burnt on a square brandreth, supported by four legs, the embers lying on flat pieces of iron about as wide as the " strakes " of a cartwheel.[1]

According to Valtýr Gudmundsson the typical old Norse house was a long building with the *búr*, or store-room, at one end, and the *stofa*, or women's room, at the other, the *skáli*, or fire-house, being in the middle.[2] This, as we have seen, is the form taken by the houses at Westward and Burscough already described. It will, however, be readily understood that when the ox-house in an English dwelling

---

[1] Information by JAMES RUSSELL of Hornsea, aged 84. Compare " plate, of a fyyr herthe. *Lamina repocilium.*"—*Prompt. Parv.*, p. 403.
[2] *Privatboligen paa Island i sa atiden, samt delvis i dat övrige, Norden*, Köbenhavn, 1889, p. 76 ; MEITZEN, *Wanderungen, Anbau, und Agrarrecht, etc.*, Berlin, 1895, iii. 491.

was placed at one end of the fire-house, and the women's apartments and store-room were placed at the other, these last-mentioned rooms would be readily included under one name.[1]

In Ireland the length of the houses occupied by the different ranks of *aires*, or landowners, was fixed by the ancient laws. The following are the lengths of the " houses " and of the store-rooms of the eight respective classes of these landowners[2] :—

No.	Length of " House."	Length of Store-room.
1	19 feet	13 feet
2	20 ,,	14 ,,
3	27 ,,	15 ,,
4	(Not given)	(Not given)
5	27 feet	12 feet
6	27 ,,	" A proper store-house "
7	29 ,,	19 feet
8	30 ,,	20 ,,

The first two sizes of " house " correspond to the size of the booth near Horncastle already described. It is possible that each of the remaining six " houses " was divided into two " bays," one for men and the other for women. If so, these last-named dwellings were composed, like the houses of the ancient Norsemen, of three parts, viz. (1) a room for men, (2) a room for women, and (3) a store-room.

[1] For the identity of chamber and kitchen see Richthofen, quoted in HENNING, *ut supra*, p. 133. The old Frisian laws have no separate word for kitchen.

[2] Tabulated from O'CURRY'S *Manners and Customs of the Ancient Irish*, iii. 26 *et seq.*

CHAPTER IV

THE LARGER RECTANGULAR HOUSE WITH AISLES

The " winter house "—The length of the bay fixed by
the space required for four oxen—The modern English
cow-stall corresponds to the Roman ox-stall—Statements
of Vitruvius and Palladius about ox-stalls—The " perch "
was an architectural as well as a land measure—The combined house and " shippon "—Great width of farm buildings which contain aisles—The *camera*, or *kell* annexed to
the Welsh *bostar* or " shippon "—Farm building at
Bolsterstone built on " crucks," with an aisle—Combined
houses and " shippons " in the sixteenth century—
Harrison's statement in 1577—Pigs and cows in London
houses in the fourteenth century—Oblong houses with
aisles in Ireland and Wales—Sleeping in the hall.

WE have already seen that the Welsh " summer
house " consisted of a single room. But the
" winter house," as it was called, or permanent
abode in the valley, consisted of several bays joined together
in a line. It was more substantially built than the " summer
house," for whilst the " summer house " was only regarded
as worth twelve pence, the " winter house " was estimated
at the rate of twenty pence for every " fork " that it contained.[1] Sometimes the " winter house " had upright columns (*columnae*),[2] and it then appears to have been built in
the basilical form, or with a central nave and aisles.

We have also seen that sixteen feet, or a little more or less,
measured in the direction of the long axis of the building,
was the length of the bay. So widespread and uniform was
the practice of building in bays of a fixed length that it cannot
have had an arbitrary origin. There must have been a reason
for it, and before we can understand the construction of our
larger and older dwellings it will be necessary to ascertain
what that reason was.

We shall find that the length of the bay was determined

---

[1] *Leges Wallice (Ancient Laws, etc.)*, ii. 802. And see also p. 864
for the value of the roof.

[2] *Ibid.*, ii. p. 863.

by the space required for the accommodation of two pairs of oxen. And inasmuch as the " shippon " or ox-house frequently was, together with the barn, under the same roof as, and in a line with, the dwelling-house, the practice arose of making all the bays, whether of the " shippon," the barn, or the dwelling-house, of uniform length. Let us examine the evidence on which this statement rests.

To begin our proofs with modern times, it is well known that English farmers regard a width of 7 ft. as the minimum amount of standing space necessary for a pair of cows. " When stalls are put up," says a writer on farming, " they seldom exceed 4 ft. in width ; more frequently two oxen are put into a double stall of 7 ft."[1] Taking 7 ft. as the space required for a pair of oxen we get the width of the stall, exclusive of partitions, as 14 ft. Taking 8 ft. as the full space required we get the width, exclusive of partitions, as 16 ft. In either case we have to add something for the width of partitions. Vitruvius, who is said to have written about 10 B.C., says that "the breadth of ox-stalls should not be less than 10 ft.[2] or more than 15 ft. As regards length, the standing room for each pair of oxen should not be less than 7 ft."[3]

Palladius, whose work is ascribed to about A.D. 210, says " 8 ft. are more than sufficient standing room for each pair of oxen, and 15 ft. for the breadth [of the ox-house]."[4]

Now we have seen from these two writers that whilst the breadth of the Roman ox-house varied from 10 ft. to 15 ft., its length was determined by the space required for each pair of oxen, viz., from 7 ft. to 8 ft. This is exactly analogous to the English practice ; for whilst the length of the English

---

[1] STEPHENS, *Book of the Farm*, 1855, vol. i. p. 254.

[2] The breadth of a cow-house at Bolsterstone, described hereafter is 10 ft. 8 in.

[3] " Bubilium autem debent esse latitudines nec minores pedum denum, nec majores quindenum. Longitudo, uti singula iuga, ne minus occupent pedes septenos."—*De Architectura*, 6. 9. See also COLUMELLA, 1. 6. 6. This author fixes the breadth at 10 or at least 9, feet.

[4] " Octo pedes ad spatium standi singulis boum paribus abundant, et in porrectione xv."—*De R. R.*, 1. 21 *Porrectio*, " extension," must mean " breadth " here.

bay is rigidly fixed in farm buildings by the standing room required for two pairs of oxen,[1] considerable variation occurs in the breadth of the ox-stall. In the thirteenth century English buildings were measured by the linear perch of 16 ft. Thus " the great barn of Walton was 10½ perches in length (a perch being 16 ft.) and 3 perches and 5 ft. in breadth."[2] Another barn was 64 ft., or exactly 4 perches in length.[3] Now if we turn to land measures we find that the linear rod or perch is now 16½ ft., as it was in the year 1222,[4] a rod of this length being still used for measuring purposes by builders.

It appears from an old German book on surveying that the linear perch or rood was the unit of measurement. The way in which this length was determined is very curious. " To find the length of a rood in the right and lawful way, and according to scientific usage, you shall do as follows :— Stand at the door of a church on a Sunday and bid sixteen men to stop, tall ones and small ones, as they happen to pass out when the service is finished ; then make them put their left feet one behind the other, and the length thus obtained shall be a right and lawful rood to measure and survey the land with, and the sixteenth part of it shall be a right and lawful foot."[5] In the measurement of English land the perch was also the unit. For, says an old writer on surveying, " when ye measure any parcell of land, ye should painfullye multiply the breadth of the perches thereof with the length of the perches of the same."[6]

---

[1] Compare *Chron. Monast. de Melsa*, 1396–9 (Rolls Series), iii. 242. " In vaccaria insuper de Felsa unam novam domum vaccariae, lxxx pedum in longitudine, fecit de novo aedificari." This was exactly 5 bays of 16 ft. each. On the next page we read of a berchary 160 ft., i.e. 10 bays, in length.

[2] " Magnum orreum Walentonie habet x. perticas et dimid' in longitudine (et pertica est de xvi. pedibus) et in latitudine iii. perticas et v. pedes."—*Domesday of St. Paul's* (Camden Soc.), p. 130.

[3] " Apud Torpeiam est orreum, habens lxiv. pedes in logitud'."—*Domesday of St. Paul's* (Camden Soc.), p. 131.

[4] *Ibid.*, p. 92.

[5] Jacob Koebel's *Geometrei*, Frankfurt, 1556. *Notes and Queries*, 9th S. i. 306.

[6] Valentin Ligh's *Surveying*, 1592. (Table at the end.)

If we ask ourselves how it was that the perch became the unit we shall see that it was so because 16 ft. was the standing-room required for four oxen in the stall, and also the standing-room for four oxen in the field, inasmuch as they ploughed four abreast. Accordingly the length of the bay, viz. 16 ft., corresponds to the breadth of a rod or rood of land, the acre being composed of four roods, each 16 ft. broad and 640 ft long, lying side by side. This was the origin of the bay, as well as of the normal width of a rood of land.[1]

The testimony of the Welsh laws supports this theory, for they state that there were 8 ft. in the field yoke and 16 ft. in the long yoke.[2] They also speak of " a rod, equal in length to that of the long yoke, in the hand of the driver."[3]

To what extent the normal length of bay was carried into great buildings, such as churches, remains to be determined. An inquiry on this point would be curious and interesting, but no opinion on it can be given here. The author has measured the bays of the great Roman building lately found in Bailgate, on the west side of Lincoln Cathedral, and found them, when measured from the centre of each pillar, 14 ft. 6 in. apart. He has also measured the bays of a few churches and found them about fifteen feet apart. In cathedrals they are much wider.

We are now in a position to describe a " coit," or combined dwelling-house and " shippon," which may be taken as a type of the kind of dwelling described in the Welsh laws as a " winter house." The example chosen is in the basilical form, and is built in bays of approximately fifteen feet in length. It is plain enough to look at, but it forms a striking illustration of our subject.

At Rushy Lee,[4] about a mile from the house at Midhope

---

[1] The Romans measured their land by the *decempeda* or ten-foot rod. The *actus*, however, was four feet wide, and this, on the English system, was the full standing-room of a single ox. Strictly the English *land* measure is 16½, and not 16, feet.

[2] *Leges Wallice*, i. 187. See also ii. 784, where we read, " Sexdecim pedes et dimidium iugum faciunt longum, id est, hyryeu," and also ii. 852, " Pedes xv. et dimidium faciunt longum jugum."

[3] *Ibid.*

[4] The site is now covered by the Langsett Reservoir.—*Reviser's note.*

Building on crucks at Langsett, West Yorks., in process of demolition. The outshot or aisle is probably an addition to the original construction.

described in the last chapter, is one of those rather numerous buildings known in Yorkshire as " coits."[1] In the plan will be seen a building with a small dwelling-house at one end of it. The main part of the building on the north side, with the larger door, is the " shippon." This contains the cow-

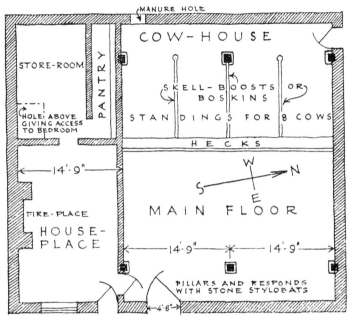

Plan of a " coit," formerly existing at Rushy Lee, Upper Midhope, West Yorks

stalls and a large " fodderum," or storehouse for hay or other food, from which the cows were fed. The larger door, 6 ft. high and 4 ft. 8 in. wide, is the main entrance to the building, and the " shippon " can be entered from an inner door in the house. The plan will show the arrangement of the building and the relative size of its divisions. Its length is 44, and its breadth 37 ft. Four cows stood between each

[1] Combined houses and barns of small size, and forming dependencies of a larger farm-house or " capital messuage," are known on the Yorkshire wolds as " barns." Each of these buildings is, or was, occupied by a " hind." The house is divided from the barn by a wooden screen.

pair of wooden pillars, two in a stall. The stalls are separated
from each other by wooden partitions called " skell-boosts."[1]
The cows entered by a separate door at the end, and stood
with their heads to the east or towards the centre of the
building, and they were fed from the " hecks " inside. Thus,
during the snows of winter, the occupier of the " coit " had
only to open the inner door of his house, go into the " shippon," and throw hay from the floor into the " hecks."[2] His
house can hardly have been a cheerful place to live in. It
contains a single bedroom approached by a ladder in the
inner and smaller room, with a window looking out at the end
of the building. The interior walls of the house are coloured
throughout by " archil," as is usual in the neighbourhood—
a cold, bright blue. Many of these " coits " have only one
aisle. A house in Bradfield called Half Hall seems to have
derived its name from the fact that it had only one aisle.[3]

The building consists, like a church, of a nave and aisles,[4]
the house at the end corresponding, as it were, to the chancel.
The plan shows the position of the pillars which support
the roof, and which divide the nave from the aisles. Each
pillar rests on a stone stylobat or block of stone. There are
three bays, the one in the south forming the house. There
are no wooden pillars or responds in the wall next to the
fire-place. Altogether there are four wooden pillars, with
two wooden responds in the north wall. The space between
pillar and pillar, measured in the direction of the length of
the building, or in other words the length of each bay, is
14 ft. 9 in., which is exactly the distance between the

[1] Compare *skeeling*, for which BAILEY's *Dictionary* (1726) gives
" an isle or bay of a barn, *Suff.*" See also p. 199 *post.*
For *boost* see under *banse* in KLUGE (*ut supra*), who gives A.S.
bôs, O.N. *bâss*, Engl. dial. *boose*, meaning a cow-stall, as well as
Engl. dial. *boosy*, meaning beast-trough.
[2] JORNANDES (c. 2), speaking of the Bretons, mentions that they
" virgeas habitant casas, communia tecta cum pecore."
[3] Aisles or partitions on one side only were common in ancient
times. See HENNING, *ut supra*, p. 110, who refers to a passage in
Galen.
[4] 1519. " Unum magnum orrium. Lez hiles standis stayd w[t]
proppes haldyng up ye pannes."—*York Fabric Rolls* (Surtees Soc.),
p. 271. Here the barn was out of repair.

" crucks " in the house at Midhope already described. The building is about twenty yards from a brook, and there are no other buildings near.

J.N.S. MARCH 1932

BARN AT
GRINDLEFORD
DERBYSHIRE

SECTION

FACE OF FRAME ABOUT 9"
BACK FROM WALL-FACE

JAMBS 5" DEEP AT
THICKEST PARTS

INCHES 12 6 0   1   2   3   4   5   6 FEET

Winnowing door and section of a barn at Grindleford

" Coits " of a similar kind may still be found in the wilder parts of Yorkshire. Usually they have an aisle on one or both sides, and therefore present a great extent of sloping roof, so that their breadth is often nearly as great as their length. The side walls are always about a man's height, and the doors in such walls go up to the eaves. There is always a door in one of the side walls which forms the chief entrance to the building, and there may be one or two other smaller doors. This combination of house and " shippon " is not always built in the form of nave and aisles ; sometimes there is a nave without aisles, and the building is then usually " built on crucks." The shell of a stone building of this latter kind exists at Grindleford in Derbyshire. Here there was a " shippon " with a house at one end of it. The inside partitions have been removed, but the windows of the house, now built up, still remain *in situ*. The main entrance is by a doorway containing an old semicircular wooden arch, shown in the illustration, opposite a pair of folding barn doors. [Visited in March 1932, this building was found to be in good condition. It stands not far from Grindleford Station on the left of the road leading to Eyam. It now consists of two and a half bays, but the plinth-stones appear to extend further in the direction of the half-bay, and it is possible that the building was formerly of three whole bays but that one end has been rebuilt. The old door-frame has a slight rebate on the inner side to take a door of semicircular shape. The walls are about 2 ft. 6 in. thick.]

The house at the end of the " coit," which corresponds, as it were, to the chancel of the building, seems to be identical with that part of the dwelling mentioned in the Welsh laws as the *camera* or *kell*, the value of which was the same as that of the *bostar* or "shippon."[1] *Kell* is cell," and this word is said to be a doublet from the same root as " hall."[2]

We know from forms which have survived to this day that the nave which was supported by " forks " or " crucks," instead of by upright pillars, had sometimes one or more aisles. Examples of this sort of construction are rare, but they are still to be found in old farm buildings. The nave

[1] " [Pretium] camere ante frontem domus xxxᵃ denarii."—*Leges Wallice* (*Ancient Laws, etc.*), ii. 803. " Kell [camera] ante frontem domus, xxx denarii."—*Ibid.*, p. 864. " Bostar uel bouiale, scipen." —Wright-Wülcker, *Vocab.*, 185, 5.
[2] Skeat, *Etym. Dict.*

of a barn at Bolsterstone in South Yorkshire, consisting of four " bays," is supported by " crucks " of the usual kind, extending down to the ground, and resting on stone bases. The inside width of the nave is 19 ft., and the length of each " bay," measured from the centres of the " crucks," is exactly 15 ft. The span of the " crucks " is from 16 to 18 ft. On the south side of the building two contiguous bays are extended outwardly[1] by means of an elaborate and massive framework shown in the section.[2] This extension of aisle forms an ox-house 30 ft. in length, and, measured from the feet of the " crucks," 10 ft. 8 in. in width. In the ox-house there is room for eight oxen and no more. Four oxen stood in a bay, a length of nearly fifteen feet, two in each stall. Now in this case it is obvious that each bay was intended to give the exact accommodation required for two pairs of oxen. As usual, the oxen faced inwards, and were fed from the main floor. Rather more than six feet above the ground floor of the ox-house are the remains of an upper floor, showing that there was a loft or gallery above.[3] The oxen entered by a door in the east end of the " aisle." To the west of the four " bays " which formed the original building is some newer work which bears the date 1688 in two places. At the west end is the inscription, " William Couedell : Sarah his wife," and over one of the dates the letters $^C_{WS}$. At right angles to the ox-house are some ox-stalls in the newer part of the building. These face the old main floor, and the oxen in them were fed from that floor. The barn doors are, as usual, on the opposite sides of the nave, and the threshing-floor between them, paved with stone, occupies the whole of the second bay from the east. It is impossible to fix the date of the older part of the building. The walls are of stone, which is plentiful in the neighbourhood, and they are built without mortar. The building here described should be carefully compared with the description of the Saterlander's house on page 101. [The Green is now

---

[1] The author has a deed, dated 1617, which relates to a cottage (*cotagium*) at Crookes, near Sheffield, containing " duas baias structure ex se." Compare the " little bays " *ante*, p. 33.
[2] Copied from a drawing by Mr. THOMAS WINDER.
[3] Compare the Saterlander's building, *postea*.

in the parish of Stocksbridge. The barn was visited in March 1932 and found to be in good condition.]

Buildings like this were not always slated with stone, though farm buildings were so slated at an early period. The great wooden framework was often completed by an interlacing of twigs, and then roofed with turf or moss.[1] Vertical holes near the feet of the " crucks " will be noticed

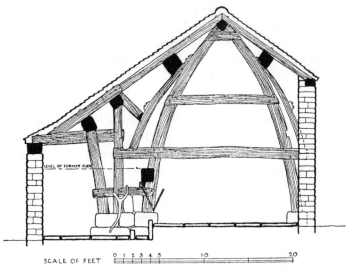

SCALE OF FEET   0 1 2 3 4 5   10   20

Section of a barn at the Green, near Stocksbridge, West Yorks

in the drawing. Such holes are usually found in these timbers. What they were for is unknown, but builders think that they were used for lifting or carrying the wooden framework. If so they would hold the ends of " levers " or lifters. Cow-houses in barns were frequent,[2] and they usually formed aisles.

We have historical evidence that in 1577 there were in the north parts of England buildings which enclosed the

[1] 1586. " Item payd to Nicholas Atkinson and Wm [Turner] for mossing ij bayes and bygging j baye with wrastlers at Sheffield mannor let to them by great, iijs. iiijd."—*MS. Steward's Accounts of Sheffield Manor.* " Wreston', plecto."—*Prompt. Parv.*

[2] 1605. " The payver, iij days payvinge both the cowhouses in the new barne, xijd."—*Shuttleworth Accounts* (Chetham Soc.), p. 170.

house and other offices under a common roof. According to William Harrison " the mansion houses of our countrie townes and villages (which in champaine ground stand altogither by streets, and ioining one to an other, but in woodland soiles dispersed here and there, each one vpon the seuerall grounds of their owners) are builded in such sort generallie, as that they haue neither dairie, stable, nor bruehouse annexed vnto them vnder the same roofe (as in manie places beyond the sea and some of the north parts of our countrie), but all separate from the first, and one of them from an other. And yet for all this, they are not so farre distant in sunder, but that the goodman lieng in his bed may lightlie hear what is doone in each of them with ease, and call quickly unto his meinie[1] if any danger should attach him."[2] Notice should be taken of the last sentence of this quotation, for we shall see further on how the " goodman " or *hausherr* in Frisian and Saxon houses " from the hearth and from his bedstead can superintend the whole management of the household, and hear every sound." In these still-existing Frisian and Saxon houses the master and his family sleep under the same roof as the cattle in one common building. We should take particular notice that Harrison speaks of houses " beyond the sea," as well as in " some of the north parts of our country," in which men and cattle occupied the same building.

Before the year 1419 there were people in London who kept pigs and cows in their houses, for the practice was forbidden by an order of the civic authority made in that year.[3] One still occasionally hears of pigs being kept in English houses.

In Ireland the oblong house was divided, " in the direction of its length, into three parts by two rows of pillars, which supported the roof," the fire being placed in the central division.[4] The large Welsh house was built in the same

---

[1] Household or family.
[2] HARRISON's *England*, ed. Furnivall, pp. 233, 237.
[3] RILEY, *Munimenta Gild. Lond.*, i. p. 335.
[4] SULLIVAN's Introduction to O'CURRY's *Manners and Customs of the Ancient Irish*, p. cccxlvi.

way, with beds of rushes along the aisles and the fire-place in the nave.[1] Aubrey, writing in 1678, says that in English houses " the beds of the men-servants and retainers were in the hall, as now in the grand or privy chamber."[2] Aubrey's recollections only apply to men-servants and retainers. But there was a time when the entire family lived and slept in one room, though the men and women were separated. This custom was common not only to the English, Welsh, and Irish, but also to the Germans and Scandinavians. " When night came, straw, dried rushes, heath, or dried ferns were spread upon the floor ; and those unprovided with beds or couches laid themselves down, each under the bench or table upon or at which he or she sat."[3] It is probable that in many houses the men slept over the cattle stalls in one aisle, and the women over the cattle stalls in the other.

In Denmark, according to Henning,[4] " three-naved " buildings were usual, and he explains this by the fact that the whole of the inner room was lighted by a hole in the roof : aisles could thus be added without blocking out the light. But this explanation admits of doubt.

[1] Seebohm's *Village Community*, p. 239.
[2] In Hone's *Table Book*, i. 391.
[3] Sullivan, *ut supra*, p. cccliii.
[4] *Ut supra*, p. 128.

CHAPTER V

FOREIGN PROTOTYPES : STATEMENTS OF ANCIENT WRITERS

Frisian and Saxon houses—Beds in English ox-houses—
The " balk "—Main difference between the German and
the English farm-house—The Roman country house compared to the Germanic—Horses not to face the fire in
Roman farm buildings—The typical farm-house in Schleswig, Hanover, and Westphalia—Galen's description of
the Greek peasant's house—The *aedificia* which Cæsar
saw in England—German houses in the time of Tacitus.

AS we are closely akin both in blood and language to
the Frisians and Saxons, it is fair to suppose that
the early forms of our houses resembled theirs. The
combination of house and " shippon " which we have just
described is found to this day in Friesland and Saxony in
an older and more elaborate form than with us. A German
writer shall describe one of such combinations :—

" Its chief characteristic is that it unites in one body the
space necessary for a very considerable establishment under
one and the same roof, and therefore represents an extremely
large building. Its ground plan is that of a basilica with nave
and aisles. The middle always forms the so-called ' floor '
(*diele*) (*a*), which is entered at the gable end through a large
gate, and which goes through the whole house as far as the
dwelling-rooms at the end. Owing to the want of an exit
this floor is used for backing wagons out. . . . In the forms
of the Frisian and Saxon house generally in use the horses
(*b*) and cows (*c*) are always so placed on both sides of the
' floor ' that they are foddered from it. Over the ' floor,'
over the cattle stalls, and over all the other rooms up to the
ridge of the roof the corn harvest and hay harvest are stored
on boards and poles laid between the joists. In the Saxon
house (Figs. 1 and 2) the back ground of the ' floor ' ends
in a low hearth (*d*), on both sides of which are the bedsteads
of the family arranged in a kind of narrow and rather high
cupboards, whilst over against them, and near them, the

men-servants sleep over the horses, and the maids over the cows. To the right and left of the hearth extends the space used for the household, which is uninterrupted as far as the two opposite side walls of the house. This part of the house is lighted by high and broad windows, and on either side a glass door forms an exit into the open air. Usually, too, the well is inside the house at the side of the hearth.[1]

Thus the master of the house can superintend the whole

FIG. I

FROM MEITZEN'S "DAS DEUTSCHE HAUS"

FIG. 2

A SAXON HOUSE

management of the household from the hearth and his bed-stead, and hear every sound. So he exercises the fullest supervision, and so long as the smoke of the great hearth fire, which had no chimney, permeated the whole building, insects and the bad stench of the cattle were driven away, so that not till the most recent times was the need felt for building additional rooms behind the hearth-wall (*heerd-wand*). Of these rooms, shown in Fig. 2, *f* is usually the best room, *h* a living-room, and *g* a store-room, kept dry by the fire on the hearth."[2]

The above passage treats of the Frisian and Saxon houses

[1] There are wells in some English houses and castles. Usually the well is 4 or 5 feet from the threshold or entrance.

[2] MEITZEN, *Das deutsche Haus*, p. 10. In the plan are also seen two "chambers"; the pigsty and calf-house are near the entrance.

as if they were identical in type. Henning,[1] however, points
to a radical difference between them. The central feature
of Saxon planning was the provision of a great covered space
for cattle. The Frisian house, on the other hand, was
primarily a structure to protect the fruits of the harvest.
Hence the long, low lines of the Saxon house and the higher,
bulkier forms of the Frisian.

People are still living who remember how farmers' men-
servants in England used to sleep on the hay in a gallery or
hay-loft over the cows. Some of them have been known to
sleep there for a year together. It is said that they often
did so to save money to be spent in drink! When Irish
labourers came over in the autumn to assist in getting the
harvest in they usually slept on the hay or straw in the barn
or in the " balk." In the sixteenth century ox-houses in
Yorkshire still contained beds, blankets, sheets, mattresses,
pillows, bolsters, and happings, or coarse coverlets.[2] As no
bedsteads are mentioned, we may presume that the mattresses were laid on the floor of the loft over the ox-stalls.

It appears from a passage in Ovid that Roman husband-
men sometimes lived in stables or ox-houses.[3]

In Saterland, in Oldenburg, are buildings, said to be of
the sixteenth century or a little earlier, which have the dwelling-house, cattle stalls and store-rooms under the same roof.
The side walls are so low that the thatch reaches nearly to
the ground. The walls are made of timber framework filled
in with bricks, or, in the smaller houses, with wattles and
mud. They are thatched with straw and heather. There are
upright pillars (Fig. 2, *a*) with beams (Fig. 2, *b*) stretched

[1] *Die Deutschen Haustypen*, p. 1.
[2] 1556. " In the oxen housse viij coverletts, iij blanketts,
xiijs. iiijd."—*Richmond Wills* (Surtees Soc.), p. 92.
1567. " Servannts bedes in the oxhousse, iiijs. iiijd."—*Ibid.*,
p. 203.
1567. " The oxe howse. One mattres with a happin, ijs., ij
codds with a window clothe, xijd. One pare of shetes, xijd.
Summa iiijs."—*Ibid.*, p. 209.
1569. " In the cowe house, iij olde coverlets, a paire blanckets,
a paire sheits, a matteras, and a bolstar, xs."—*Ibid.*, p. 218.
[3] " In stabulis habitasse, boves, pavisse, nocebat,
Iugeraque inculti pauca tenere soli."—*Fasti*, iii. 191.

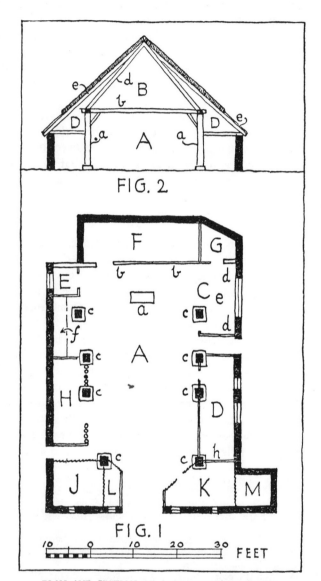

FIG. 2

FIG. 1

PLAN AND SECTION OF A HOUSE IN SATERLAND

across them. Both rows of pillars are overlaid by horizontal beams extending the whole length of the building, which is about sixty-five feet long by forty-nine broad. Upon the oblong so made (A), which forms the inner room of the building, rafters (Fig. 2, d) are fixed. The garret or loft (Fig. 2, B) is called *bölke*. Now the low side walls are erected, and long rafters (Fig. 2, e) laid from them to the ridge of the roof. By this means a sort of outer room going round the building is obtained, divided by a floor. Upon the floor are cattle stalls and rooms. The upper portion (Fig. 2, D), lying immediately under the long rafters, is used as a place to store fodder for the cattle, and for a gallery.

A HOUSE IN SATERLAND

Entering the great door we find ourselves on a spacious main " floor " (Fig. 1, A). The smaller partitioned rooms on both sides usually serve for cattle stalls. On the left of the entrance lies the turf nook (L) where turf for the fire is stored, and by the side of it the calf-house (J). Then crossing over a little passage which leads to a side door in the building, we come to the cow-house (H). There, separated from the " floor " by the great pillars (c) and by small posts, stand the cattle, their heads facing inwards. On the right of the entrance, divided from the " floor " by a narrow partition wall, is the stable (K), and next to it the pigstyes (M). Adjoining the pigstyes is the weaving-room (D), made light by a large window and containing a loom (h) and weaving apparatus. A smaller apartment, used as a washing-room, lies near, with an exit to the yard.

The whole domestic life of the Saterlander is spent on the spacious " floor." In the background, about 6½ feet from the back wall (Fig. 1, *b*), burns the open fire (Fig. 1, *a*), the centre of domestic intercourse. It is continually kept burning, for there is no lack of turf. In many houses it even serves for giving light, and by its dark red glow people work and amuse themselves. The older dwellings have no chimneys. The smoke of the turf fire spreads through the whole building. That has its advantages, for it scares vermin away and makes a very big smoke chamber. Meat and bacon are well preserved on the beams of the roof over the hearth. The space on both sides of the fire serves for kitchen, diningroom, living-room, and bedroom alike. On the right of the fire, in a room (*C*) made light by a broad window, stand a table and a chair (*e*), which at meal times are sometimes brought up to the fire. There are also two large clothes chests (*d*) by the walls near the windows, which are commonly used as settles. On the opposite side of the " floor " are four alcove beds (*f*) one over another. They are concealed by a curtain, and sometimes by a sliding partition. Near the sleeping-place a room (*E*) is screened off, to which fresh air is conveyed by a separate window. The corn harvest lies in the cock-loft or *balk* (Fig. 2, *B*).[1] For the hay an additional room (Fig. 1, *F*) is made, which in many houses has a separate entrance. Under the hay-room the potatoes are laid in a cellar ; a little side room (*G*) is used as a sleeping room.[2] It will be noticed that the aisles of this German building resemble the aisle of the farm building at Bolsterstone already described.

The main difference between the combined house and " shippon," as still found in England, and the German dwelling just described lies in the position of the " floor " or barn floor. In the German dwelling the great doors are at the gable end of the building, and the " floor " extends longitudinally from the great doors through the building as

---

[1] In Yorkshire a hay-loft, and also a ceiling of a room, is known as " the balk."

[2] From a paper by Prof. THEODOR SIEBS entitled " Das Saterland," in the *Zeitschrift des Vereins für Volkskunde*, iii. p. 257.

far as the hearth-wall. But in the English buildings the great doors, otherwise the great barn doors, are at one of the sides, and the threshing-floor intersects the building transversely so as to separate the dwelling-house from the " shippon." In the English, as well as in the German, building, the corn harvest appears to have been stored in the " balk " above the cattle, and to have been thence thrown down upon the " floor " to be threshed. On one side of the " floor " of the typical old English farm building is a wall reaching up to the joists of the " balk," and dividing the " floor " from the " shippon." On the other side of the " floor " the wall goes up to the ridge-tree, and behind this last-named wall the chimney-stack of the " house-place " or fire-house is often found. In one case which the author has seen,[1] the corn harvest was said to have been stored over the house-place, open spaces being left on each side of the chimney-stack for loading or unloading the sheaves. The open spaces are still there, and the outer side of the wall which divides the " house-place " from the " floor " has been plastered and whitewashed, as though it had been the " entrance hall " as well as the threshing-floor of the building. In Lancashire the " balk " has a complete partition wall, and is called the " scaffo'd," hay being thrown through a hole in such wall called the " scaffo'd hole."

In advising upon the plan of a Roman country house Vitruvius says :—" The great hall (*culina*)[2] is to be placed in the warmest part of the court ; united to this are the ox-stalls, with the cribs towards the fire and the east, for oxen with their faces to the light and the fire do not become rough-coated. Husbandmen, who do not understand aspects, think that oxen should look towards no other quarter but the sunrise. Stables, especially in the villa, should be placed in the warmest places, so long as their aspect is not towards the fire. For if horses are stalled near the fire they become rough-coated. Hence stables are not without advantages

---

[1] At Fulwood, near Sheffield.
[2] LANGE renders the word as " hauptraum."—*Haus und Halle*, 33. The basilica, too, was to be placed on the warmest side of the forum.—VITRUVIUS, v. I.

when they are placed in the open space outside the great hall and towards the east."[1] A reminiscence of the notion that horses should not face a fire seems to be preserved in England in the proverb :—

> " A lantern on the table
> Is death in the stable."

In a Yorkshire farm-house the lantern was hung over the kitchen door. In the west of Ireland it is kept in a hole in the wall. Columella advises that " a big and lofty hall be built, of such size that the domestics may conveniently inhabit it during every season of the year."[2]

Giraldus Cambrensis, a twelfth- to thirteenth-century writer, gives an account of the sleeping arrangements in a Welsh house :—

" But at last, the hour of sleep approaching, they lie down all together on a place thinly strewn with rushes and covered with hard rough cloth which the country produces and which in common parlance is called *brachan*. And they are clad by night as by day : for they keep off the cold at all times with only a thin and transparent cloak ; they are, however, much comforted by a fire at their feet and likewise by the near heat of their sleeping companions. But when their underside begins to weary of the hardness of the mattress or their upper side to get cold from exposure, they instantly jump up to the fire, from whose benefit they seek the promptest relief for their discomforts ; and thus, going back to lie down and constantly turning over when discomfort prompts them, they expose, alternately, one side to the cold and the other to the hardness."

Of houses still existing in Schleswig, Hanover, and Westphalia, Lange says, " The great ' floor ' (*Deele*), with the hearth at the back end (*auf der Fleet*),[3] on the right and left

---

[1] VITRUVIUS, vi. 9.

[2] " Magna et alta culina ponetur . . . ut in ea commode familiares omni tempore anni morari queant."—COL. i. 6.

[3] For " fire and flet," with the meaning " fire and house-room," see *Hist. Eng. Dict.*, s.v. " Flet." Ducange (s.v. " Flet ") cites a passage from " Leges Burgorum Scotic.," which mentions " interiorem partem domus capitalis quæ dicitur *Flet*."

Photo : S. O. Addy

"Balk" or "scaffold" at Fulwood.

the cattle stalls, behind the hearth three dwelling-rooms, the middlemost of which is the state-room, laterally in a line with the fire-place doors, through which the smoke also escapes—these are the chief characteristics." " The great covered middle room," he continues, " with smaller rooms round it, and with the dwelling-rooms at the back divided into three parts, seems to have been a common type of all the dwelling-houses of Aryan peoples at a certain stage of their evolution."[1]

Again Lange, following Galen, describes the old Greek peasant's house as it existed in Asia Minor in the second century of our era. " It was divided by Galen into two kinds, the poorer and the richer. The former consists of a single big room with the hearth in the middle, and the cattle stalls on the right and left, or on only one of the two sides. Before the hearth, towards the door, stand stove-benches. The chief room serves at the same time for kitchen and living-room. And as no separate rooms are mentioned besides the chief room, one may suppose that it served at the same time as a sleeping apartment for the inmates, who prepared in it their simple bed by the side of the fire.

On the other hand the better kind of peasant's house has an *exedra* at its back end, and always a sleeping-room at the side of it. Over these in an upper story are likewise three rooms, which are used for household purposes, and especially for storing wine. At the sides, however, over the cattle stalls there are rooms which, following the arrangement of the cattle stalls, probably also extend to the entrance side. What their use was we are not directly told, but it is plain that they served partly for the purposes of husbandry and partly for sleeping rooms for the servants. . . . If the smoke of the hearth could be made of use for the store of wines in the chambers over the *exedra*, it may be argued that in the better

---

[1] *Haus und Halle*, pp. 32, 33. In England, about the end of the thirteenth century, we find the following account of a house built by the Abbot of Malmsbury. " Apud Fouleswyke fecit unam aulam, et mediam cameram inter duas cameras ad gabulum illius aulae."—*Registrum Malmsburiense*, (Chronicles and Memorials, etc.), ii. 367.

kind of farm-houses the hearth stood more towards the back end than towards the middle of the hall."[1]

We have thus seen that the basilical form of house is widespread, and that it was a common type of dwelling-house in Asia Minor as far back as the second century.

When Cæsar came into England he found both an extremely large population and a great abundance of houses (*aedificia*) almost exactly resembling those of the Gauls.[2]

The Belgic or Germanic people who emigrated to England before Cæsar's time would naturally continue their own method of building, and Tacitus has left some account of what that method was. " It is sufficiently well known," he says, " that none of the Germanic peoples dwell in cities, and that they do not even tolerate houses which are built in rows. They dwell apart, and at a distance from one another, according to the preference which they may have for the stream, the plain, or the grove. They do not lay out their villages after our fashion, with the buildings contiguous to each other and in close contact. Every man surrounds his house with a space, either for protection against the accident of fire, or from ignorance of the art of building. They do not make use of stone cut from the quarry, or of tiles ; for every kind of building they make use of unshapely wood, which falls short of beauty or attractiveness. They carefully colour some parts of their buildings with earth which is so clear and bright as to resemble painting and coloured designs."[3] When Tacitus says that no cities were occupied by the Germans, he means that they had no cities to be compared with those of Italy and Greece. He can hardly mean that they had no towns. We should notice that he speaks of houses (*domus*), not of mere huts or cabins. The words which he uses would have served to describe an English, as well as a German, village. " He finds," says

---

[1] LANGE, *ut supra*, p. 32. GALEN, *De Antidotis*, i. 3, vol. xiv. p. 17 (ed. Kuhn).

[2] " Hominum est infinita multitudo creberrimaque aedificia, fere Gallicis consimilia."—*B. G.* v. 12. MEITZEN, *Das deutsche Haus*, pp. 24, 28, thinks that Cæsar would have used such a word as *tuguria* or *casae* had he meant " huts."

[3] *Germ.* xvi. (ed. CHURCH and BRODRIBB).

Meitzen, " the difference between German and Italian villages in that wherein it consists to this day, viz., that the houses in Italian villages, as also in the town, are built wall to wall, so that for every one of them a wall-thickness can be spared. In Germany, however, they were built in the country not in contiguous buildings, but the houses stood alone."[1]

We shall not, perhaps, be far wrong is supposing that the " space " by which the German village house was surrounded was the " toft "—the ground or place on which the house stood—of the old English village. Nothing is more frequent among old English deeds than grants or conveyances of a messuage *cum tofto et crofto*. The size of the toft was proportioned to that of the arable holding ; in what manner, we shall see in a later chapter. Hence such phraseology as the following, in a charter of the 15th century :[2] " ij bovatas terrae in Edene, cum j tofto, quantum ad ij bovatas pertinet in eadem villa." That is to say " two bovates of land with as much toft as goes with two bovates." Elsewhere in the same charter we find that a certain toft is made over to the monastery of Durham " cum domibus quae factae sunt in eodem topht." Elsewhere again we read of four bovates being disposed of, " cum omnibus mansuris propriis."

In the English village street each house stood in its own " toft " adjoining the street, with a croft behind it, the " toft and croft " forming together a long and rather narrow strip. We learn from Tacitus that the German houses were built of rudely-shaped wood, and it has already been shown that English houses built of wood which was split by wedges, or which retains the bark, still exist. We have also seen that English farm-houses were often coloured throughout by the bright hues of " archil." When, in addition to these resemblances, we consider the close parallel which is known to have existed between the ancient German and the English methods of agriculture, it can hardly be doubted that the arrangement of the houses and their construction were very much alike in both countries. It is improbable that either

---

[1] *Das deutsche Haus*, p. 24.
[2] *Feodarium Prioratus Dunelmensis* (Surtees Soc.), pp. 132, 134.

the German or the English village house of the first century was round. It is far more likely that it resembled the still-existing German houses which have been described, as well as the smaller existing wooden houses of which examples have already been given.

CHAPTER VI

THE TOWN HOUSE

Foreign influence—The " rows " of Chester—" Taverns "
or shops below the street—Carriage traffic not permitted
in narrow streets, as in Roman times—" Wints " or
" wynds " and " turnpikes "—Different trades in different streets or quarters—Appentices, booths, and shops
or sheds—The height of appentices fixed by law—The
projecting upper story of Roman origin—Its use—
" Solars "—In the twelfth century town houses had only
one upper floor—The " garret "—Height of rooms—
Stone party walls in wooden houses—Size of rooms—
Probable early use of decorated woodwork in fronts of
houses—A goldsmith's house in York in 1490.

AS regards the great country houses, and many of the
houses built in cities, we have no reasons for believing that the chain which still links us with the old
Roman civilization was ever broken.[1] The forms of such
houses were largely modified by foreign influence.

At Chester, for example, the two main streets intersect
each other at right angles, as though the city had sprung
from a Roman stationary camp.[2] " The streets, being cut
out of the rock, are several feet below the general surface,
which circumstance has led to a singular construction of the
houses ; level with the streets are low shops or warehouses,
over which is an open balustraded gallery with steps at
convenient distances into the streets. Along the galleries, or,
as they are called by the inhabitants, ' rows,' are houses with
shops ; the upper stories are erected over the row, which
consequently appears to be formed through the first-floor of
each house and at the intersection of the streets are additional

---

[1] On the Continent this applies more forcibly. A fourth-century
writer, Ammianus Marcellinus, speaking of the dwellers on the
Main, says (xvii. ii. i.) that their houses are " accuratius ritu romano
constructa."

[2] The streets of Lincoln are nearly on the old Roman lines ;
even the Roman sewers are there. York, Gloucester, and Exeter
are also good examples of Roman quadrangular towns.

flights of steps."[1] Here we have a distinctly Roman method
of building. For the " open balustraded gallery " is the *pergula* or covered balcony which in some Roman towns rested
on the top of the *tabernae* or shops.[2]

On the other hand, in Pompeii and other Roman towns,
" the street front on the ground-floor, even of large and
handsome houses, was usually occupied by a row of shops.
In some cases these shops have no doorway or passage communicating with the main house, and were probably rented
by the owner to independent tradesmen ; in others the shops
could be entered from the house."[3] This Pompeian arrangement of shops resembles that of mediæval and modern Italy,
and is like our modern arrangements.[4]

In England shops in front of town houses were sometimes
known as " taverns," from the Latin *taberna*, and were below
the surface of the street, like cellars. They were even known
as " cellars." Thus by a statute passed in the reign of Henry
VIII, merchant gilds were heavily fined if they bound an
apprentice by oath or bond not to " set up, nor kepe any
shop, house, or *seller*."[5] Cellars were used as places of business in London as early as the first half of the reign of Henry
III.[6] We learn from a very full account[7] of the building of
a house in Sheffield in 1575 that down to a late time
" taverns " or underground shops were dug out in front of
town houses. The following entries show this :—

> " Payd to ij dykers for casting earth furth of the
>   taverne iiij daies   .   .   .   .   . ij*s*. viij*d*.
> Item paid to Roades and Batley for workeinge and
>   castinge earth ij daies in my taverne   .   . xxij*d*.

[1] LEWIS, *Topographical Dictionary of England*, 1831, vol. i. p. 429.
[2] SMITH'S *Dictionary of Greek and Roman Antiquities*, ii. 368.
The Corpus of Latin Inscriptions, iv. 138, mentions " tabernae cum
pergulis suis." Halliwell gives " tavern " as a Yorkshire word for
cellar. In Chester the *tabernae* must have been below the " rows."
There are cellars or store-rooms beneath the " rows " yet.
    Compare *Rot. Hundr.* ii. 101b. " . . . sex cesteria cervisie de
taberna dicte Thome."
[3] SMITH'S *Dictionary of Greek and Roman Antiquities*, i. p. 679.
[4] Compare the *Dings* of York, p. 36.
[5] RASTELL'S *Statutes*, 1557, f. 77b.
[6] RILEY, *Munimenta Gild. Lond.*, vol. i. p. xxxii.
[7] MS. in the author's possession

Then follow some payments for walling the " tavern," which
seems to have been built of stone and covered with boards.
Assuming that the accounts are in chronological order, the
" tavern " was dug out and finished after the house was
" reared."
These taverns were entered by stairs, which sometimes
encroached on the public street, and the old accounts of the
Burgery or municipal corporation of Sheffield show that the
burgesses exacted a small rent or acknowledgment for such
encroachments.

Thus in the year 1566 this entry occurs : " William
Tomson for his taverne stare iiij*d*."[1]

The whole question of encroachments throws an interesting light on the building methods of the Middle Ages. The
Hundreds Rolls (*Rotuli Hundredorum*), which consist of inquisitions taken in pursuance of a special commission set up
in 1273, are full of records of encroachments by private citizens on the public way. Thus, in a London parish, we read
that John de Northampton *fecit quemdam gradum super regia
via*.[2] At Richmond several persons were stated to have built
steps to the detriment of the King's highway,[3] while at Stamford one Richard Wardele built some steps *ad introitum unius
celarii* measuring 8 ft. in length by 4 ft. in width.[4]

In London during the thirteenth century, steps frequently
led into shops from the street ; " they seem to have seriously
encroached upon the footway at times, for at later periods
they are the subject of frequent enactments."[5] Sir Walter
Scott, near the beginning of *The Antiquary*, describes a
" ' laigh shop,' *anglice* a cellar, opening to the High Street
by a straight and steep stair." At the bottom of the stair
the shopkeeper " sold tape, thread, needle, skeans of worsted,
coarse linen cloth and such feminine gear to those who had
the courage and skill to descend to the profundity of her
dwelling, without falling headlong themselves or throwing
down any of the numerous articles which, piled on each side

[1] LEADER, *Records of the Burgery of Sheffield*, p. 14.
[2] *Rot. Hundr.*, i. 428a.
[3] *Ibid.*, i. 133a.
[4] *Ibid.*, i. 351b, 355a, 395b.
[5] RILEY, *ut supra*, vol. i. p. xxxii.

of the descent, indicated the profession of the trader below."
It is interesting to find the same practice on the other side
of the English Channel.[1] " In some towns of Flandérs,"
says Viollet-le-Duc,[2] " the shops were sometimes below the
ground ; to get into them you had to go down a number of
steps, and these steps even encroached on the public street.
By the side of the balustrade were benches, on which samples
of merchandise were displayed ; an awning protected these
as well as the benches from the rain. It is well to observe
that in trading towns the shopkeepers did all they could to
block the public way, to stop the wayfarer by putting
obstacles to traffic. This custom, or rather this abuse, lasted
for a long period ; it became absolutely necessary to estab-
lish footpaths and rules for the inspection of the highways,
which were rigorously enforced under a heavy penalty for
disobedience. During the Middle Ages, trading streets, with
their open shops and their display of goods in the public street,
were like bazaars. The street, then, became the merchants'
property, and foot passengers could hardly make their way
through it during business hours; as for horses and carriages,
they had to abandon all attempts to pass through narrow
streets impeded by displays of merchandise and buyers.
During meal times business was suspended, a considerable
number of shops were shut up. When curfew sounded, and
on holidays, these streets became silent and almost deserted."

When many " tavern stairs " were made in a narrow street
it is obvious that vehicles drawn by horses could not pass
through. To remedy such inconvenience two courses were
possible. One was to remove the stairs and fill up the holes
in the streets, leaving mere cellars beneath the *pergula*, to be
entered by steps inside the houses instead of outside. The
other was to excavate the whole street down to the floors of
the " taverns," and this seems to have been the plan adopted
at Chester.[3] The numerous cellars still found under the

[1] In Copenhagen at the present time many shops are below street
level and approached by steps cutting into the street.—*Reviser's note*.

[2] *Dict. de l'Architecture*, ii. p. 239.

[3] The floors of the cellars in some of the old houses in Bailgate,
Lincoln, are on a level with the Roman road, the modern road
being on a level with the first-floor.

Reproduced from *Turner and Parker's "Domestic Architecture in England," by permission of Messrs. Parker and Sons, Ltd.*

Shops in Butcher Row, Shrewsbury. The wares were formerly set out on hinged flaps projecting outside the ground-floor window openings

Photo: H. Dan

West Street, Rye, Sussex. The steps and chimney-stack, though not in this case actually of mediaeval date, illustrate the kind of obstructions often referred to in the Hundreds Rolls.

footpaths of streets in old towns which contained shops show that the expedient of filling up the holes was also adopted.

Steps, as the Hundreds Rolls show, were by no means the only obstruction likely to be encountered in a mediæval street. We read of the erection of *traves, ubi equi ferrantur*, erected in a street near Aldgate. In another place it is a chimney (*chymeneya*) which causes trouble,[1] while occasionally we find houses and shops built in the public way. One Adam de Basing built a house on the highway at Aldermanbury which was pulled down by the citizens. Adam's son and heir, however, appropriated the site and built an enclosing wall, thus continuing the obstruction. No fewer than six accounts of this occur in the Hundreds Rolls.[2] Elsewhere we hear of a man paying rent for a shop (*unam shoppam*) built on the street.[3] Narrow passages were sometimes blocked by privies[4] (*camerae privatae*) and even hermitages became a nuisance, as in the case of " Lucia la Ankereswomman," whose cabin stood out into the road 2 ft. towards the west and $1\frac{1}{2}$ ft. towards the east.[5] At Lincoln some houses held by an ecclesiastic were described as being built on the King's wall to the danger of the city's defence.[6]

To this day English shopkeepers prefer narrow streets, as, for instance, New Bond Street in London. Experience has shown them that more business can be done in such streets. The practice of touting at the shop door for custom was of long duration. An English poet[7] of the fourteenth century laughed at the noises they made in the streets, as when cooks and their servants cried " hot pies, hot ! "

Such was the narrowness of the streets, and such the importunity of the shopkeepers, that if a man got into a

---

[1] *Rot. Hundr.*, i. 420b. In another entry, i. 426a, a *forgia* is instanced as an obstruction.

[2] *Ibid.*, i. 407a, 409a, 410b, 412a, 425a.

[3] *Ibid.*, i. 426a. Another entry, i. 413b, refers to a shop as *selda* and another as *soppa* (ii. 79b).

[4] *Ibid.*, i. 433b.

[5] *Ibid.*, i. 426a. A hermitage is also mentioned in i. 414b, and in i. 426a a hermitage (*hermitagium*) is described as projecting into the street from a tower in the city wall.

[6] *Ibid.*, i. 397b.

[7] LANGLAND, *Piers the Plowman*, Prologue, 225.

H

street at one end he could hardly get out at the other without buying something. It was the old way of advertising.

In English towns there were streets closed to all but foot passengers. The hundred and fifty-six " rows " of Yarmouth, each about eight feet wide, are an example of this, and it is said that in later years vehicles called " trollies " or " harry-carries "[1] were specially built to traverse them. Such names as Waingate and Fargate in Sheffield imply that in ancient times there were streets in that town which could only be traversed by foot passengers. For Waingate is " wagon street," and is the road which leads to the old bridge crossing the river. The name implies that there were other streets through which wagons could not pass. Fargate means[2] " public street " or " driving street," and implies the same thing. It is obvious that in old cities the larger streets would lead to the bars or gates, as they do, for instance, to the four gates of York and Chester. Here the plan of the Roman camp, with its *via principalis* and its four gates, is followed.

In the Roman provincial towns there were also streets which could only be traversed by foot passengers. At Pompeii " the narrow streets are practically blocked by single large stones in their centres ; the broader streets are crossed by rows, containing from two to five stones." Some twenty-five years before the destruction of Pompeii Claudius forbade travellers to drive in carriages through provincial towns. " Heavy burdens were carried on the backs of horses, mules, or cattle. . . . In the case of Pompeii horses and carriages were, beyond a doubt, confined to certain streets." Occasionally these streets were closed by iron gratings.[3]

In England, smaller streets were often closed to traffic by means of posts or chains. From several items in the Hundreds Rolls it appears that such obstructions were sometimes set up by private citizens on their own initiative. Thus in Grimsby one Symon Wacket was reported as having blocked

[1] THORNBURY, *A Tour Round England*, 1870, ii. 36.

[2] From O.N. *far*, means of passage, and *gata*, a road. Compare O.N. *far-vegr*, a track, road, Swedish *farwæg*, via publica ; O.E. *fær*, passing, transit. The author here desires to correct a former opinion on this point. Compare the German *fahren*, to drive.

[3] SMITH'S *Dict. of Greek and Roman Antiq.*, ii. 952.

the public street with an iron chain (*per cathenam ferream*) and levied a toll without warrant.[1] In the city of London several people are recorded as having set up posts before their houses, presumably in order to keep their entrances clear of traffic.[2]

The smaller streets of English towns were, as we have seen, mere alleys leading into the wider or public streets. In Warrington they are known as " wints " ; over the portal of one of the alleys in that town is inscribed the name " Little Weint."[3] In Edinburgh they are called " wynds," in Yarmouth " rows." " Row " is also found in London, as in Paternoster Row. " Wint," or " went,"[4] is equivalent to the Latin *angiportus*, and was a vent or exit leading to the public street, to the gates, or the walls. In some northern towns such a passage is known as a " jennel."[5] At Market Weighton it is called a " galing " or " goaling."[6] In other parts of East Yorkshire it is called a " rent." At Scarborough the streets in the old part of the town are on the slope which leads up to the castle, and are extremely narrow. Some of these streets, like those at Clovelly in Devonshire, contain steps by which the slope can be ascended, and have a very un-English appearance. It was easy to close such streets if necessary by barriers at either end, and the spiked contrivances known as " turnpikes " were everywhere used for this purpose.[7]

A striking feature of the old English town was that each craft had its own quarters or street. Everybody has heard of the Jewry or Jews' quarter of the larger towns, where the business of money-lending was carried on. In London a great number of old street-names are associated with particular trades—Goldsmiths' Row, Needlers' Lane, where

[1] *Rot. Hundr.*, i. 292a.

[2] *Ibid.*, i. 415b, 428b.

[3] " Weind " (formerly weint) occurs in Wigan, while in Preston there is Anchor Wend.—*Reviser's note.*

[4] HALLIWELL'S *Dict. of Archaic Words.*

[5] In Edinburgh a passage leading up to the Castle is called the Vennel. *Cf.* med. Lat. *venella*, a passage.—*Reviser's note.*

[6] Probably connected with Icelandic *geil*, a narrow passage, and thus also with English *gill*, a little chasm.

[7] " Torne pyke, suche as lyeth over away—*rouliz*."—PALSGRAVE, 1530. Compare Cheyne Row, lane barred by a chain.

needles were made or sold, Carriers' Row, Stockfishmongers' Row, Paternoster Row, where the " paternoster makers " lived—these may suffice for examples. The same divisions are found in the smaller towns. Baxtergate in Pontefract, Whitby, and Doncaster was the bakers' street. Fishergate in Doncaster and Ripon was the street where the fish dealers carried on their trade. There is a Butcher Row with interesting old shops in Shrewsbury. (See illustration opp. p. 112.)

Other examples are : Ropergate in Pontefract, where ropes were made ; Salter Row in the same town, and Saltergate in Chesterfield, which were occupied by the salt dealers or the meat-salters ; and Packers' Row, Irongate, Knifesmithgate, and Glumangate in Chesterfield. The last-named street was the abode of gleemen or minstrels. Such minstrels were employed by old municipal corporations, and the part of the town which they inhabited was generally known as St. Julian's quarter.[1] The same arrangement of trades in various quarters was the rule in German towns.[2] It also prevailed in England during the Roman occupation, as we may see by the *insulae* at Silchester, occupied by dyers.[3]

It was long before the practice of making the shop within the house itself began to be usual. The booth, open shed, or shop in front of the dwelling-house, like the Lucken Booths of Edinburgh, began at first to take the place of the underground " tavern." In the year 1258 there were 120 booths (*selde*) in Pontefract, and of these 42 were occupied by cobblers and persons who sold salt. Beside these there were 60 stalls.[4] In Scotland booths are known as *krames*. At Winchester in the twelfth century, we read that " Osbert, the son of Thiard, a tenant of King Henry, had set up 5 bordells, partly in the King's way, and had made them for the love of God and a refuge for the poor."[5] These bordells

---

[1] ROWBOTHAM, *The Troubadours*, p. 189 *et seq.* Compare Gilly-gate in Pontefract, Durham, York, and other towns.

[2] A long list is given by FOERSTEMANN, *Die deutschen Ortsnamen*, p. 167.

[3] *The Builder*, vol. lxx. p. 378.

[4] *Yorkshire Inq.* (Yorkshire Arch. Record Series), i. 50.

[5] *Bishop of Winchester's Survey*, 1148, quoted in J. F. MORGAN, *England under the Norman Occupation.*

seem to have been sheds or booths of some kind. In the
same document we read of "estals," "escheops," and
"eschamels" in Winchester High Street. In London the
stalls on which goods were offered for sale were fixed to the
walls in the streets by means of hinges, so that they could
be taken up and let down. They were ordered to be $2\frac{1}{2}$ feet
in breadth.[1]

In A.D. 1419 it was declared that if a man fixed "appentices" to a house either by iron or wooden nails, such
"appentices" were to be regarded as landlords' fixtures,
even if the lease were for a considerable period.[2]

It was also ordered that "appentices" should be so high
that a man could easily ride or walk beneath them.[3] Again,
it was declared that "appentices," rain gutters, and "jetties"
(i.e. projecting stories) should not be less than nine feet high,
so that people could ride under them.[4]

The Hundreds Rolls provide an instance of four shops
adjoining a London house which were formerly in the nature
of an "appentice" but were subsequently incorporated in
a masonry gable.[5] Elsewhere we read of a shop (*soppa*)
belonging to the Abbot of Shrewsbury but forming part of
the house of one Gilbert Meverel.[6]

The projecting stories which, with their quaint and decorated fronts and their many gables, make some old English
towns so beautiful, were not born of a mere freak or of an
artist's fancy. They were intended for use, namely, to give
shelter from the sun or rain to stalls and booths, and to goods
displayed in the streets. The evolution of the projecting

---

[1] STOW's *Survey of London*, ed. 1633, p. 678.

[2] RILEY, *Munimenta Gild. Lond.*, vol. i. p. 432. Compare COT-
GRAVE, 1632 : "*Soupenduë*. A penthouse ; iuttie, or, part of a
building that iuttieth beyond, or leaneth ouer the rest." The
appentice seems to have been fixed at the *end* of a house. "Pen-
tyce, of an howse ende."—*Prompt. Parv.*

[3] "Item, qe lez appentices soient si hautz qe home puisse aise-
ment alere et chivalere southe ycelles."—*Ibid.*, vol. i. p. 336. These
appentices must have been mere shelters.

[4] "Qe Pentis, Goters, et Getez soyent sy hautz, qe gens puissent
chivacher dessouz, et a meyns ix pees haut."—RILEY, *Munimenta
Gild. Lond.*, vol. i. p. 584.

[5] *Rot. Hundr.*, i. 407a.

[6] *Ibid.*, ii. 79b.

" solar " or upper room can be traced by reference to Roman practices. In Rome the tops or roofs of the colonnades in front of the houses, or of the *insulae*, were known as *solaria*, meaning literally " places for basking in the sun."[1] Hence when rooms began to be built over these colonnades such rooms were knows as " solars," so that the sense of " basking-place," or " sunning place," originally applied to the tops of the colonnades, was afterwards transferred to the rooms built over them. Projecting stories may still be seen in some of the houses at Pompeii, and the Roman Emperors forbade their erection in narrow streets.[2] In England they belong to town houses, though occasionally they may be found in the country. In such cases the country house is a copy of the town house, as there could be no actual need in the country for such projections.

In the twelfth century it appears that the houses in London had only one story above the ground floor.[3] In the original sense of the word a garret was a watch-tower or look-out. When it was first added to the " solar " does not appear, but in the early part of the fourteenth century we find houses in London of two or three stories mentioned, and each of these stories, as also the cellar beneath, occasionally formed the freehold of different persons.[4] As the " solar " projected beyond the room beneath, so the garret projected, though only to a slight degree, beyond the " solar." This projection of the garret would afford some little additional shelter to the stalls below. The " solar " was the chief dwelling-room of the family, the garret being often used as a store-room for corn and other provisions.[5] " From a deed bearing date 1217 or 1218, it appears that the corbels or joists for support-ing the upper floor were inserted at a height of eight feet from the ground."[6] It is a common thing nowadays to find

[1] SMITH'S *Dictionary of Greek and Roman Antiquities*, i. p. 672.
[2] *Ibid.*, i. p. 666, where see the engraving.
[3] RILEY, *Munimenta Gild. Lond.*, vol. i. p. xxxi. The existence of an Anglo-Saxon phrase *þri-flére*, three-storied, is worth noting.
[4] *Munimenta, etc., ut supra.*
[5] TURNER and PARKER'S *Domestic Arch. of England* (fifteenth century), part i. p. 34.
[6] *Munimenta, ut supra*, p. xxxi.

in houses of the sixteenth and seventeenth centuries rooms
not more than six feet high, and this is especially the case in
the smaller houses. So long as a man of average height
could walk in them without knocking his head against the
ceiling everybody was satisfied.

The document known as " Fitz-Alwyne's Assize," dated
A.D. 1189, shows that the party-walls of London houses
" were of freestone, 3 ft. thick and 16 ft. high, from which
the roof (whether covered with tiles or thatch) ran up to a
point, with the gable towards the street."[1] These stone walls
were built as a protection against fire, the rest of the building
being of wood and plaster. From the height of this wall we
may conclude that both the upper and lower rooms were
less than 8 ft. high. The length and breadth of the rooms
we do not know, but we have already referred to a room
without Ludgate which in 1352 measured 16 ft. in length
by $12\frac{3}{4}$ ft. in breadth,[2] this being the " bay " to which we
have so often referred.

The earliest timber buildings of our old towns have
perished, but they must have been as well carved and as
picturesque as any of the later examples which yet remain.
A gable over the north doorway of Cormac's chapel in Ireland,[3] which is said to date from the year 1120, is an imita-
tion in stone of the fine carving which decorated the gable
of a wooden house. The transition from wood to stone was
gradual. Just as the early printers copied the manuscripts,
so, we may be sure, the first builders of stone houses and
churches copied the wooden ones.

In 1490 a goldsmith's house in York consisted of a hall,
parlour, bolting house for sifting bran, kitchen, buttery, great
chamber, another chamber, and a shop. The hall was hung
with tapestry embroidered with flowers. The parlour contained a bed, with its tester ornamented by a figure of the
Blessed Mary. The walls were hung with tapestry, embroidered with figures of St. George and the Blessed Mary.

[1] *Munimenta, etc., ut supra*, p. xxx.

[2] *Ante*, p. 56.

[3] STOKES, *Early Christian Architecture in Ireland*, 1878, Plate xli.
LORD DUNRAVEN, *Notes on Irish Architecture*, ii. p. 75.

Amongst other things, the great chamber contained two feather beds and a " sprosse " chest, this being apparently identical with what was afterwards known as a Flanders chest. The other chamber contained a parclose,[1] or wooden partition, which probably separated it from the great chamber. This smaller chamber contained, amongst other things, a bed, a basket, and a bushel of coals. We may infer from this that the great chamber with the small separated chamber were in the upper floor, these rooms being approached by a ladder passing through a hole in the floor of the smaller chamber, as in the house at Upper Midhope already described.[2] The contents of the great chamber show that it was used for a bedroom only. The shop contained stithies, a forging hammer, and the usual tools of a goldsmith's trade.[3]

It frequently happened that all the wood-and-plaster houses in a street fell into decay. Such a street was then called Rotten Row, or " ruinous street."[4]

[1] " Parclos to parte two roumes, *separation*."—PALSGRAVE.
[2] *Ante*, p. 78.
[3] *Test. Ebor*. (Surtees Soc.), iv. 56 *et seq*.
[4] See the Author's account in *N. & Q*., 9th S., i. 470.

CHAPTER VII

BUILDING MATERIALS—CHIMNEYS—WINDOWS—MURAL
DECORATIONS—ROOFS

Wood the commonest building material for ordinary
houses—The " reared " house—The rich man's house
sometimes built of stone—The wattled house—" Parging "
—Sod houses—Use of bricks—The evolution of the chimney—Remarkable chimney at Warrington—Flues and
louvres—The " reredos "—The " room in the chimney "
—Chimneys of wood or wicker work—Comparison of the
chimney in the megaron at Tiryns—The window or
" wind-hole "—Small size of the oldest windows—Window frames covered by linen dipped in oil—Early glass
windows—Dearness of glass—Decoration of walls—The
usual colours were blue and yellow—Wattled posts imi-
tated in the mural decorations of the peasantry—The
painting of leaves on walls—Squares drawn on the floor
—The serpentine mark at the entrance—Decorated hearth
in lake village near Glastonbury—Whitewash a protection
against fire—Universal use of plaster and whitewash in
churches—Roofs of turf, rushes, and heather—Houses
without fires.

IN historic times the houses of the English peasantry
were mostly built of wood, stone being only used where
wood could not be obtained. We have seen that the
houses in the Glastonbury marsh village were built of wood
and clay, and also that these materials were used for building houses which still exist. The Hundreds Rolls record
that a village (*que vocatur Ravenesodd*) was built of sand and
stones thrown up by the sea.[1] The old English word for
build was *timbran*, to " timber,"[2] and the man who built
the house was called the *treowwyrhta* or carpenter.[3] The

---

[1] *Rot. Hundr.*, i. 402a.

[2] Compare an entry in *Rot. Hundr.*, ii. 126b, where a certain
Gervase Godling is noticed as having cut down twelve oaks, taken
them to his house, and had houses built of them.

[3] ALFRIC'S Colloquy in WRIGHT-WÜLCKER, *Vocab.*, p. 100. In
mediæval Latin timber for building was known as *meremium*. In
the fourteenth century a good deal of timber for building purposes
was brought from Norway.—*Priory of Coldingham* (Surtees Soc.),
Appendix, p. lvii.

Old Frisian for " house " was *timber ;* the German *zimmer*, a room, is from the same root, and the Old High German *zimbar* meant " wood for building." Basically connected with these is the Latin *domus*.

Houses were built of wood even in places where stone was most abundant, and this kind of building continued to the close of the sixteenth century. A very full account of the building of a house in Sheffield in the year 1575 has been preserved.[1] The builder begins to enter up his payments thus :

" First paied to Johne Ronksley for gayting me xxx c
  slate stones . . . . . .   xxx*s*.
Item paied to my Lord for the delph yre of the said
  stone . . . .   x*s*.
Item paied to my Lord for viij trees after x*s*. the tree   . iiij*l*.
Item paied to Mr. West for vij trees and he gave my
  wiffe one tree besydes . . . . .   xvj*s*."

So the builder paid thirty shillings for 3000 " slate stones," and £4 16*s*. for fifteen trees, another tree being given to his wife for luck. He tells us further on that he paid £2 6*s*. 8*d*. " for meat and drink that day the house was reared "[2]—a large sum considering the rate of wages at that period. The " rearing " of the house was the setting up of the timber framework of which it was composed, a wooden house, or house built of wood and plaster, being still known in Yorkshire as a " reared house " to distinguish it from a stone house. The rearing of a house, described in mediæval Latin as *levatio*, was the lifting or setting up of the timber-work or skeleton structure which supported the whole building.[3] The timber-work was prepared and made ready before it was set up. That such was the case is shown by the statute 37, Hen. VIII, which recites that certain novel outrages had of late been practised, such as " the secret burnynge of frames of tymber prepared and made, by the owners thereof, redy

---

[1] MS. in the Author's possession.
[2] 1349. " In iiij lagenis cervisiæ empt. et expenditis circa. levacionem meremii, 4*d*."—Appendix to *Bishop Hatfield's Survey* (Surtees Soc.), p. 234.
[3] In Borneo the parts of a house are made ready for putting together, and on a given day, when the omens have been consulted, the work of erection is started.

to be sett up, and edified for houses." This misdemeanour
was made felony.[1] We have already alluded to the mortise
holes at the feet of old " crucks," which seem to have held
levers, and the considerable sums of money spent in ale when
the timber-work was reared show that the assistance of many
men was required.

The builder of the house in Sheffield paid two shillings
" for gayttinge basinge stone," i.e. foundation stone. The
house was " mossed " and slated.[2] It was completed by the
plasterers and " dobers " (colour-washers), these two classes
of workmen being separately paid. Sixteen stones of lead
were used for the gutter, the cost being 13s. 2d. The builder
paid :

> " to Dewk the glasyer for
> xvi foots of glasse for my windows viijs."

No other payment for glass is mentioned, so that the windows must have been few or very small. The house seems to
have adjoined the street, for it was " next unto Mrs. Braye's,"
and the yard was paved at the back. As gable ends faced
the street in town houses, the mention of the leaded gutter
shows that there were two gable ends facing the street in
this house. Below the ground, in front of the house, was a
" tavern " or shop.

In the houses of the wealthy stone was used at an early
period ; we do not know how early.[3] In such houses it may
have been used continuously, though by no means frequently,
since the Roman occupation. Where in existing houses the
lower part of the wooden framework is filled in by stone or
bricks, such houses are said, in common phraseology, to be
" half-timbered." But they are really " whole-timbered " ;
they are essentially wooden houses, built of wood from the
foundation, the interstitial spaces having been filled in by

[1] See the note in *Prompt. Parv.*, p. 176. In the seventeenth
century the framework or skeleton of a house was known as " the
carcass."—*Hist. Eng. Dict.*

[2] " Payd in parte of a recconing for mossing of and slating my
howse, xxs."—Were the slates laid over the moss or the moss over
the slates ? Probably the former, lead being used for the gutter.
In Denmark the walls seem to have been stuffed with moss.

[3] Under the name of *estland* boards, or *estrich* boards, much
wood for building purposes was brought from Norway and Sweden.

the material nearest at hand, whether that material were clay, mud, stone, or brick. The oldest way was to weave twigs or brushwood in and out of the posts. After that came laths, which were fitted into " slots " in the posts by a process known as " shooting." In a house at Warrington examined by the author, wattle and daub, stone and brick are filled into the woodwork of different parts. Here the wattles are rods of hazel,[1] with the bark on, laid close together in an oblique direction, and covered by a thick coating of clay mixed with cow-dung. The act of throwing this material on is still known in South Yorkshire as " parging," and in Derbyshire as " sparging," from the Latin *spargere*, to sprinkle ; the term is now only applied to the rough plastering of the inside of a chimney. Many of the poorer houses were built of mud or sods. Thus when Grimm the fisherman, as the old tale goes, founded Grimsby :

> " Bigan he þere for to erþe,
> A litel hus to maken of erþe."

> " Began he there for to dwell,
> A little house to make of earth." [2]

There was a place called " Sodhowses "[3] in Yorkshire which seems to mean " turf houses." Some of the Scotch " summer huts " were built of sods, or of turf upon a foundation of stones, and roofed with turf and straw. Sometimes a dry stone wall " was lined with turf and wattled with twigs, which kept the earth from falling."[4] Many houses in Cambridgeshire are built entirely of " clunch," a kind of hard chalk marl.

The word " brick " does not occur in English literature before the middle of the fifteenth century, and " perhaps the earliest true brick-building existing is that of Little Wenham Hall,"[5] believed to date from the end of the thirteenth cen-

---

[1] " A hartheled wall, or ratheled with hasill rods, wands or such other. *Paries craticius*."—WITHALS' *Dictionarie*, 1616, p. 191. Compare German *reitel*, the stem of a young tree.

[2] *Havelock*, l. 739.

[3] *Yorkshire Fines*, part ii. p. 127.

[4] JOHNSON, *A Journey to the Western Highlands of Scotland*, ed. 1886, p. 44.

[5] PARKER, *Concise Glossary of Arch.*, 4th ed., p. 45.

tury. But we are not to suppose that the art of brick-making, so commonly used by the Romans, was ever lost in England. Such a loss would have been exceedingly improbable. The old name for a brick was *tigel*, or " tile,"[1] and the tiler was the brickmaker. Formerly bricks were much thinner than they are at present, and there was little to distinguish them from tiles. Though they were not much used in the Middle Ages, the art of making them was not lost. It is a curious fact that the walls known in Yorkshire as " parpoint " walls, consisting of thin and rather small stones, resemble walls faced with Roman bricks.

The evolution of the chimney is one of the most interesting questions which concern domestic architecture. We have seen that in the English prehistoric hut the open hearth stood in the middle of the floor, and that in a German house already described it stood at a distance of several feet from the nearest wall. Having regard to the central position of the prehistoric hearth, it is on that ground likely that the fireplace of the Middle Ages did not adjoin an outer wall, as the custom now is, but stood at some distance from the outer wall. Henning,[2] quoting Gladbach, describes a house in the Bernese Oberland which had a central fireplace and a smoke-hole in the roof with moveable flaps to keep out snow and rain. Another Swiss house[3] had louvres in the gable to let out the smoke.

Till very lately a central chimney existed at a house known as Oughtibridge Hall, near Sheffield, " where a large stone chimney-stack from the kitchen passed through the middle of a bedroom, rendering the room useless. A length had been cut out of the heavy ridge-tree to make room for this stack, and the ends were left without support, excepting such as they derived from the pins of the spars."[4] A remarkable chimney in an ancient timber house at Warrington in Lanca-

[1] " *Luteres*, tigelan."—WRIGHT-WÜLCKER, *Vocab.*, 434, 5. (For *luteres* read *lateres*.)
[2] *Ut supra*, p. 150.
[3] *Ibid.*, p. 19.
[4] T. WINDER, in *The Builders' Journal*, vol. iii. p. 41.
Often there were seats or shelves within the chimney. 1575. " j burde within the chymney, jd."—*Richmond Wills* (Surtees Soc.), p. 255.

shire, shown in the illustration, is nearly in the centre of the building. The jambs and lintel, as well as the whole framework of the deep fireplace, are of wood, and " that part of the framework of the flue, if framework it were originally, which is on a level with the sleeping shelf or chamber, is of wood to the height of about a foot, but above that the curving structure is of brick. Whether or not this was the original condition it is difficult to say."[1] The present stove, with its modern surroundings, fills up the cavity of the ancient hearth and wide fireplace, whose sides were hung with hams and flitches. [The house where this fireplace existed was pulled down in 1898. It stood at the corner of Cockhedge Lane and Brick Street.]

In 1538 Leland expressed his wonder that the chimneys, otherwise the flues, in Bolton Castle were carried up the sides of the walls. " One thinge," he says, " I muche notyd in the haulle of Bolton, how chimneys were conveyed by tunnells made on the syds of the wauls, betwyxt the lights in the haull ; and by this means, and by no covers, is the smoke of the harthe wonder strangly convayed."[2] He means that, in his time, the practice was to erect a sort of " cover," to use his own word, over a fire, such a cover being a canopy made usually of wood and plaster. Carew, in his *Survey of Cornwall*, published in 1602, says that " the ancient maner of Cornish building was . . . to set hearths in the midst of the roome for chimneyes which vented the smoake at a louer in the toppe."[3] Unless " chimney " in this passage is to be taken as meaning a portable fire-grate, Carew's statement confirms that of Leland, who, as we have just seen, uses " chimney " in the sense of " flue." A later writer, Aubrey, who was born in 1626, speaks to the same effect. " Antiently before the Reformation, ordinary men's houses, as copyholders and the like, had no chimneys, but fleus like louver holes : some of them were in being when I was a boy."[4] Aubrey is here using the word " chimney " in the sense of

---

[1] From a note by Dr. CHARLES WHITE of Warrington. The " sleeping chamber " is problematical.

[2] *Itin.* (1710–2), viii. ii. 66b.

[3] *Survey of Cornwall*, ed. 1723, f. 53.

[4] In *Antiq. Repert.*, i. 69.

a stone passage in the side of a wall. He is recalling a time when no such passages existed in ordinary houses, and when flues like that at Warrington were used instead. William Harrison, writing in 1577, uses " chimney " in the same sense. After telling us that in the " young days " of old men who lived in his own village in Essex there were not above two or three chimneys " in most uplandish towns," he says that " each one made his fire against a reredosse in the hall where he dined and dressed his meat."[1] The " reredosse " seems to have been the canopy made of wood and plaster, which so often stood over the open fire-hearth and received the smoke. In an old bailiff's roll, dated 1337, and relating to Auckland in Durham, we read of a tree being sawn to support the chimney in the lord's chamber.[2] This record is rendered more interesting by the fact that Richard de Bury, Bishop of Durham, author of *Philobiblon*, then resided at Auckland. One wonders how a book-lover and collector could preserve his treasures unless they were protected from soot and smoke.

The structure which Leland calls a " cover," and which Aubrey calls a " flue," seems to have been known in mediæval Latin as *mantellum camini* and also as *fumarium* or *epicaustorium*,[3] and in English as a " fomerel "[4] or " tuel."[5] In German it is called *rauchmantel*. In *Gawayn and the Grene Knight*, written about A.D. 1360, " chalk whyt chymnees " are described as appearing on the roof of a castle. These may have been the summits of whitewashed flues made of wood and plaster. Bequests of chimneys are not uncommon

---

[1] HARRISON'S *England*, ed. Furnivall, pp. 239, 240.

[2] " In j arbore sarranda, pro camino in camera Domini supportando, 2d."—*Bishop Hatfield's Survey*, ed. Greenwell (Surtees Soc.), p. 204. Probably it was the mantel-tree.

[3] " Papias the grammarian, who wrote about 1051, explains the word *fumarium* by *caminus per quem exit fumus*; and Johannes de Janua, a monk, who about 1268 wrote his *Catholicon*, printed at Venice, says, ' Epicaustorium, instrumentum quod fit super ignem caussa emittendi fumum.' "—BECKMANN, *History of Inventions* (English ed.), 1846, i. p. 311.

[4] " Fomerel of an halle, *fumarium*."—*Prompt. Parv.*

[5] " *Epicausterium*, a thuelle."—WRIGHT-WÜLCKER, *Vocabularies*, 777, 13.

in old wills, but it is doubtful whether or not the term refers to wood or metal flues which could be removed, or to portable fire-grates. The summits of the oldest stone chimneys resemble louvres, and the smoke did not escape from the top, but from one or more holes in the sides.

We hear of a stone chimney (*caminum lapideum*), projecting a foot or more into a passage, in the Hundreds Rolls.[1] But as early as 1172 the castle at Newcastle-on-Tyne had flues in the walls running up to the parapets.

When, therefore, we read in old authors of the absence of chimneys in England, we are not to suppose that the open hearth, except in the hovels of the poorest inhabitants, was without a funnel of some kind to convey the smoke. It is true that stone or brick flues which formed tubes " in the sides of the walls " were only to be found in castles or large buildings, but wood-and-plaster canopies or " covers " to convey the smoke were commonly used from a very early period.

Where there was an original upper story, or where an upper story was made in a room which was originally open to the roof, the floor of that upper story was often level with the mantel-tree of the canopy which covered the fire. Such, as we have seen, was the case in the mud house at Great Hatfield, already described. As the canopy itself was large, covering stove-benches, and even cupboards beneath, the effect was that there was a large chimney-breast, receding like a cone from three sides, in the room above. This chimney-breast often projected four or five feet into the interior of the upper room. It was in this way that the so-called " room in the chimney," about which so many tales have been told, grew up. This " room " was not " a priest's hiding-hole," but a survival of the old way of building a chimney. As there was a great open hearth below, the canopy which covered that hearth was necessarily very large, and protruded a long way into the upper room.[2]

---

[1] *Rot. Hundr.*, i. 406a.

[2] HENNING, *ut supra*, p. 14, gives a plan of a house in the Böhmerwald which shows a small square *rauch-kammer* off the living-room, behind and to one side of the hearth.

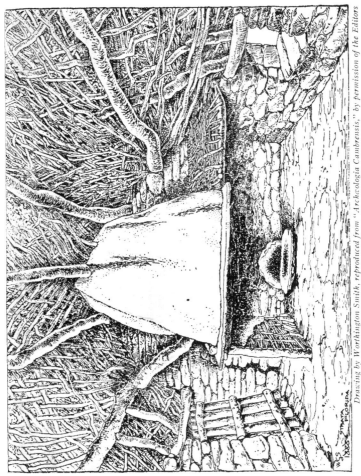

Drawing by Worthington Smith, reproduced from "Archæologia Cambrensis," by permission of the Editors

Fireplace in a cottage (now destroyed) at Strata Florida. The chimney was of wickerwork daubed outside with clay. The lattice shelf on the right was for the poultry. (For exterior and plan see pp. 48 and 49 *ante*.)

" At Derwent Hall, Kimberworth Hill Top, and Worksop, flues from ground-floor fireplaces were found corbelled
out at the first-floor so as to form a small room 6 ft. or 8 ft.
long by about 4 ft."[1] That at Worksop is shown here in
elevation and section. Here the canopy of the chimney—

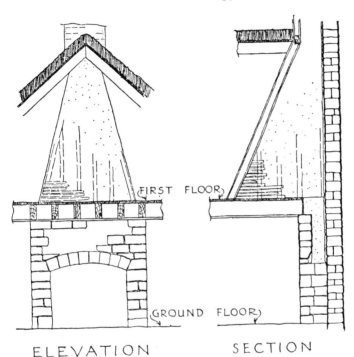

ELEVATION   SECTION

A ground-floor fire-place with lath and plaster " flue "
projecting into upper room.

a wood-and-plaster framework—rested upon the chamber
floor, the actual opening for the smoke being a comparatively small hole adjoining the wall. As there was no door
leading into the so-called " room in the chimney," and no
opening into it except the small hole, that " room " was of
course useless. It was so much wasted space. It has been

<hr>

[1] T. WINDER, in the *Builders' Journal*, vol. iii. p. 41. Compare
the description of the chimney in the mud house at Great Hatfield,
ante, p. 62.

I

remarked that " many of the earliest flues were of wicker,
which is said to account for the disappearance of them from
many of our castles. The writer removed one of stud and
mud from a farm-house at Hill Top, Grenoside, last year."[1]
We have express evidence that at the beginning of the
fifteenth century chimneys were built of wood, for it was
declared by the ordinances of the city of London, compiled
A.D. 1419, that no chimney should thenceforth be made unless
it were of stone, tiles (i.e. bricks), or plaster, and not of wood,
under pain of being pulled down.[2] It is obvious that chimneys built of timber and mud[3] would be easily destroyed, or
would fall down and leave no trace of their existence.

A primitive arrangement of grate and chimney is mentioned by Pennecuik in his *Description of Tweeddale* (1815
ed.). He describes " a circular grate placed upon the floor
about the middle of the kitchen, with a frame of lath and
plaster, or spars and matts, suspended over it, and reaching
within about five feet of the floor, like an inverted funnel,
for conveying the smoke, the whole family sitting round the
fire within the circumference of the inverted funnel." Pennecuik calls this a " roundabout fire-side." Jamieson, quoting
Pennecuik in the *Scottish Dictionary*, remarks : " I do not
recollect having seen the grate carried so far out as the middle
of the kitchen : it is usually on one of the gable ends, the
wall forming a back of the seat which is immediately behind
the fire. In many instances the *roundabout* is formed by a
square projection from the gable."

Some writers have maintained that Greek and Roman
houses had no chimneys except in the kitchens. We are
also told that in Greek houses the chimney " seems only to
have been used in the kitchen."[4] And as to the Romans
it has been a subject of much dispute whether they " had

[1] T. WINDER, *ut supra*, p. 41.

[2] " Item, qe nulle chimenee soit desore en avaunt fait, sinoun
de pier, tielles, ou plastre, et nemy de merisme, sur peyn destre
abatuz."—RILEY, *Munimenta Gild. Lond.*, vol. i. p. 333.

[3] " Dalbura camini lutei ac murorum."—Account, dated 1482,
of the Prior of Finchale in *Priory of Finchale* (Surtees Soc.),
p. ccclv.

[4] SMITH's *Dict. of Greek and Roman Antiq.*, i. p. 664.

Photo: J. E. Birtles, Warrington

Chimney in a house (now destroyed) at Warrington, Lancs.

chimneys for carrying off the smoke, except in the baths and kitchens."[1] If the Roman, like the early English, chimney were made of wood or wicker-work, one could not be surprised at the absence of all traces of its existence. It is probable, as we shall see, that chimneys made of wood existed in large Greek houses in very early times. In the centre of the megaron or men's hall at Tiryns Schliemann found round hearths, about 3·30 m. in diameter, within a space enclosed by four pillars, which were shown to have been of wood. The hearth at Tiryns "was surrounded by an upright rim of plaster. . . . The hearth, being in the middle of the hall, could be approached from all sides to obtain warmth in the winter. The four pillars surrounding the hearth are so far apart as to allow a convenient passage between them and the hearth, and even room to sit there. The smoke, too, did not fill the room, but found a convenient outlet through the openings of the central dome."[2] It is very interesting to compare this account of the hearth at Tiryns with the hearths which we have described, and especially with the central hearth and wooden chimney posts of the old house at Warrington.

It may be taken almost as an axiom that the smaller the window the older the house. It is true that there are many houses belonging to the sixteenth and seventeenth centuries in which very small windows may be found. But these are never the chief windows in the house, though they may represent survivals from older types. The smallness of the oldest windows may be inferred not only from extant examples, but also from the dearness of glass. Another proof is to be found in the fact that the word window means " wind eye "[3] or " wind hole," as though its main use was to admit air rather than light. Another old English word for window was egþyrl, meaning " eye hole." What the oldest forms of English mural windows were like may still be seen in the various " lowp-

---

[1] *Ibid.*, i. 686.
[2] *Tiryns*, ed. 1886, pp. 222, 223.
[3] O.N. *vind-auga.* Gothic, *augadaurô*, means " eye-door."
" In Egyptian houses, when it was decided to open windows on the street, they were mere air-holes near the ceiling."— MASPERO, *Manual of Egyptian Archæology*, 1895, p. 11.

holes," loop-holes or apertures found in the walls of old barns. Here we have narrow, vertical slits, triangular, and sometimes round holes. It is probable that the orginal loop-hole or " lowp-hole " was a " leap-hole " or aperture, through which light or air could enter, or through which smoke could escape.[1] In a much more ornate condition all these forms of " lowp-holes " are to be found in churches. With the Romans, as with us, holes in barns were for ventilation.[2] Amongst the Norsemen " the ancient halls and dwellings had no windows in the walls, but were lighted by louvres and by round openings (*gluggr*) in the roof, covered with the caul of a new-born calf."[3]

In David Loggan's time (1675), college rooms in Oxford had often extremely small windows, these having remained unaltered in the seventeenth century. " Glass windows," says Aubrey, " except in churches and gentlemen's houses, were rare before the time of Henry VIII. In my own remembrance before the Civil Wars, copyholders and poor people had none in Herefordshire, Monmouthshire, and Salop : it is so still."[4] There seems to be no evidence that the small windows of English houses were ever covered with the cauls of new-born calves, as in Iceland. But a good substitute for these was supplied by framed blinds of cloth or canvas, called " fenestralls."[5] In the time of Henry VIII they used linen dipped in oil, as well as glass.[6] Glass, however, was used in great houses from the days of the Romans. At the recently-discovered Roman villa at South Darenth, in Kent, there were found " broken sheets of window glass, having on one surface the iridescence characteristic of all Roman glass, and on the other traces of staining in brilliant colours."[7] It was the comparative dearness of glass which prevented its more

[1] See *Academy*, May 30, 1896.
[2] " Fenestras habere oportet ex ea parti unde commodissime perflari possit."—VARRO, *De Re Rustica*, i. xiii. 5.
[3] CLEASBY and VIGFUSSON's *Icelandic Dict.*, s.v. *gler*.
[4] In *Antiq. Repert.*, i. 72.
[5] *Prompt. Parv.*, p. 155. Compare the " harden " windows in the house at Great Hatfield, *ante*, p. 64.
[6] *Antiq. Repert.*, i. 273.
[7] *Daily News*, December 13, 1894.

frequent use in early times. When it became cheaper in the sixteenth century a fashion arose of making the windows in great houses as numerous and big as possible. A good example of this was Hardwick Hall in Derbyshire, of which the people said :

> " Hardwick Hall,
> More glass than wall."

It is a curious fact that, as late as the sixteenth century, glass windows did not pass to the heir as part of the freehold estate, but to the personal representatives. They consisted of a series of moveable casements, which could be easily taken out.[1]

In the north of England it is the custom to decorate the inner walls of houses, and occasionally the outside stonework, by means of a colour obtained from the plant liverwort. This substance, known as " archil," or " orchil," is mixed with limewash to give it a deep blue colour. Phillips, the author of a dictionary printed in 1678, describes it as " archal, otherwise liverwort, because it groweth upon the freestones of the mountain Peak."[2] Unpleasing as this colour is to the eye of good taste, the practice has been very common till late years. In the north of Yorkshire it is usual to wash bedroom walls with a drab colour, and where they join the slanting roof to put waving lines of dark blue, with spots

of the same colour in the folds. The pattern itself is a reminiscence of the old wicker house,[3] with twigs or pliant boughs woven between the posts. In Derbyshire it is called the *witch-worm* pattern. Sometimes dots only are used. If we

---

[1] " Notices of Past Times from Law Books," by W. Two-PENNY, in *British Magazine*, iii. 650 ; *Northumberland Household Book*.

[2] Compare Latin *glastum*, Irish *glaisin*, woad. Prof. Sullivan thinks there must have been an Irish word *glas*, meaning " blue." Does the place-name Glassby mean " blue dwellings," in allusion to the colour of the houses ? *Cf.* Whitby, or " white dwellings."

[3] O.N. *vanda-hús*, Edda, 52.

may believe an illuminated manuscript, the Anglo-Saxons painted their houses in various hues. " The colours most frequent are yellow and blue."[1] These two colours continued, as we have seen, in use to a comparatively late period. In stripping the plaster off an old house it will usually be found to consist of various layers of blue and yellow colourwash. In the north of Yorkshire yellow-ochre sometimes competes with archil, and it is interesting to notice that the latter substance was also used by the Romans for decorating walls.[2] Clay wash and umber are also used. The floors of houses are commonly flagged with sandstone or blue slate, and after they have been washed on Saturday the edges next the wall, and also the hearth, are decorated by waving lines and dots about a thumb in width, the pattern resembling the upper mural decoration just mentioned. This is done by means of a sharpened piece of whitening.[3] About Wakefield floors are occasionally washed with milk " to fetch a gloss on."

In Derbyshire the ceiling and the walls were sometimes decorated by a light green colour. This was done by putting copperas into the limewash. Before the introduction of wallpapers it was usual to decorate the walls with patterns, such as green leaves with rather indistinct stems.[4] This was done by means of a contrivance resembling a large stencil plate. The practice is ancient, whether the stencil plate was used anciently or not. The regulations of the *Feste de Pui* in London provided that the room for the feast was not to be hung with cloth of gold, or silk, or tapestry, but decorated with leaves and strewed with rushes.[5] In Derbyshire " pot

---

[1] WRIGHT'S *Essays on Arch. Subjects,* vol. i. p. 193. The buildings of the Anglo-Saxons " in many cases, if not always, have been plastered on the outside."—PARKER'S *Glossary of Arch.,* 1850, p. 405. Compare what TACITUS says about the German houses in *Germ.* xvi.

[2] VITRUVIUS, vii. 7.

[3] Information by the Rev. W. Slater Sykes.

[4] The canons of Beauchief had a room called " grenlyf chawmbur " (greenleaf chamber).—ADDY'S *Beauchief Abbey,* pp. 58, 141. The room may, however, have been hung with tapestry, decorated with green leaves.

[5] RILEY, *Munimenta Gild. Lond.,* vol. ii. pt. i. p. 226.

moul " and " rubbing stones " are used for the decoration of floors. Some women make spots on the hearth. This is done by dipping a piece of rag into a basin of " pot moul," or pipe-clay, moistened with water. Either the whole or part of the stone floor is covered by squares drawn by means of a sharpened piece of pipe-clay used like a crayon, and sometimes a small flower is drawn in the middle of each square. So the *megaron*, or men's apartment, at Tiryns had squares produced by scratched lines on its concrete floor.[1] The threshold is usually sanded, and a serpentine line or letter S made in the sand. This decoration is done by a brush, and women rarely omit it. They are very particular about keeping these patterns clean from one Saturday to another, on which day they are renewed.

It is interesting to compare these still-existing customs of decorating floors and hearths with a discovery made in the Glastonbury lake village. In one of the houses there a hearth made of clay was found beneath four other hearths which had been superimposed. " Its shape was, roughly speaking, a square of 5 ft. 3 in., with the corners rounded ; it was raised 4 in. above the surrounding floor level, and its edges bevelled off ; the surface was smooth and flat, and covered with an impressed decoration of circles measuring $5\frac{1}{2}$ in. in diameter, arranged in rows parallel to the edges."[2]

English houses were plastered and whitewashed from the earliest times of which we have any record. The Romans too had their *dealbatores*, whitewashers, or " dawbers." After the great fire of London in the year 1212 the civic authorities ordered that the cookshops on the Thames, as well as all bakeries and breweries, were to be whitewashed and plastered inside and out, as a protection against fire. They also ordered that all houses covered with reeds or rushes which could be plastered should be plastered.[3] Whitewash and fresco-painting were universally applied to the stone walls of ancient

[1] See the illustration in SCHLIEMANN's *Tiryns*, 1886, p. 209.
[2] Report of meeting of the British Association in the *Manchester Guardian*, 2 Sept. 1896.
[3] RILEY, *Munimenta Gild. Lond.*, vol. ii. pt. i. pp. 86, 87.

churches,[1] though modern " restorers " always strip them
off as a late innovation. At Deerhurst the Saxon chapel was,
with the exception of the dressed quoins, " originally plastered, both inside and out, with a thin coat of hard white
stucco, only thick enough to hide the projecting inequalities
of the blue lias rubble-work."[2] Limewash was used by the
Germans,[3] and probably by us, in the days of Tacitus. The
fresco-painter could exercise his art on the moist plaster, and
the " dauber " could cover it with various colours. The
whitewashed house which here and there adds a charm to
the English landscape was anciently a very common object.
In wooden buildings whitewash was intended, as we have
seen, as a protection against fire, and not as an ornament.
In the Kentish villages there are " noggin houses " with
white flowers worked into a red or black foreground of
plaster.

When the roof of a whitewashed house was covered, as
it often was, with green moss or turf, its appearance must
have been very striking. Although stone, slates, straw, reeds,
rushes,[4] and other materials were used for roofing, yet moss
or turf, on account of its cheapness, was much used for farm-
buildings and the cheaper kinds of houses. In the fifteenth
century the turf used for this purpose was known in the
north of England as " dovet," and it seems to have been
laid on a foundation of ling or heather.[5] Turf roofs were
common amongst the Romans. In Iceland the roofs of farm-
buildings are still covered with " green fresh grass-covered
turves," as they were long ago.[6] Old accounts often mention the heather and the moss which were used for covering

[1] LANGLAND, *P. P.*, Passus III. l. 61. TURNER, *Domestic Arch.*,
p. xxvi.

[2] *Archæologia*, vol. 50, p. 68.

[3] *Germ.* xvi.

[4] 1614. " For one thrave of spartes [rushes] to the bull house
and for lainge on of them, vij*d.*"—*Memorials of St. Giles's, Durham*
(Surtees Soc.), p. 44.

[5] 1478. " In reparacione murorum, tecturæ de le cothous et le
yowhous, cum le watlyng et factura murorum ejusdem, et adquisi-
cione de le lynge et dovet pro eisdem domibus, etc."—*Inventories
of Jarrow and Monk-Wearmouth* (Surtees Soc.), p. 120.

[6] *Laxdæla Saga* in VIGF. and POWELL's *Icel. Reader*, pp. 53, 354.

Photo: H. Dan

Reproduced from " Old English Household Life," by Gertrude Jekyll, by permission of B. T. Batsford, Ltd.

Fireplace at Bex Farm, Kent.   The oven is of a similar type to that in the house at Burscough (p. 71).

Fresco (date, 1719) on a house at Newnham, near Faversham.   The groundwork is a pale brick-red.

Photo : H. Dan

or thatching buildings.[1] The practice continued in England
to the middle of the last century, if not later. It is obvious
that in such cases some contrivance was necessary to prevent
the turf from falling down, especially before it had grown
together. Such a contrivance was known amongst the Norsemen as a *torf-völr*, a thin plank which ran along the eaves.
Moss and stonecrop still continue to grow on the thatched
roofs of old cottages.

" Many churches in Norfolk are still covered with thatch,
and some of the high-pitched, ornamental roofs would hardly
bear a heavier covering."[2] It appears from the writings of
an Ulster poet, who flourished between the years 1220 and
1250, that the walls of Armagh Church, in Ireland, were of
polished stone, covered with whitewash :

"Well hath its polished sides been warmed
With lime as white as plume of swans."[3]

We have seen that there were cottages in Yorkshire in
which fire was not used daily, or perhaps not used at all.[4]
The occupants of such cottages must often have sought
warmth at some place of common resort, like the village
smithy or like the *lesche* or public inn of the ancient Greeks.
The place-name Cold Harbour, which occurs so often in
England, and is found in Germany as Kalteherberge, seems
to refer to an inn of this kind.

[1] 1370. " In c travis de hathir emptis pro coopertura domorum
xs."—*Inventories, ut supra,* p. 56. 1605. " A laborer, for gettinge
mosse for the great barne and the newe stable, vppon his owen
chardges xs. viijd. (and he must have ijs. viijd. more when the
stable ys covered)."—*Shuttleworth Accounts* (Chetham Soc.), pt. i.
p. 169.
[2] PARKER, *Glossary of Architecture,* 1850, p. 461.
[3] O'CURRY'S *Manners and Customs of the Ancient Irish,* iii. 58.
[4] *Ante,* p. 81, note 1.

CHAPTER VIII

THE MANOR HOUSE

Rooms of manor houses in the twelfth century, and their
dimensions—The " house "—The " woman house "—
The " bower " and " hall " correspond to the *gynæconitis*
and *andronitis* of a Greek house—Quadrangular arrangement of the manor house and its outbuildings—Great size
of the barns, which contained whole stacks—" Hall and
bower " the two essential parts of a manor house—Con-
tinuance of this form to recent times—The British manor
house as described in the Eddic Songs—Description of
Padley Hall—The hall and buttery—The " trance " or
entry—Outside stairs—Chapel containing fire-place—Its
use—The bower over the buttery—The pigeon-cote over
the chapel window—The curtilage—Manor houses at
Charney Basset and Beaurepaire—The inner chamber—
Furniture—The windows faced inwards to the court—
Apparent absence of upper rooms in the oldest manor
houses.

IN the twelfth century the manor house of Sandon, in
Essex, consisted of a hall, a bower, and a latrina. Adjoining it were ample storehouses for grain, an ox-
house, a washhouse in which clothes were trodden in vats
by the feet, a brewery, a pig-cote, and a hen-house.[1] In the
same century the manor house of Kensworth, in Hertford-
shire, consisted of a hall 35 ft. long, 30 ft. broad, and 22 ft.
high, viz. 11 ft. to the tie-beams, and 11 ft. from the tie-
beams to the ridge-tree. There were two other rooms, viz.
the " house " (*domus*)[2] and the bower, or women's apartment (*thalamus*), the " house " standing between the hall and

---

[1] " Numerus domorum Sandune . Aula . Camera . privata .
Grangiæ due magnæ . Grangiæ ii. minores . Bovaria . Bateressa .
Bracinum . Porcaria . Gallinaria." Appendix to *Domesday of
St. Paul's* (Camden Soc.), p. 134. The editor explains *bateressa*
as a " washhouse."

[2] Here *domus* is equivalent to " entrance hall " or " entry."
Compare BARET's *Alvearie*, 1580 : " an entrie, a porch, or portall
before an house, wherein sometimes men use to dine, and therefore
is taken for a hall . . . *Atrium*."

the bower. The " house " was 12 ft. long and 17 ft. broad ;
it was 17 ft. high, viz. 10 ft. to the tie-beams, and 7 ft. from
the tie-beams to the ridge-tree. The bower was 22 ft. long
and 16 ft. broad ; it was 18 ft. high, viz. 9 ft. to the tie-
beams, and 9 ft. from the tie-beams to the ridge-tree. The
annexed plan, drawn to scale, shows the relative size and
position of the three rooms, the three doorways being conjectural. Besides these rooms there was an ox-house 33 ft.

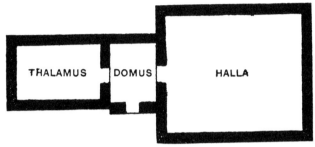

CONJECTURAL PLAN OF KENSWORTH MANOR HOUSE

long, 12 ft. broad, and 13 ft. high. There was also a sheep-
cote, 39 ft. long, 12 ft. broad, and 22 ft. high, with a lamb-
cote, 24 ft. long, 12 ft. broad, and 12 ft. high.[1] From the
above measurements we learn that the " hall " at Kensworth
was nearly twice as big as the " house " and bower put together. At a later period the bower was known in the north
of England as " the woman house."[2] The bower and hall
of this manor house correspond, both as regards relative size
and position, to the *gynæconitis* and *andronitis* of a Greek

---

[1] Compare the Frisian house described by CADOVIUS-MÜLLER
in 1730. Here the *domus* corresponds to the *middelhues*, the *halla*
to the barn, and stalls and the *thalamus* to the kitchen and parlour.
The plan of this house is given in HENNING, *ut supra*, p. 43. Compare also the plan of a house at Ginheim near Frankfort-on-Main,
HENNING, p. 10.

[2] " Halla hujus manerii habet xxxv. pedes in longitud', xxx.
ped' in latitud', et xxii. in altit', xi. sub trabibus, et xi. desuper.
Domus, que est inter hallam et talamum, habet xii. pedes in longitud', xvii. in latit' et xvii. in altitudine, x. sub trabibus et vii. desuper.
Thalamus habet xxii. pedes in longit', xvi. in latitud', xviii. in
altitud', ix. sub trabibus et ix. desuper."—*Domesday of St. Paul's,*
ut supra, p. 129.

house as described by Vitruvius.[1] According to him the principal entrance led at once into the women's room, the men's room being by its side. The dwelling of the Irish *aire*, the man who possessed twenty cows, had also its hall or " living house," and its bower or " woman house." The aire, says Prof. Sullivan, " had the living house, in which he slept as well as took his meals ; the women's house, in which spinning and other domestic work was carried on ; the kitchen, the barn, the calf-house, the pigsty, and the sheep-house.[2] In the residence of chiefs and flatha a sun-chamber or *grianan* was also provided for the mistress of the house, which in the large dúine appears to have been put on the rampart, so as to escape the shadow of the latter."[3] The sun-chamber corresponds to the English solar.[4]

The buildings of these manor houses were so arranged as to form a quadrangle or courtyard, and often their barns, which contained the whole crop, were of great size. Thus in the twelfth century, the great barn of the manor house at Walton was 168 ft. long, 53 ft. wide, and 33½ ft. high, viz. 21½ ft. to the tie-beams, and 12 ft. from them to the ridge-tree.[5] A large barn with a nave and two aisles adjoining Gunthwaite Hall, near Penistone, still remains (see photograph). It is 165 ft. long, 43 ft. broad, and 30 ft. high, viz. 15 ft. to the tie-beams, and 15 ft. from them to the ridge-tree.

[1] 1569. " In the woman house." *Richmond Wills* (Surtees Soc.), p. 219. The same wills also mention, in 1579, " the maydens house " and " the woman's house " (p. 285). Compare *kvenna-hús*, women's apartment, in *Fornaldar Sögür*, ii. 162.
[2] " Conjunguntur autem his (*i.e.*, the Gynæconitis) domus ampliores," *i.e.*, the andronitis, vi. 7 (10).
[3] In *Encyclop. Brit.*, 9th ed., xiii. 256.
[4] Compare *Rot. Hundr.* i. 534a, where it is recorded that the king's baileys were chased out of the village of Watton (Norfolk) to the house of John de Gymingham and that the pursuers broke the windows of John's solarium (*fenestras solarii ejusdem Johannis fregerunt*), entered and ill-treated the officers.
[5] " Magnum orreum Walentonie habet x. perticas et dimid' in longitudine (et pertica est de xvi. pedibus) et in latitudine iii. perticas et v. pedes, et in altitudine sub trabe xxi. ped' et dimid', et desursum trabe xii. ped'."—*Domesday of St. Paul's, ut supra*, p. 130.
There was formerly a barn at Cholsey, in Berkshire, 303 feet long and 51 feet high. The pillars were four yards in circumference.—PARKER'S *Glossary of Arch.*, 1850, p. 241.

It consists of 11 bays of 15 ft. each in length. It has two rows
of wooden pillars, each measuring 14 in. by 9, and standing on
stone pedestals. The length of the tie-beams from one pillar to
another is 23 ft. The roof is in a single span extending across
the whole breadth. The building is of timber framework
filled up with stonework to the height of 8 ft. 9 in. There
are six barn doors. Vast and church-like as this building
seems, as we watch the barn-swallows flitting across its
ancient timbers, it is smaller than that at Walton. In different parts of these large barns stacks of wheat, barley, beans,
peas, and other farm produce were stored, up to the ridge-
tree if necessary.[1] Such buildings resembled the *nubilaria*
of the Romans.

In the twelfth century the manor house of Ardleigh consisted, like that at Sandon, of a hall with a bower annexed.
In this hall there were two moveable or reversible benches,
a fixed table, and a " buffeth." There were also a kitchen,
a stable, a bakehouse, two storehouses for grain, one at the
manor house itself, and the other at the " berewick," and a
servants' house.[2] The " chamber " and " hall " of such
houses are the " bower and hall " of Chaucer,[3] and other
old writers.

If we may take the buildings of Kensworth as our guide,
the manor house of the twelfth century consisted of a central " house," with a *thalamus* or bower on one side, and a
" hall " on the other. That such was the usual arrangement
may be inferred from the typical manor house of later times.
We know from many extant examples of the sixteenth and
seventeenth centuries that the typical country house of the
larger and better kind consisted of a " house-place," or central room, with a large room on either side of it ; entrance

[1] See *Domesday of St. Paul's, ut supra*, where full details are
given.
[2] " Quando autem recepit manerium hæc fuerunt ibi edificia,
quæ cum manerio reddet. Scilicet una aula, et una camera appen-
dicia, et una coquina, et unum stabulum, et i pistrinum, et due
grangie, una ad curiam, altera ad berwicam, et una domus servien-
tium. In aula fuerunt duo bancha tornatilia, et una mensa dor-
miens, et unum buffeth."—*Domesday of St. Paul's, ut supra*, p. 136.
[3] 1386. " Ful sooty was hir bour and eek hir halle."—*Nonne
Prestes T.*, 12.

to the building being obtained by a central door opening into the " house-place." This threefold arrangement was not, however, followed in the smaller houses. In these there was nothing more than a hall and a bower, so that the "house" and the " hall " became synonymous terms, and, as we have seen, this room was sometimes called the " hall house."

The Eddic Songs, which range between the ninth and the twelfth centuries, exhibit a striking picture of family life in the British Isles, and much may be learnt from them about the houses occupied during that period. They tell us of the " salr," or great hall, and of the " búr," bower, or women's room. In the bower " the lady sits with her maids, working the tapestry with figures of swans and beasts, and ships and heroes, fighting and sailing, precisely like the toilette of Bayeux." The hall and bower stand in a court, and " there is a ' ta ' or forecourt, a broad platform probably on which the great hall stands, or the space just before it." In the court " games go on and ceremonies take place."[1] In describing the " salr " the author of *The Lay of Rígh* says that it had " doors turned to the south ; the door was down, there was a ring on the lintel." The meaning is that the door moved up and down in a groove like a portcullis, the ring being used as a knocker. The floor was strewn. The poet gives us a glimpse of the life led within. " Then *mother* took a broidered cloth of bleached flax and covered the table. Then she took thin loaves of white wheat and covered the cloth. She set forth silver-mounted dishes full of . . . . . . old [well-cured] ham, and roasted birds. There was wine in a can, and mounted beakers. They drank and talked whilst the day passed by."[2]

Let us now turn to the ruins of an ancient manor house. The remains of Padley Hall, near Hathersage, in Derbyshire, will supply us with as good an example as can now be obtained.[3] In their original state the buildings formed a

---

[1] VIGFUSSON and POWELL, *Corpus Poet. Boreale*, i. p. lviii.

[2] *Ibid.*, i. p. 239.

[3] " Padley Chapel," as it is locally known, has recently been acquired by St. Mary's R.C. Church, Derby, and it is proposed to restore it. It is described and illustrated in J. C. Cox, *Notes on the Churches of Derbyshire*, 1875–9.—*Reviser's note*.

Padley Hall, Derbyshire. Outer view.

Padley Hall, Derbyshire. Inner view.

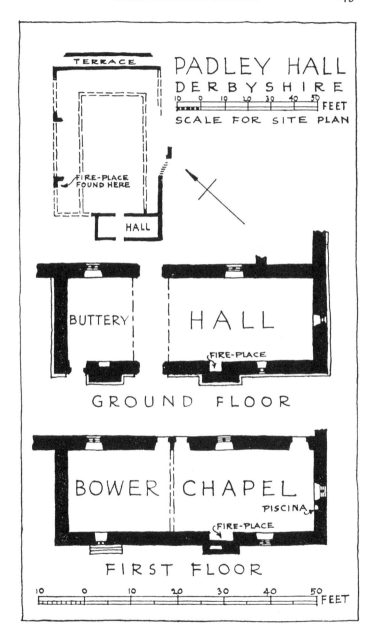

TERRACE

PADLEY HALL
DERBYSHIRE
10 0   10 20 30 40 50
FEET
SCALE FOR SITE PLAN

FIRE-PLACE
FOUND HERE

HALL

BUTTERY

HALL

FIRE-PLACE

GROUND FLOOR

BOWER · CHAPEL

PISCINA

FIRE-PLACE

FIRST FLOOR

10   0   10   20   30   40   50 FEET

quadrangle. Judging from the remains of a buttress, there seems to have been an entrance gateway in the south-east side. On this side, as well as on the opposite side, pieces of walls, dressed stones, and hillocks indicate the site of destroyed buildings. The north-east side appears to have contained no buildings, and to have been bounded on that side by a massive wall, built of large blocks of stone, which is now standing, and is of the height of about twelve feet. On the top of this wall was a terrace or walk, originally approached by a flight of stone steps. On the remaining or south-west side the main walls and roof of the buildings are complete.

The buildings on the south-west side comprise on the ground floor a hall and a buttery, divided from each other by an entry or passage, which goes through into the quadrangle. This entry, which appears to take the place of the *domus* at Sandon, is a little more than 6 ft. wide, and the arches at each end of it are 8 ft. 4 in. high.[1] The buttery measures 15 by 17 ft., and, measured up to the original beams of the floor, is 12 ft. high. It contains one window, 2 ft. 7 in. by 2 ft. 5 in., looking into the quadrangle. Like the hall, it was separated from the entry by a wooden screen, of which no traces remain, and this screen probably contained a hatch for serving provisions, like the buttery hatches in the colleges of Oxford and Cambridge, and in some old houses. Against the south-west wall of the buttery is a buttress, which dies into the wall, and which seems to have been intended to give strength and support to the building. Within the buttress, about two feet from the ground, is an opening 2 ft. 4 in. square, finished by dressed stones, which may have served for an ambry. It cannot have been a fireplace, for there is no flue leading upwards. The north-east wall of the buttery is fractured at its north-west end, as though it had continued further in that direction. The buttery is now occupied as a cow-house, and one of the door-

---

[1] " At Appleton in Berkshire there remains the entrance doorway to the hall of a Norman house of this period, opening at one end of the vestibule or ' screen,' as it was often called ; the two small dorways opening into the kitchen and buttery also remain." TURNER, *Domestic Arch.*, p. 5.

Photo: J. Bradbury

Reproduced from ' The Lure of Midhope-cum-Langsett," by Joseph Kenworthy.

Interior of Gunthwaite Barn, near Penistone.

ways in the south-west wall, shown in the photograph but not on the plan, is modern. The other doorway in the same wall is ancient, so that there was an original doorway leading into the buttery from the outside of the quadrangle. As the buttery had only one rather small window, and was surrounded on its outer sides by walls nearly three feet thick, it was very suitable as a store-room for bread, ale, and wine. We have already seen that in old farm-houses the buttery was placed in the north-west corner of the building. It was so here.

A fire-place, much blackened by smoke, has been found in the north-west side of the quadrangle, at the place marked on the plan. As this was not far from the buttery, the kitchen may have been there.

The arches at the two ends of the entry are partly built up, but there seems to have been no door at either end. On the outer side, however, in the wall next to the hall, is a hole about three feet from the ground and 10 in. square and 1 ft. 2 in. deep, as though a wooden pole had been inserted there to bar the entrance. Such a pole would have served to keep cattle out. An entry or entrance of this kind was known in Scotland as a " trance," and in England as a " traunce,"[1] " tresawnce,"[2] or " tresaunte." These words are derived from the Latin *transitus*, a passage. In the twelfth century such a passage leading to the hall, and dividing the hall from the buttery, was known in the Latin of that period as *trisantia*.[3]

The way into the hall was through a doorway in the screen, which once divided the hall from the entry. This room is 32 ft. in length and 17 ft. in breadth. Like the buttery it was 12 ft. high. It has a square-headed window in each of its three outer walls. The largest window, which faces inwards, is 2 ft. 7 in. by 2 ft. 4 in. The two other windows are only 2 ft. 6 in. by 1 ft. With such small windows the room must have been badly lighted. The hall is now occupied

[1] 1599. " *Tránsito*, a passage ouer from one place to an other, a traunce."—MINSHEU's *Spanish Dict.*
[2] 1440. " Tresawnce, in a house.—*Transitus, transcencia.*"—*Prompt. Parv.*
[3] *Domesday of St. Paul's* (Camden Soc.), pp. xcix. 136.

K

as a stable, and there is a modern doorway in the south-east wall not shown in the plan. There is a fire-place immediately under the fire-place in the chapel above. The buttress or outside chimney-stack of the hall and chapel has lately fallen and been rebuilt with the old stones almost from the foundation. Its summit is a conjectural " restoration." Before this alteration, the top of the chimney-stack was slated like the roof of the building by old slates, and the chimney-stack did not rise above the eaves.

Over the hall is a chapel,[1] and over the buttery is a chamber or bower. These upper rooms were divided from each other by a massive wooden partition which extended from the floor to the ridge-tree, and the part above the tie-beams, with its lath-and-plaster work, still remains. Access to the chamber, as well as to the chapel, was gained by outside steps,[2] probably of wood, in the quadrangle. These have been removed, but the separate doorways still remain.[3] The old floor of the chapel and bower has also been removed, and replaced by a floor three feet below the original floor. On removing the old floor some of the beams or joists were found to be so firmly fixed into the walls that they had to be sawn asunder, and a few of the ends, of hard oak, yet remain *in situ*. The original beams, which were thick and very numerous, were laid in and then built over, so that they served to hold the building firmly together. This lowering of the original floor was done in recent times to give greater height to the two upper rooms, which are now used for storing hay. No traces of inner stairs can be found. Existing remains under the blocked-up doorway in the chapel show that the original floor was of thick oak boards.

The bower was lighted by a square-headed window of considerable size looking into the quadrangle. It had for-

---

[1] The popular, but erroneous, name for the whole of the remains is now " Padley Chapel." Old people speak of it as " the hall."

[2] The upper rooms of an ancient Egyptian house were reached by an outside staircase.—MASPERO, *Manual of Egyptian Archæology* (English ed.), 1895, p. 11.

[3] In the old Norse hall the men's door or chief entrance was in the east gable. At the opposite end there was frequently a second or women's door. See HENNING, *ut supra*, p. 155.

merly also a square-headed window of about the same size on the south-west side, near the wooden partition. The stonework of that window remains in the wall, but there is no trace of it outside, and it must have been built up at an early time. It would appear that some early alterations were made in this wall, and possibly the builder changed his plan whilst the building was being erected. On the summit of the buttress which dies into the wall is a narrow window or pair of small loop-holes. These loop-holes have lancet-shaped heads, and are high up, near the junction of the wall and roof. They are contained within a recess, splayed inwardly, whose top is surmounted by a covering of wooden beams. Both the loop-holes have shallow rebates, as if to hold shutters or the framework of small glass windows. In the wall between the blocked-up window and the loop-holes are two large stones which seem to have been inserted to fill up a recess. Near to these stones the corbel on which one of the pendant posts supporting the roof rests is merely roughly " boasted " or blocked out, as if it was not intended to be exposed to view ; the other corbels, which support pendant posts, are carefully moulded and finished. Accordingly the two loop-holes may have been intended to give light to a small inner apartment or closet.[1] There is no fire-place in the walls of the bower. Although the bower was, properly speaking, the women's apartment, it was " very accessible to the other sex."[2]

It is not known whether any inner communication existed between the chapel and the bower, though the fact that these rooms were approached through separate doors on the outside is some evidence that there was not. The chapel contains three square-headed windows, and was better lighted than any other room in the building. The upper part of the south-east window, now walled up, retains a part of its tracery. This window served for the east window of the chapel, beneath which an altar may have been placed. On its southern side is a small water-drain, lavatory,

[1] " One doore taken from the priuie in the said parlor."—MS. of WM. DICKINSON, 1572, in the author's possession.
[2] WRIGHT'S *Homes of Other Days*, p. 272.

or piscina, about a foot square and a foot deep, and nearly two feet from the window. The sill of the south-east window is ornamented beneath by pellet-moulding, exactly like that under the eaves. In the south-west wall is a fire-place 5 ft. 9 in. wide, which is over the fire-place in the hall below. The fire-place in the chapel[1] may be accounted for by the purposes to which such a room was formerly applied. " We find that when our sovereigns did not attend to public business in the hall, or give audience in their chamber, they used the chapel for that purpose. In the chronicles of the twelfth, and even of the thirteenth century, there are frequent notices of the transaction of secular business in the domestic chapel."[2] There is no reason why the chapel at Padley should not have been used, except in service time, as an ordinary dwelling-room.[3] The *Boldon Buke*[4] of 1183, and *Bishop Hatfield's Survey*,[5] of the fourteenth century, setting forth the duties of villeins at big hunts, state that the villeins find a bed (*lectica*) in the hall, the chapel, or the chamber. The chapel must also have served often as a library. In the will of Hugh Trotter, treasurer of York Minster, who died in 1503, it is stipulated that various books, including Ovid and Vergil, which Trotter leaves to St. Barnard's Hospital, Canterbury, shall be chained in the chapel of that hospital at the testator's expense.[6]

The roof of the chapel, as well as of the bower, contains a single pair of hammer-beams with one tie-beam in the lath-and-plaster screen which divided the chapel from the bower.

---

[1] At Heybridge, in Essex, about 1271, there was a " solarium cum capella de constructione Herveii de Borham cum duobus caminis de plastro Paris."—*Domesday of St. Paul's* (Camden Soc.), p. cxix. Here then was a chimney, made of plaster of Paris, in the chapel.

[2] TURNER, *Domestic Arch.*, p. 17, and the authorities there cited.

[3] At Caddington, in Herefordshire, in 1181, mass was performed three times a week, if required, in the domestic chapel of the manor house.—*Domesday of St. Paul's* (Camden Soc.), p. 147.

[4] Pub. SURTEES SOC., p. 29.

[5] *Ibid.*, p. 69.

[6] *Testamenta Eboracensia* (pub. SURTEES Soc.), vol. iv. p. 220. " Ut hi libri cathenentur in capella ejusdem hospitii sumptibus meis."

In the chapel the ends of the hammer-beams are ornamented by rude figures of angels whose arms support plain shields. In the bower the ends of the hammer-beams are ornamented by plain shields surrounded by cable moulding. No traces of painting or gilding now remain. On the north-east side of the chapel, near the large window, was a doorway leading from the chapel into a long upper room or rooms, which stood on the south-east side of the quadrangle. The south-east wall of this range of buildings yet remains to the height of about twelve feet. In it are very numerous holes for the reception of the beams which supported the floor.

Returning to the outside of the building, there is a pigeon-cote consisting of four rows of pigeon-holes in the gable end above the chapel window. These are part of the original building, and they do not go through into the chapel. Only lords of manors had the right to keep a pigeon-house.[1]

It is probable that the inner walls of the destroyed buildings which surrounded the court were built of wood. This would account for the total destruction of those walls, and the partial preservation of the outer walls. Examples of great houses yet remain in which the walls facing the court are of wood, whilst the outer walls are of stone.

The outside of the chapel and bower is ornamented just below the eaves by a course of pellet-moulding, reminding us of the *guttae* of a Doric entablature. This is an interesting example of " wooden construction translated into stone," for it represents the ends of the poles or spars which supported the roof. The slates of the roof are modern. The masonry of the outside wall is of large smooth ashlar stones, very well dressed and jointed. At the gable ends, and on the side facing the quadrangle, the masonry is not quite so good, the stones being smaller and less carefully dressed. In the walls are a number of " putlock holes," or *columbaria*, for the scaffolds when the house was being built.

The other rooms or offices, such as the kitchen, brewery, stables, and farm-buildings, were contained in the two sides of the quadrangle which adjoined the hall and buttery.

There are no signs of a moat or any kind of defence, but

[1] ROGERS, *Six Centuries of Work and Wages*, 1884, p. 75.

the house has been completely surrounded by a strong wall which, in some places, is five feet thick. This wall enclosed a quadrangular area of about six acres. It seems to have been a sort of barmkyn, or outer fortification, into which cattle were driven for safety. Quite lately the wall has been sold to a railway company, and the greater part of it removed. The stones in the portion which remains are large ; some of the removed stones are said to have been much more so. The outer courses were of stone without mortar. The interior was filled up by grout and rubble.

A little distance up the hill to the east of the house was a small, deep pond, now dry, which may have served for a reservoir to supply the house with water. About 500 yards to the west were the stews or fish-ponds. The railway has gone straight through them.

A house at Charney-Basset, near Wantage, in Berkshire, has a hall and buttery on the ground-floor, with a chamber and chapel on the floor above them.[1] In this case the chapel, which is only 12 ft. 5 in. by 9 ft. 10 in., is over the buttery, whilst the chamber, containing a fire-place, is over the hall.

The chapel is separated from the chamber by a stone wall with a small doorway through it. The hall beneath the chamber is 30 ft. by 16, and has an original fire-place in it beneath the fire-place in the chamber, and three original windows. It has a door leading into the courtyard. In place of windows the buttery has small loops. As at Padley both the chamber and the chapel have an open timber roof. The chapel, which has two windows, has a piscina and a locker in the wall. As at Padley, too, the entrance to the chamber and the chapel was by steps from the yard.[2] The arrangement of this building, which is ascribed to the end of the thirteenth century, closely resembles the building at Padley in other respects.

---

[1] At Sutton in Middlesex there was " Una aula cum boteleria ad unum caput, cum parva capella ad aliud caput " ; and also " unum solarium cum parva capella tegulis coopertum."—*Domesday of St. Paul's* (Camden Soc.), p. cxix.

[2] TURNER, *Domestic Arch.*, p. 153, where see the drawings and plans.

A third example may suffice to show that this was a common type of the manor house when built of stone. In 1464 the manor house of Beaurepaire near Durham is described in an inventory of that date. There was a chapel, an outer chamber (*camera exterior*), an inner or withdrawing chamber (*camera interior*),[1] a hall, a buttery (*promptuarium*), and a kitchen. The outer chamber contained two sheets, two " dormonds," and three bolsters filled with feathers. Its walls and windows were hung with a delicate woollen cloth covered with a tissue of silk. It had a long dining-table with two trestles, a shovel and poker (showing that there was a fireplace), two brass candlesticks, and an iron candlestick fixed to the wall. The inner chamber contained three chests, an old chair, and a stool near the bed (*juxta lectum*). From this we learn that the outer chamber was a women's sitting-room, elegantly furnished and draped, with an inner chamber, i.e. a bed-chamber, adjoining. Such may have been the case at Padley, and possibly also at Charney. The hall at Beaurepaire, which was hung with variegated red say, contained five dining-table leaves (*tabulae mensales*), and four pairs of trestles. There were four long forms and four stools for the high table. As an iron poker is mentioned there must have been a fire-place. The buttery contained four candlesticks, used doubtless in the hall. The kitchen contained a large number of household utensils. In the chapel was a clock with two bells, one of them being larger than the other.[2]

The larger windows at Padley face inwards to the quadrangle or court. Though the country around is very beautiful, the builders of the house did not regard the scenery. Two little windows, 2 ft. 6 in. high and 1 ft. broad, in the hall looked outwards, and through them glimpses of the surrounding hills and woods might have been had if the glass were good enough to admit of a view at all. The only view to be had from the bower or women's apartment was through a

[1] 1567. " The chambre within the greate chambre."—*Richmond Wills* (Surtees Soc.), p. 201. 1444. " Lego eidem optimum bordetbed in le withdrawyng chaumbre. . . . Item lego eidem j lectum plumarium . . . in le forchaumbre."—*Test. Ebor.* (Surtees Soc.), ii. p. 101.

[2] *Feodarium Prioratus Dunelm.* (Surtees Soc.), p. 190.

window which faced a blank wall, or a row of buildings, on the opposite side. Such was the usual way of erecting these houses. Richard Carew, writing of his own county in 1602, says, " The ancient maner of Cornish building was to plant their houses lowe, to lay the stones with mortar of lyme and sand, to make the walles thick, their windowes arched and little, and their lights inwards to the court."[1]

The pleasure of seeing was sacrificed for the advantage of not being seen. Moreover, when glass was rare, or not used at all, country gentlemen could not think of prospects, and they continued to follow the example set by their predecessors. The practice of building in this way was the result of historical tradition. The large Roman villas " at Lydney, Woodchester, Chedworth, and many other places have an extensive cloister or *peristylium*, round all four sides of which the rooms are arranged very like the plan of a mediæval monastery."[2] The Roman house, with its quadrangle, and its rooms facing inwards, was the type which the builders of such houses as that at Padley unconsciously followed, unsuitable as that type was for the English climate. The house at Padley was not expressly built to keep out the sunshine, but it would have served well for that purpose.

It will have been noticed that in the description of the manor houses of Sandon, Kensworth, and Ardleigh nothing is said about upper rooms, and as the descriptions are careful, we may with probability conclude that there were none. At Kensworth the hall was 35 ft. long ; at Padley it is 32 ft. At Kensworth the hall was 11 ft. high when measured to the tie-beams ; at Padley it was 12 ft. to the ceiling. At Kensworth there was a *domus* between the hall and the bower ; at Padley there is an entry or " trance " between the hall and buttery. At both places the relative position of hall and bower was the same, though the bower at Padley was placed over the buttery. It should be noted that the word *búr*, bower, in Old Norse meant buttery. The changes which the word underwent are interesting, for the buttery and kitchen were on the women's side of the house. It is most likely that

[1] *Survey of Cornwall*, ed. 1723, f. 53.
[2] SMITH's *Dict. of Greek and Roman Antiq.*, i. p. 683.

in early times the word " bower " included the buttery, and was used to describe the whole of the women's side of the house. Even in the thirteenth century " hall and bower " were the essential parts of a manor house, other rooms being mere adjuncts or " appurtenances."[1]

[1] Thus about 1250 the villeins of Blackwell had to provide a wooden house for the Prior of Worcester, built on " forks " or " crucks." " Invenient de suo postes, furcas, ticna, et alia ligna necessaria præter Waldlure ad faciendum aulam, cameram cum pertinentiis, grangiam, boveriam, et coquinam Prioris."—*Registrum Prioratus Wigorn* (Camden Soc.), p. 65b.

CHAPTER IX

THE CASTLE AND WATCH-TOWER

Public character of the English castle—The " keep "—
" Toot hills " and the oldest watching-places—Towns
built at the feet of castles—The castle at Castleton,
Derbyshire, described—Concrete walls of the keep—The
angles of the keep directed to the cardinal points—The
two rooms of the keep—The concealed roof—Beacons
lighted on the summits of towers—Elevated entrance to
the keep—The living room of the keep—The garderobe
and mural chamber—Curtain rods of the windows—The
watchmen employed by the Crown at this castle and elsewhere—No fire-place extant in the keep—The window-
like aperture above the concealed roof—Its possible uses
—The room in the basement—The cave beneath the keep
—The offsets and the lead work—Date of the keep at
Castleton—English round keeps compared to Sardinian
núraghs—Scottish brocks compared—Church towers used
as watch-towers—Elevated position of their doors—
" Lanterns " and fire-places in church towers—Church
towers used as lighthouses—Church tower at Newcastle
controlled by the burgesses—Meaning of " belfry "—
Watchmen inhabiting German church towers—Detached
bell towers—Circular church towers—Windows facing the
cardinal points—Irish and Scotch " round towers " compared—These towers used as watch-towers.

THE public character of an English castle is shown
by the fact that it was maintained by a local tax,
known as ward-silver, ward-penny,[1] castle-guard, or
" waite-fe," levied on those who dwelt within a defined distance from its walls. We know that, in one case at least,
different tenants contributed towards the maintenance of different parts of the building.[2] Entries in the Hundreds Rolls
contain frequent mention of the taxes due for the upkeep of
castles and garrisons. In Essex, certain dependents of the
earl-marshal of Chesterford " solebant vigilare *wardestaf* bis
per annum et dabant viij*d.* per annum ad *wardpeny.*"[3] In

---

[1] *Domesday of St. Paul's* (Camden Soc.), p. lxxviii.—RASTELL'S
Statutes, 1557, f. 47 *b.*; *Magna Carta*, s. 29.
[2] See GALE'S *Registrum Honoris de Richmond.*
[3] *Rot. Hundr.*, i. 155a.

a Shropshire entry[1] we read of somebody who " dat *motfey* iiij^{ord}. stretward iiij^{ord}." The Earl of Oxford, says another entry,[2] " reddit per annum *ad ward* Castr. Dovor xxs." On the same page we find a mention of *letefe*. The Abbot of St. Edmunds held a certain manor from the king " pro servicium xxs. annuatim solvendi ad *waytefe* castelli de Norwich."[3]

It may be noted, by way of comparison, that " Latium was anciently divided into a number of clan-settlements or villages which were an aggregate of dwellings gathered round a central enclosed or fortified space, an *arx* or *castellum*."[4] In England the different villages made separate contributions of castle-guard rent to the castle of their district.[5] A castle was an Acropolis, or place of refuge for the neighbours when plundering enemies invaded the land. It contained a watch-tower, usually known as a keep,[6] and it was always built, if possible, on a hill or rock. This watch-tower was, evidently, not always of stone. The Hundreds Rolls record that at Shrewsbury Castle " unus magnus turris ligneus," which fell down, was never rebuilt.[7]

On the tops of many English hills there are enclosures, surrounded by walls of earth, some of which, in early times, were the sites of villages. These are sometimes known as " castles," and they are often called " camps." The ancient inhabitants of Great Britain found that some kind of fortification was necessary for the preservation of their lives and property, and they tried to make themselves safe in pile dwellings or lake dwellings, and, as an alternative to these, on eminences strengthened by art. Like the prehistoric villages in the Po valley, the earth walls of these fortified villages were surmounted by wooden palisades. There were

[1] *Rot. Hundr.*, ii. 55a.
[2] *Ibid.*, i. 516a.
[3] *Ibid.*, i. 502a.
[4] Smith's *Dict. of Greek and Roman Antiq.*, s.v. *pagus*.
[5] *Notes and Queries*, 8th S., x. 351. In the *Welsh Laws*, ed. by Hubert Lewis, p. 143, the repair of castles is laid down as part of the work of the tenants on a manor.
[6] An old sense of the verb " keep " was to " watch." Compare " He that keepeth Israel shall neither slumber nor sleep."
[7] *Rot. Hundr.*, ii. 106b.

huts within the enclosed villages of the Po valley, and such was the case in Great Britain. As population became more numerous, everybody could not live in an elevated stronghold or in a lake village, and so open settlements in the plain became usual, though people still liked to live within a comfortable distance from their ancient place of refuge. In the end they ceased to inhabit it permanently, but they maintained the earth-walls or substituted stone walls for them, and they threw up a mound, or built a tower, on which the warders kept watch and gave warning of approaching danger. The Roman *oppidum* was the stronghold which commonly overlooked the plain. It was so in ancient Greece. " To detached towers, courts surrounded by masonry were sometimes added as places of refuge for the inhabitants of the neighbouring country and their goods."[1] It was so, too, with the ancient Israelites : " He is my high tower and my refuge." In England the earliest form of watch-tower was an artificial mound known as a " ward-steal," " toot hill," or " touting hill," these words being equivalent to the Latin *specula*, Italian *specchia*, Greek σκόπιά, a watch-tower.[2] Such artificial mounds, with their surrounding ditches, still exist in considerable numbers. Some are found adjoining enclosed areas or castle yards. Often these mounds are found close to old churches, and then in addition to their use as watching-places they were sometimes used as moot-hills, or places on which the moot or local assembly met.

Three entries in the Hundreds Rolls are worth noting because of their bearing on the thirteenth-century castle. One of these is a deposition to the effect that in Hereford the

---

[1] GUHL and KONER, *Life of the Greeks and Romans* (Eng. trans.), 1875, p. 68, where a plan of such a combination in the island of Temnos is given. Compare " *refugium*, geberg," in WRIGHT-WÜLCKER, *Vocab.*, 43, 14.

[2] " *Specula uel conspicilium*, weardsteal."—WRIGHT-WÜLCKER, 180, 3. " *Specula*, a totynghylle,"—*Ibid.*, 797, 20. " Totyng hole or place, or a hyghe hyll to espye all about, *specula*."—HULOET, *Abcedarium*, 1552. The word occurs in German place-names as *spiegel*. Compare the German place-name Wartberg (watch-tower), Spanish *miradéro*, a viewing-place, watch-tower ; O.N. varð-berg, a " watch-rock " ; also O.E. *scēawere*, O.H.G. *scouwa*, watch-tower.

King possesses " magnam partem civitatis . . . cum *castro et haya*,"[1] meaning literally " with camp and hedge " but doubtless implying " castle and walls." Another entry[2] refers to " castrum Bristoll et *berton castrum* Glouc' cum *berton* Winchecumbe & Newenham." *Berton castrum* perhaps implies a castle with a farm adjoining.

The third entry[3] is a curious one. It states that William Belet constructed and raised a castle (*castellum*) at Marham to the prejudice of the King and his castle at Norwich and the country at large, in that, should war break out, the enemy could have a base (*receptaculum*) there and lay waste the whole country-side and the adjacent religious houses.

Many English towns are built at the feet of castles. A good example may be seen at Castleton, in Derbyshire, where a castle, anciently known as Peak Castle,[4] protected the neighbourhood for many miles round. Bounded on the west side by a nearly perpendicular abyss, at whose base lies the great Peak Cavern, and on the two remaining sides of a triangular space by steep and all but inaccessible declivities, few strongholds have possessed better natural advantages. Ascending the hill by a zigzag path on the north side next to the town, we enter the triangular area or castle yard by a ruined gateway, on one side of which are some remains of a porter's lodge. The area forms a sloping platform, in whose southern angle stands the watch-tower or keep. The keep is on the highest part of the area, and it is usual for such a building to occupy the highest ground. The wall which still surrounds the area on the north and west sides contains some herring-bone work on the west side. It is a little more than six feet thick, and is now of an average height of nine feet. The wall on the south-east side is modern, and seems to

---

[1] *Rot. Hundr.*, i. 185a.
[2] *Ibid.*, i. 175b.
[3] *Ibid.*, i. 519b.
[4] The entry in Domesday is " Terram castelli Will'i peurel in pechefers tenuerunt Gernebern et Hundinc," the words " in pechefers " being written over " castelli." Pechefers may be " Peak forest." The place is called Nordpech in 1173. (" Pipe Rolls.")
[Prof. Ekwall, in *Place-names of Bucks*, p. 175, suggests that Pechefers is a mistake for Peches ers, *i.e.* Peak's arse, from the proximity of the cavern.]

SECTION C-D

10   10   10   20   30   40   50

PEAK CASTLE, DERBYSHIRE

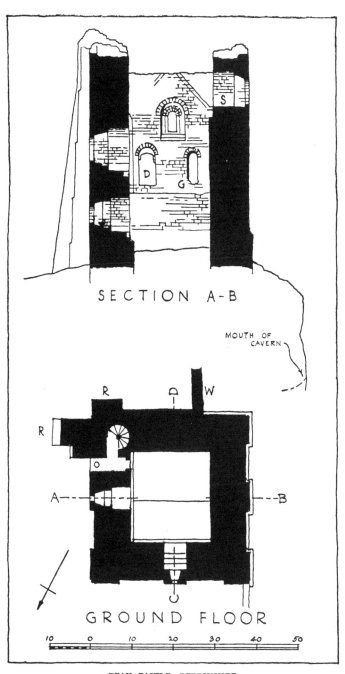

SECTION A-B

MOUTH OF
CAVERN

GROUND FLOOR

PEAK CASTLE, DERBYSHIRE

have replaced an ancient wall like that on the other two sides, though, for the purpose of defence, a wall on that side would hardly have been necessary. There is no mound or earthwork of any kind within the castle yard, but the ground has been "levelled up" next to the north wall to a height of about eleven feet. Besides the remains of the porter's lodge at the entrance there are some slight remains of a barbican or house on the north wall, as well as of a tower in the northwest angle. It is said that on digging into the area some years ago the "tops of some arches" were discovered.

On the basement floor the walls of the keep are eight feet thick. They are built of concrete made of broken pieces of limestone, which is found on the spot, mixed with mortar. Both the outside and the inside of this concrete wall have been faced with fine and well-jointed blocks of gritstone ashlar, which were brought from a considerable distance. Much of this gritstone facing has been stripped off, or has fallen from two of the outer sides, so that on those sides the concrete is laid almost bare. The concrete is of intense hardness, and holds so well together that little harm has been done to the stability of the building by the removal of its outer facing. We are reminded of the thick Roman concrete walls made of broken stones and lime-faced with thin burnt brick. "Walls thus formed were stronger and more durable than even the most solid masonry. Blocks of stone could be removed, one by one, by the same force that set them in place; but a concrete wall was one perfectly solid and coherent mass, which could only be destroyed by a laborious process, like that of quarrying hard stone from its native bed."[1] In the oldest of these walls the concrete was poured into a wooden framework, which was raised as the wall proceeded.

The four angles of the quadrangular keep are directed to the four cardinal points. In other words, if we bisect those angles by two imaginary lines which intersect each other, those lines will point to the north, south, east, and west.

The keep contained two rooms, one above the other. The

[1] Prof. MIDDLETON in SMITH'S *Dict. of Greek and Roman Antiq.*, ii. 188.

upper room was surmounted by a roof of good pitch, and, as was usual in rectangular keeps, this roof was concealed by the walls which rose above it. When we consider that these buildings were watch-towers as well as fortresses the reason for this concealment becomes apparent. As the roof was below the rampart walk the watchman's view was un-interrupted, and beacon fires could be more safely lighted, and signals be more easily seen from a distance. Amongst the Romans such fires were lighted on watch-towers to give warning of the approach of freebooters,[1] and the practice was continued through the Middle Ages. In Caxton's *Cronicles of Englond*, printed in 1480, we read " that men shold tende the bekenes that the countrey myght be warned."[2]

The keep was entered not by the opening broken into the lower room on the north-east side (ground plan, O), as it is at present, but by an arched doorway (D in the plan of upper floor) opening into the upper room on the south-east side. This doorway, 4 ft. 9 in. wide, is surmounted on the outside by a relieving arch and tympanum. It is 8 ft. 6 in. above the present level of the ground outside.[3] The wall (W) at right angles to the south-east wall seems to be modern.

Passing through the arched doorway we enter the upper apartment or living-room. The height of this room was 17 ft. to the " square," and 27 ft. to the ridge. The length is 22 ft. and the breadth 19 ft. Probably the floor was of wood, but in some castles it is supported by a stone vault. In the thickness of the south-east wall is a gardrobe (G),[4] well concealed from view by a tortuous passage, and having

---

[1] " Praedonum adventum significabat ignis e specula sublatus." CICERO, *Verr.*, ii. v. 35.

　　　　" . . . dat signum specula Misinus ab alta
　　　　aere cavo."—VERGIL, Æn., l. 239.

[2] In *Hist. Eng. Dict.*, s.v. beacon.

[3] The entrance to old Scotch houses was " very often by a flight of steps which reaches up to the second story ; the floor, which is level with the ground, being entered only by stairs descending within the house."—JOHNSON's *Journey to the Western Highlands*, ed. 1886, p. 28.

[4] It is engraved in *Arch. J.*, vol. v. 214. An account of this castle by Mr. W. H. ST. JOHN HOPE is given in *Derb. Arch. J.*, xi. 124.

L

formerly a door at its entrance. The gardrobe projects, like an oriel window without a corbel, over the precipice below, and is lighted by a small window or opening. On the outside it is concealed from view by the later, and apparently modern, wall marked " W " on the plan. A narrow doorway, formerly closed by a door, in the north-east wall leads to a mural chamber (M), which has two little windows, one in the north-east and the other in the north-west. It is not known for what purpose this chamber was used, but it would have made a convenient watching-place,[1] bedroom, or store-room.[2] Both the gardrobe and the mural chamber have barrel vaults. The living-room is lighted by three narrow windows, the highest of which is in the south-east gable, and twelve feet above the floor.

The other windows are in the north-east and north-west walls, and, like the windows in the mural chamber, afford a view on one side of the town beneath, and on the other side of the porter's lodge. The morning and midday sun fell on the gable window, but the other windows are small, and the room was not well lighted. The apertures of the two lower and smaller windows were concealed in the night-time by curtains, for the holes which contained the ends of the curtain rods are there, just below the semicircular arches which surmount the sides or jambs. There was sufficient room in these recesses to hold beds, but it is more likely that curtains were drawn to make the room warmer by night.

From what has been said it will be seen that this room was intended to be permanently occupied. Fortunately we know from historical records that this keep was used as a watch-tower in the year 1158, and for many years afterwards. The public records show that a porter and two watchmen

---

[1] " Towtynge hoole to look out at in a walle or wyndowe."—HULOET's *Abcedarium*, 1552.

[2] In a description of this castle by Mr. HARTSHORNE in *Arch. J.*, vol. v. 214, it is described as " a small chamber inaccessible," and the plan of it is wrong. The keep has been carefully surveyed by Mr. Edmund Winder, junr., architect, and by Mr. Barton Wells. For their assistance in examining the building at various times the author is much indebted.

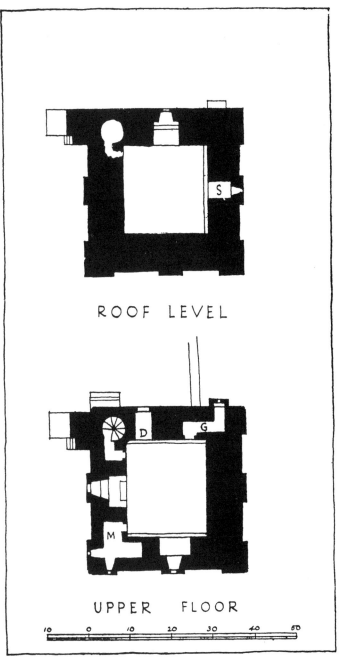

ROOF LEVEL

UPPER FLOOR

PEAK CASTLE, DERBYSHIRE

(*vigiles*)[1] were employed by the Crown at this place, and received together the yearly salary of £4 10s., which is about £150 of our money. The salaries of the porter and watchmen at other castles are of similar amounts.

At Rockingham Castle in A.D. 1160 a porter and two watchmen got together the yearly salary of £4 11s. 4d. At Worcester in 1163 the only watchman employed received a yearly salary of £1 10s. 5d., and the porter a yearly salary of £2 5s. 7d. At Hanton in 1160 the capellanus, watchmen, and porter got £4 11s. 3d. These salaries were paid to the sheriff of each county out of the Royal Treasury. In 1173 the sum of £45 8s. was paid to twenty knights (*milites*) and sixty foot soldiers at the castles of Nottingham, Peak, and Bolsover, 160 bushels of wheat having been stored at the Peak in the previous year. But this was an extraordinary occasion, and the regular yearly salaries paid to the porter and watchman at Peak Castle—no payments being made to any other persons—show that they were the only officials permanently maintained there.[2] The porter of Peak Castle occupied the lodge at the gate of the enclosure, whilst the watchman lived in the upper room of the keep. They probably watched in turns, giving signals of approaching danger by hoisting a flag, blowing a horn, or lighting a fire on the rampart walk. The view from the top is wide and beautiful.

In such a place life would hardly have been bearable in winter without a fire, but there is no trace of either chimney or flue in any part of the building. It will be noticed, however, in the section A B, that the wall on the southwest side of the living-room is unpierced by any window, in order, it may be, that a wooden, or perhaps leaden,[3] flue might stand near it. We have already seen in a previous

---

[1] " In liberatione . ii . vigilum et . i . portarii de Pech' iiii . li . et . x . s."—*Great Roll of the Pipe* (Pipe Roll Soc.), i. p. 52. Etymologists may consider whether Peche or Pech is cognate with *pagus*, πάγος, in the sense of hill-fort. Compare " beach," cognate with "*fāgus*."

[2] There was a castellan, or constable, but no mention of him is made in the Pipe Rolls.

[3] 1507. " To the plommer for casting and working my fummerel of lede," at Little Saxham Hall.—Account in *Prompt. Parv.*, p. 169.

chapter how frequently the flues of ancient fire-places were made of wood and plaster. Such a flue may have been carried through the roof near the opening on the south-west side above the roof, which looks so like a window. Unless such a flue existed we are driven to the conclusion that a fire was burnt in an open brazier, thereby filling the room with smoke.

The window-like aperture (S) in the south-west wall above the roof may have been a sheltered watching-place. It may have been what Cotgrave calls " a sentrie, or little lodge for a sentinell, built on high," the origin of our modern sentry box.[1] It will be noticed in the plan that, unlike all the windows below, the floor of this window-like aperture is flat. It is about 6 ft. 5 in. in depth and 4 ft. 1 in. in breadth. The narrow loophole at the outer end of the aperture has been crossed horizontally by two bars, one at the height of 4 ft. 7 in. above the floor, and the other a little above the floor. The adjacent country is highest on this side of the keep, and it was therefore necessary that the watchman should stand, when occasion required, at a greater height than on the other sides, where the country is much more open. It is possible that a cresset light was burnt in this aperture, the flame being protected by a wooden door or shutter kept in its place by the iron bars. The aperture can hardly have been a dormer window.

We may now descend by the circular staircase in the thickness of the wall into the basement or apartment on the ground floor. As usual this basement is at the exterior ground level, whilst the natural slope of the ground within remains unaltered. The height of this room, measured from the highest part of the ground within to the ledges which supported the floor above, was 12 ft., and 17 ft. measured from the lowest part of the ground. The entrance to the stairs was closed by a door at the bottom of the staircase, as

[1] *Dictionarie of the French and English Tongues*, ed. 1632, s.v. *garite*.

" Sentry " is probably from Lat. *sentire*, to perceive.

A writer in the *Gentleman's Magazine*, May 1781, observes that in many Cornish parishes there is a field known as the " sentry." But this is probably a corruption of " sanctuary."

well as by a door in the living-room above. In the basement
there are two narrow windows, deeply splayed, " slipped up
to," and admitting very little light. Such rooms as this are
the rule in keeps of this period, and are regarded by the best
authorities as store-rooms.[1] No well has yet been discovered
in the basement, as is usual in these buildings, but its pipe
may yet be in the wall at the bottom. Strange to say, a small
natural cave extends beneath the building, with openings in
the cliff on the south-east and south-west sides. A few pieces
of zigzag moulding, which seem to have formed part of
some earlier structure, are built into the inner walls of the
keep.

There is an offset or ledge on two adjacent sides of the
basement, and also beneath the " sentry," not to support a
floor, but to diminish the thickness of the wall as it rises.
The circular staircase goes from the bottom to the top of
the building, so as to supply each floor. At the top it ended
beneath a roofed turret, from which a door opened out on
the rampart walk. The outer edge of this walk was protected
by a wall, now rather less than two feet high. There are no
ledges or other evidence of the existence of a storey in the
roof. The roof itself is entirely gone, but its position is
clearly marked by projecting courses of stone or weather-
mouldings, which supported the ends of the spars. Remains
of the lead which composed the two lateral gutters exist,
and it is probable that the roof was made of that material,
more especially as lead was found in great abundance in the
neighbourhood. Parts of the leaden tube (T) or casing
through which the water from the roof was discharged on
the north-east side remain in the wall.

The positions of the broad pilaster strips at the angles, as
well as in the centres, of the outer facing will be seen on
the plans. At each angle of the building was a cylindrical
shaft with a neat capital in the Norman style, the shaft at
the south angle being very well preserved. Altogether this
keep was designed with great ingenuity, and its workman-

[1] Compare the store-rooms in the basements of many old lofty
quadrangular houses in Thessaly, the habitable part being the top
storey.

ship is excellent. As a fortress it was impregnable. A few necessary repairs have been done at the east angle of the keep, the two buttresses (R) at that angle shown on the plan of the ground floor being new. They are intended to support the building, which seemed weakened by the windows of the staircase and the removal of the outer facing. It appears from entries in the Pipe Rolls that during the years 1172 and 1173 the sum of £113 was spent on works (*operationes*) done at the king's castle of Peak and Bolsover ; but the payments made to the watchmen of the Peak at an earlier time seem to indicate that the keep was built before the year 1172. At any rate it cannot be of later date.

Besides the rectangular keep there are in England round keeps, the finest example being that at Conisborough (king's fort), near Doncaster. If we take Mr. Clark's admirable plans and sections of this building[1] and compare them with published plans of those strange round towers, known as núraghs, in Sardinia,[2] the resemblance will be seen to be most striking. These núraghs, like the typical English castle, have walls of great thickness. Their upper stories are reached by staircases in the walls, which wind round the body of the structure as at Conisborough, and " which start either from the ante-room or entrance passage, or from the central hall or chamber." These chambers are " oblong domes " ; the lowest room or basement at Conisborough is a " domed vault." As at Castleton and Conisborough, the staircases of the núraghs lead to terraces or rampart walks on the top, and nearly all the doors point south-east. Such is the case, as we have seen, at Castleton ; it is the same at Conisborough. This southern position of the doorways may be a mere chance, and of no importance ; but the likeness in other respects is far too strong to be accidental. The Sardinian núraghs, according to the better opinion, were places of refuge and also watch-towers. From the commanding position of their terraces " the eye could travel over the whole country. At the least sign of danger fires were lighted as

[1] *Mediæval Military Architecture*, i. 431 *et seq.*
[2] PERROT and CHIPIEZ, *History of Art in Sardinia*, etc., trans. by GONINO, vol. i. pp. 26, 27, 28.

signals, which were immediately repeated from one hilltop to another, until the whole country was ablaze with lights."[1]

It is also interesting to compare the thick walls and mural chambers of some English castles with the Scottish " brochs " or " broughs." These are round towers, common in Orkney and Shetland, and also on the adjacent mainland. They have " an outer and inner wall of dry stone, the interstitial space containing little chambers for human habitation, whilst the open central area might be used for cattle."[2] The top is usually reached by a stone staircase which supplies each floor. The tower in the island of Mousa has seven of these chambers, one above the other.[3]

We are so accustomed to regard church towers as bell-towers that we are apt to overlook their other uses. They were often used as watch-towers. For example, the imposing tower of Bedale Church, near Richmond, in Yorkshire, " was constructed purposely for defence. As in the keep of Richmond, the enemy might come into the ground-floor by the huge western door, but there they were stopped. The staircase retains its portcullis groove. The existence of the portcullis itself was unknown till it fell, from the effects of a stroke of lightning. All communication with the clock and bells was stopped until it was hacked away. The chamber above is fitted with a fire-place, and even a *templum Clausinæ* (? *Cluacinae*) in stone."[4]   In that part of Glamorganshire known as Gower, twelve of the sixteen churches " have towers evidently built for defence. The exterior doors, where they occur, are usually insertions."[5]   At Salkeld, in Cumberland,

---

[1] Perrot and Chipiez, *ut supra*, p. 38.

[2] *Hist. English Dict.*, s.v. *broch*. The word is from O.N. *borg*, O.E. *burh*, a castle, stronghold. About two miles from Castleton are the remains of a Roman town called Brough.

[3] Hibbert's *Shetland ;* Worsaae's *Danes and Norwegians*, 1852, p. 234.

[4] Longstaffe's *Richmondshire*, 1852, p. 56. In the tower of Cockington Church, near Torquay, is a fire-place, etc., on the first floor.

[5] Clark, *Mediæval Military Arch.*, i. 114, 117. See also Parker, *Glossary of Arch.*, 1850, s.v. pele-tower. He says that some church towers were used for habitation and for defensive purposes.

the only entrance to the tower is from the nave and the door is iron-plated. Fortified towers exist also in Lincolnshire, but they are chiefly found in border counties such as Hereford and Cumberland. The church of Newton and Arlash, on the Cumberland coast, is more like a fortress than a church. It was built in 1309 and has a narrow door and high windows. There is a fire-place in the tower.

The church tower sometimes resembles the keep in having its doorway at a considerable height above the ground, so as to be approached by outside steps. Such, for instance, was lately the case at Norton, in Derbyshire, where the doorway, like that of the keep at Castleton, was on the southern side of the tower and six feet above the ground. Under pretence of a " restoration " this doorway has been lately made up, and the outer stairs removed, so that at present there is no outer doorway in the tower. The belfry is approached by a ladder as in the Irish round tower, and there has never been a stone staircase. At Royston, near Barnsley, there is a remarkable oriel window in the west side of the tower, a little below the belfry window. It is supported by a long stone bracket or corbel, which gradually dies into the wall, and is surmounted by a similar piece of stone work. Old inhabitants of the village speak of it as " the lantern," whilst others call it a " look-out," and say that a light was burnt in it. About half-way up the tower of Middleham Church, in Yorkshire, " is a stone fire-place, which appears to be of very late date, and is partly composed of ancient tombstones."[1] There is also a fire-place at Burgh-on-Sands.

At Melsonby, in Yorkshire, is a " fortified church tower," which has been described as " a Norman keep in miniature." There is a chimney in the church tower of Thorpe Abbots in the basement on the north side. The flue runs up the wall nine inches square, the smoke escaping from a small loophole,[2] as in the chimney of the crypt at Hornsea, described in the last chapter of this work.

From time immemorial the tower of the parish church of

---

[1] ATTHILL's *Church of Middleham* (Camden Soc.), p. xviii. See other instances mentioned in *Notes and Queries*, 3rd S., xi. 60.

[2] *Archæologia*, xxiii. 13.

St. Nicholas in Newcastle has been repaired by the corporation of that place. It is an acknowledged fact that church bells in the olden times were instrumental in guiding the traveller to his home in the dark nights. " The church of St. Nicholas was not only of service in that way, but also as an inland lighthouse. Tennant spoke of the pathless moors of the neighbourhood in the past century, and many a wayfarer who traversed them had reason to bless the lantern of St. Nicholas in the nights of old. History recorded the prominent part which the steeple played during the Civil Wars, when the Scots besieged the town, and the incidents tended to show that the mayor and burgesses had at that time the control, management, and maintenance of the lantern and tower. Again, one of the bells in the steeple was known as the ' common ' or ' thief and reever ' bell, in consequence of its having been used for the double purpose of summoning the burgesses together for public business, and, it is supposed, of informing thieves, horse, cattle, and sheep stealers on the eve of the annual fairs that they were permitted to enter the town, and that no troublesome questions would be asked. The free burgesses appear to have had some control over the bells and belfry, and they at the present time meet in guild three times in a year, and at their meetings the mayor presides, and is usually accompanied by the sheriff and town clerk. They are summoned to attend the guild meetings by the tolling of the ' common bell,' and on these occasions the ringer is not paid by the freemen, but by the Corporation. The Corporation possess, or did possess formerly, keys to the belfry, and they can require the bells to be rung when they think fit, so long as they do not interfere with divine service. For the use of the bells the vicar and churchwardens have contended, and still contend, that the Corporation are responsible for the keeping in repair of the lantern or steeple."[1]

Several Cornish churches have lanterns constructed on the towers. The most famous is " St. Michael's Chair " on the tower of St. Michael's Mount. Cressets were often used as beacons, as at Hadley, Herts (late fifteenth century), where the

[1] *Antiquary*, vol. xxxii. p. 350.

light served to guide travellers through Enfield Chase. These cressets were placed on cresset-stones, examples of which survive at Wool, Lewannick, York, Furness, and Calder.[1] The Hadley cresset, a cresset on Falkirk church tower and other places, have been lighted occasionally in recent years to celebrate coronations and other days of national rejoicing.

In Scotch towns the church steeples are often the property of the municipality and not of the church, and the bells in those steeples belong to the municipality.

According to the best authorities the word " belfry " did not originally mean a place in which bells were hung. Its earliest known form is *berfrey*, meaning, " a wooden tower, usually moveable, used in the Middle Ages in besieging fortifications." Then it came to mean " a tower to protect watchmen, a watch-tower, beacon-tower, etc."[2] Cotgrave defines *beffroy* as " a beacon or a watch-tower from which things may be discerned farre off." In German towns watchmen continued to live in church towers to a late period. " In the fifteenth century," says Beckmann, " the city of Ulm kept permanent watchmen in many of the steeples. In the year 1452 a bell was suspended in the tower of the cathedral of Frankfort-on-the-Maine, which was to be rung in times of feudal alarm, and all the watchmen on the steeples were then to blow their horns and hoist their banners. In the year 1476 a room for the watchman was constructed in the steeple of the church of St. Nicholas. In the year 1509 watchmen were kept both on the watch-towers and steeples, who gave notice by firing a musket when strangers approached."[3] In most, if not in all, cities " the town piper, or as we say at present town-musician, was appointed steeple-watchman ; and lodgings were assigned to him in the steeple."[4]

In some cases the tower, like the Irish and Scotch round

---

[1] See *Notes and Queries*, 9th S., iii. p. 477. The use of the cresset stone is described in the *Rites of Durham*.

[2] *Hist. English Dict. ;* SKEAT's *Etym. Dict.*

[3] *Hist. of Inventions* (English ed.), 1846, ii. 193.

[4] BECKMANN, *ut supra*, 191. " *Toren bewaerder, toren wachter*, watch-keeper upon a tower, or upon a steeple."—HEXHAM's *Dutch Dict.*, 1675.

tower,[1] was detached from the church. Indeed, in early times this seems to have been the general practice. " There are several examples of detached bell-towers still remaining, as at Evesham, Worcestershire ; Barkeley, Gloucestershire ; Walton, Norfolk ; Ledbury, Herefordshire ; Chichester, Sussex ; and a very curious one, entirely of timber, with the frame for the bells springing from the ground, at Pembridge, Herefordshire."[2] Half a mile from the church of Warmsworth (W. Yorks) is a detached steeple containing one bell. The *clochier* or *campanile* of St. Paul's Cathedral was a separate building.[3] Circular church towers are to be found in some parts of England, as for instance at Little Saxham in Suffolk, and in various parts of Norfolk.[4] These towers are very plain, with the exception of the topmost story, which is usually neatly ornamented. Like the Scotch and Irish round towers, the English towers have four windows in the topmost story facing the cardinal points. As we have seen, the tower of the English castle is sometimes round, like that at Conisborough, which resembles the Irish round tower in having its doorway considerably above the ground.[5]

The construction of the Irish round tower shows that it was primarily intended for a watch-tower, whatever may have been its other uses. It is more like a modern lighthouse than anything else. Seventy-six round towers still exist in Ireland. One of the best preserved of these is that on the island of Devenish in Lough Erne. Its height is 85 ft. The doorway is 9 ft. above the ground. The building is " divided into five stories of unequal height by offsets in the wall, except in the case of the topmost story, which has stone brackets for the support of the floor. . . . The upper story has four windows facing the cardinal points, which are each 4 ft. 2 in. in height. . . . This tower is a fair representa-

---

[1] In the Latin description of the plan of the monastery of St. Gall, two round towers, similar to the Irish type, are said to be *ad universa superspicienda*.

[2] PARKER, *Glossary of Arch.*, 1850, p. 104.

[3] GOMME's *Primitive Folk-Moots*, 157. The bell of this tower summoned the citizens to the folk-moot.

[4] *Archæologia*, xxiii. 10 *et seq.*

[5] The distance at Conisborough is twenty feet.

tive of the class which exists in Ireland. Their special features are that their average height is from 100 to 120 feet,
the average thickness of wall at the base $3\frac{1}{2}$ to 4 feet, and
the average internal diameter at the level of the doorway
7 to 9 feet. They taper, and the walls diminish in thickness
towards the top. The doorways are mostly at some distance
from the ground, as 4, 8, 11, and 13 feet. There are almost
always four windows in the upper story facing the cardinal
points, and there is never more than one aperture in each of
the stories underneath."[1]   There are several round towers
of exactly similar construction in Scotland. Either they are
bonded into a church, or are close to a church. When they
form part of a church the entrance is not on the outside,
but by an opening in the west gable of the nave.[2]   In all
these towers, whether English, Irish, or Scotch, the most
important part of the building, and the one on which the
builder has bestowed the most pains, is the topmost story
with its four windows. Every other part of the building is
ancillary to this room, in which the watchman could sit and
watch.

[1] ANDERSON, *Scotland in Early Christian Times*, 1881, p. 46.
The chief authority on the Irish round tower is PETRIE'S *Inquiry
into the Origin and Uses of the Round Tower of Ireland*, 1845.
[2] ANDERSON, *passim*.

CHAPTER X

THE buildings known as churches will here be considered in their character as basilicas or town-halls,
in other words as places where public business was
done and justice administered, though it is not denied that
they were also temples of religion. These buildings will gain
a new interest, or even a new charm, when we see them as
they once were—the centre-pieces of the old social life. To
understand their structure it will be necessary to glance at
their history.

A good authority on architecture has said that " one of
the most remarkable characteristics of English architecture,
though it is but a negative one, is the almost total absence
of any municipal buildings during the whole period of the
Middle Ages. The Guildhall of London is a late specimen,
and may even be called an insignificant one, considering the
importance of the city. There are also some corporation
buildings at Bristol, and one or two unimportant town halls
in the cities, but there we stop."[1] It was the same in Belgium,

---

[1] FERGUSSON, *Hist. of Architecture*, ii. 413. (1893 ed.)

where the municipal buildings surpass those of any other country. But " none of these are very old."[1]

When we first meet with " municipal buildings " in England they are usually in a churchyard. According to Anthony à Wood, the old portmoot of the burgesses of Oxford was held in St. Martin's churchyard in and before the time of Henry II.[2]

Before local councils or courts made use of roofed buildings they sat on artificial mounds in the open air. For example, at Stoneleigh, in Warwickshire, the court of the sokemen used to be held on a hill called the Mootstow-hill (i.e., assembly-place hill), near that town. It was so called because pleading was done there. But after the abbots of Stoneleigh had acquired the said court and liberty for the easement of the tenants and suitors, they made a court-house in the midst of the town of Stoneleigh.[3] There seems to be no evidence of the existence of a town-hall at Stoneleigh, and it is likely that the " court-house " was the church. To pass in another case from likelihood to certainty we find that as late as 1472 the parishioners of two parishes in Yorkshire are reported to the Archbishop of York for holding their local council in the church and churchyard.[4] The practice had been forbidden two centuries before,[5] but customs die hard, and it is not surprising to find the old practice lingering on even in the fifteenth century.

The origin of the jury of twelve and its early connection

[1] *Ibid.,* ii. 199.
[2] *Archæologia Oxon.,* i. 274.
[3] " Curia de Stonle ad quam sokemanni faciebant sectam solebant ab antiquo teneri super montem iuxta villam de Stonle vocatam Motstowehull, ideo sic dictum quia ibi placitabant sed postquam abbates de Stonle habuerunt dictam curiam et libertatem pro aysiamento tenencium et sectatorum fecerunt domum curie in medio ville."—*Stoneleigh Reg.* f. 75 in VINOGRADOFF'S *Villainage in England,* p. 367. The council of sokemen usually consisted of twelve men, as in the " Twelve Men " of St. Austell's in Cornwall, the Twelve Feoffees of Hornsea, the Twelve Capital (or Church) Burgesses of Sheffield, the Twelve Lawmen of Stamford and Lincoln, etc.
[4] " Dicunt quod omnes parochiani ibidem tenent plebisitum, et alias ordinaciones temporales, in ecclesia et cimiterio."—*York Fabric Rolls* (Surtees Soc.), p. 256.
[5] INDERWICK, *The King's Peace,* p. 13.

with religious tradition is a question which is not irrelevant at this point. The priestly character of judges is found to a very late date among the Teutons,[1] and ordeals, casting of lots, and divination are all derived from and connected with priestly justice. The twelve men of a jury, acting under a judge, may be a parallel to Christ and the twelve disciples. In the Hundreds Rolls are numerous lists of twelve jurymen,[2] known sometimes as *judices legum*, sometimes as *lagemanni*. At Norwich twelve *burgesses* held the church of Holy Trinity.[3]

" One of the canons of the Scots church," says Mr. James Logan, " prohibited the laity from holding courts in churches. This injunction was unnecessary, if meetings had not been at first held in them which were inconsistent with their sacred appropriation. From this, and some other reasons I shall adduce, I have formed an opinion that moothills were first raised for such purposes as churches were considered unfit for."[4] The truth is that moothills were the original seats of assemblies afterwards held in churches. Mr. G. L. Gomme has given instances of courts held in English churches, and he cites Ritson on *Court Leets*, who says that " the stewards or bailiffs of a leet would, in bad weather, occasionally hold courts in the church, where, notwithstanding a canon, it is in many places still held."[5]

The English parish church was known as a basilica at least as early as the seventh century,[6] and it had not ceased to bear that name in the Latin documents of the fifteenth century.[7]

---

[1] KEMBLE, *The Saxons in England*, i. 145.

[2] *Rot. Hundr.*, ii. 238 *seq.* ; i. 354a ; ii. 38a, 45a.

[3] MAITLAND, *Township and Borough*, p. 177.

[4] *Archæologia*, xxii. 200. SKENE'S *Acts of Parliament of Scotland*, 388.

[5] *Primitive Folk-Moots*, 53, 59, 115.

[6] An authentic inscription recording the dedication of Jarrow church in 685 contains the words, " dedicatio basilicae Sancti Pauli."—*Inventories, etc., of Jarrow and Monk-Wearmouth* (Surtees Soc.), p. xxvi.

[7] 1458. Commission to John Bishop of Philippolis " ad consecrandam basilicam infra villam de Colthorp . . . . . . cum cimiterio." —*York Fabric Rolls* (Surtees Soc.), p. 240. In 1480 there was a commission to the Bishop of Dromore to consecrate " basilicam, et cemiterium in villa de Lamley de novo constructam."—*Ibid.*, p. 241.

It was habitually used not only as a court of justice, but as a place in which most kinds of public business could be lawfully done. The evidence on this point is abundant, but only a brief epitome can be given here.

In 1268 the Papal Legate issued certain constitutions, one of which forbade the setting out of stalls for merchandise within the walls of the church.[1]

At Exeter in 1358 public banqueting and drinking in the church, especially in the choir, were forbidden.[2]

Grosseteste, bishop of Lincoln, directed that " markets were not to be held in sacred places seeing that the Lord cast out those who bought and sold from the temple."[3] In 1275 deeds were kept in a chest behind the high altar of St. Paul's Cathedral.[4] In 1409 we read of men and boys making an uproar and playing in York Cathedral, even while mass was being said. And it was complained that the sacristans did not thrash mad dogs (*furiosos canes*) and those who disgraced themselves or did business in the church.[5] In 1504 the accounts of certain executors were to be audited yearly in St. Mary's Church at Bury St. Edmunds.[6] Marriage settlements were executed and serfs manumitted at the church door. In 1510 pedlars sold their wares on feast days in the church porch.[7] In 1601 mortgages were paid off in the south porch of Ecclesfield church in Yorkshire.[8] In 1665 bread was stored in churches. The " walks in Paul's " are mentioned by the Elizabethan dramatists, and the nave of the cathedral was used, like a Roman basilica, as an exchange

[1] W. ANDREWS, *The Church Treasury*, p. 98.

[2] *Archæologia*, xviii. 412.

[3] " Praecipimus etiam firmiter auctoritate Evangelica et etiam de speciali indulgentia apostolica ne in locis sacris habeantur mercata ; cum Dominus ementes et vendentes de templo ejecerit."— *Roberti Grosseteste Epistolae*, ed. LUARD, p. 161.

[4] *Household Roll of Bishop Swinfield* (Camden Soc.), p. cxxx.

[5] *York Fabric Rolls* (Surtees Soc.), p. 244.

[6] *Bury Wills* (Camden Soc.), p. 97.

[7] *York Fabric Rolls, ut supra*, p. 271.

[8] Court Rolls in the possession of the Duke of Norfolk. On the Sunday before Candlemas, 1318, the execution of a deed relating to land was witnessed in Felkirk church, near Barnsley, by all the parishioners.—*Yorkshire Arch. Journal*, xii. 257.

M

mart. " Perhaps the most remarkable survival of Roman
institutions in Britain was the practice of the old order of
serjeants-at-law who assembled in the nave of old St. Paul's
Cathedral, each serjeant having been allotted a special pillar
in the cathedral at his appointment, where he met his clients
in legal consultation, hearing the facts of the case, taking
notes of the evidence, or pacing up and down."[1] Bishop
Bonner in 1552 forbade any manner of common plays to be
played, set forth, or declared in churches or chapels. As
late as the seventeenth century Yorkshire people danced in
their churches at Christmas,[2] and an injunction of Grindal,
Archbishop of York, 1571, ordered " that the minister and
church-wardens shall not suffer any lords of misrule, or summer lords or ladies, or any disguised persons or others in
Christmas or May games, or any minstrels, morris-dancers,
or others, at rush-bearings, or at any other time to come
unreverently into any church or chapel or churchyard, and
there dance, or play any unseemly parts with scoffs, jests,
wanton gestures, or ribald talk, namely in the time of divine
service or of any sermon."[3] In Manchester, at the wake,
the pageant of Robin Hood, Maid Marion, and Friar Tuck
was exhibited within the church, the priests organising it
and the churchwardens making themselves responsible for
the expenses.[4]

Notice of the holding of the Court Baron of the manor
was published in Hathersage church in 1656.[5] At Ashburton
in Devonshire, " the annual court leet and court baron of
the manor lords is held alternately by their stewards in the
chapel of St. Laurence."[6] At Dover, between 1367 and 1581,
the mayor was usually elected in St. Peter's Church. After
that date, down to the nineteenth century he was elected in
St. Mary's.[7]

" In Southampton church merchants stored grain and

[1] G. L. GOMME in *Contemp. Review*, May, 1896, p. 694.
[2] AUBREY'S *Remains of Gentilisme*, pp. 5, 213.
[3] W. ANDREWS, *The Church Treasury*, p. 100.
[4] *Ibid.*, p. 103.
[5] MS. in the author's possession.
[6] A. J. DAVY in *Notes and Queries*, 8th S., xii. p. 32.
[7] STATHAM, *History of the Castle, Town and Port of Dover*, 1879.

wool,[1] theft of which was punished by excommunication ; the overflow of markets and fairs pressed within the aisles or precincts as at Salisbury and Wells. Local lampoons were fixed to its doors, and in many places councillors met within its walls for consultation, or the commonalty assembled there to make grants of land or transact business. The Cathedral was the place chosen by the Bishop and Mayor of Exeter wherein to discuss their mutual grievances. While at Bridgewater the king's judges held trials in the Greyfriars church. We hear of seditious verses nailed to the door of St. Michael's, Coventry, and of a cloth-market in the porch, and the Coventry churches were put to a stranger use than any before noted—they were converted into hospitals in time of plague."[2]

In a will dated 1493 there is provision for the announcement, by every curate in the hundred of Hoo, of a sale of land.[3]

The ancient Welsh laws show that churches were regularly used as courts of justice. Theft was denied by the defendant at church upon a relic. " Let the judge," it is said, " require of him his oath, with that of two men nearest to him in worth ; and that in a week from the succeeding Sunday, at the church where his sacramental bread and holy water shall be."[4] If a man made a false appraisement the church proceeded against him for perjury.[5] If a man did not pay a fine which he had been ordered to pay, then " let the church proceed against him and let him pay the debt in full."[6] Relics, we are told, were not necessary " in causes carried on in the churchyard, or in the church ; because it is the place of the relics."[7] In a case of debtor and surety judgment was given in the church.[8] In many other places

---

[1] Compare the account of a man's property taken out of a Shropshire church in *Rot. Hundr.*, ii. 1ᴴ1b.

[2] HARRIS, *Life in an old English Town*, p. 319.

[3] See *Folklore*, iv. 517.

[4] *Welsh Laws*, ii. 235.

[5] *Ibid.*, ii. 35.

[6] *Ibid.*, i. 135.

[7] *Ibid.*, ii. 37.

[8] *Ibid.*, i. 115.

in the Welsh laws churches are incidentally referred to as courts of justice. But litigious business was transacted on weekdays and not on Sundays.[1] Inquisitions, however, by the king's sheriff were held in England as late as the thirteenth century on Sundays.[2]

The Welsh practices just referred to belong to the ninth or tenth century. The jurisdiction of English churches in matters of civil and criminal law extended to a much later period. At Ripon, for example, in the fifteenth century we find the chapter of the collegiate church there dealing with a great variety of questions which now are only within the cognizance of non-ecclesiastical courts of law. The chief matters with which they dealt were testamentary cases, and next to these in point of number came actions of debt. They also dealt with acknowledgments of tenure, affiliation, defamation of character, matrimonial cases, and breaches of promise of marriage, perjury, theft, etc.[3] This judicial process was similar to the practices of other ecclesiastical courts. It does not appear in what part of the collegiate church of Ripon the court sat. At Durham it sat in the galilee of the cathedral.

If we turn to north-western Spain we shall see how these earlier uses of the church have survived to modern times. The local government there " has been purely democratic ; the council, which consists of all the *vecinos* (neighbours), assembling on Sundays at the summons of the church bell."[4] It was the lord's day, *dies dominicus*, as our old charters have it, and in Spain his council met on Sundays. This Spanish case is only an accidental survival of what was once the universal practice in Western Europe. Traces of secular uses of the churches may be seen everywhere.[5] The history of the Christian Church has been, in a large measure, a history of the decline of her secular power. The transition from

---

[1] *Welsh Laws*, ii. 70.

[2] *Yorkshire Inquisitions* (Yorkshire Arch. Soc.), *passim*.

[3] Acts of Chapter of the Collegiate Church of SS. Peter and Wilfrid, Ripon, A.D. 1452 to A.D. 1506 (Surtees Soc., 1875).

[4] *Quarterly Review*, vol. clxxxii. p. 484, where much valuable information on this subject is given.

[5] See some examples in GRIMM'S *Rechtsalterthümer*, p. 805.

the basilica-temple to the temple has been going on for a
very long period, and the change is not yet fully carried out,
even though the royal arms have been removed from every
parish church in England.

On December 17th, 1524, a court was held in the church
of Kirkby Ireleth for the purpose of deciding as to the ownership of certain lands, on which occasion " divers notorious
persons " ran off with a manor roll.[1] The jurisdiction of
ecclesiastical courts was, of course, strictly limited. There
are numerous cases in the Hundreds Rolls of ecclesiastical
judges having damaged the king's interests by dealing with
cases outside their jurisdiction.[2]

The fabrics of our churches still continue to puzzle the
antiquary. Who, for instance, can explain those strange
apertures, known as " low side windows," which are found
in the chancels of so many of these buildings ? Nor is it
easy to say what is meant by the very numerous oblique
holes known as " squints." In this case, however, we have
a clue which may lead to the truth. The greatest number
of squints are in the wall adjoining the south side of the
chancel arch, and they point directly to the south door or
main entrance to the building, in such a way that a person
standing at the door can see straight through the hole to the
place now occupied by the altar or communion table. " In
Bridgewater Church, Somerset, there is a series of these
openings through three successive walls, following the same
oblique line, to enable a person standing in the porch to see
the high altar."[3] Thus wrote a good authority on church
architecture. But in ancient times " the altar was placed at
the end of the nave, on the chord of the apse."[4] It stood
directly under the chancel arch, so that " squints," if they
existed in early times, cannot have been intended to enable
people to see the elevation of the Host at the altar. The
object of the opening seems rather to have been to enable a

[1] See *Notes and Queries*, 9th S., vol. v. 329.
[2] *Rot. Hundr.*, i. 113a, 115b, 117b, 118b, 119a, 121a, 122a, b,
123a, 124a, 126a, 129a, 131a (important), 133a, b, 135b, 358a, 452b,
519b.
[3] PARKER'S *Concise Glossary of Architecture*, 1875, p. 258.
[4] FREEMAN'S *Architecture*, p. 155.

man standing within the door of the porch to see the high seat occupied by the president of an assembly sitting in the chancel. That man must have been a door-keeper, as in an old English poem written about 1330 :

" In the ealde lawe dore-ward
Lokede dore and yate.

*   *   *

So doth thes dore-wardes eke
In holy cherche nouthe." [1]

The *ostiarius* or door-ward is described by Shoreham as the first of the seven orders of the church, though the lowest in rank. It is remarkable that in the serio-comic language of the Edda a door-keeper or usher kept watch over the entrance to the hall of the gods, tossing up seven short swords at once, and from this we may perhaps infer that in public ceremonies a door-keeper with a drawn sword kept the door of an old northern hall or palace. In the church it is likely that the door-keeper stood in such a position that he could see the face of the president through the " squint," and be able to take orders from him, either directly or indirectly, through the medium of an official sitting near the inner opening of the " squint."

The " usher " of a school, not unlike the Usher of the Black Rod in the House of Commons, was originally an *ostiarius* or door-keeper. He was so called because, in addition to keeping the door of a church, he taught his pupils in the porch. A reminiscence of this practice may be found in the form of " *testamur*," which is given by the " masters of the schools " at Oxford to an undergraduate who has passed " responsions," and in which it is certified that the candidate " *quaestionibus magistrorum scholarum in parviso pro forma respondit.*" Here " *parvisus* " is the " parvis " or porch of a church or other building. The practice of teaching in the porch of a church was borrowed from the Romans ; there was direct continuity between the Roman and the English method. Amongst the Romans " the elementary schools and

---

[1] *Poems of William de Shoreham*, ed. WRIGHT (Percy Soc.), p. 46. Perhaps we ought to read " mouthe."

those of the *grammatici* were usually held in a verandah partly
open to the street, and the schoolroom is accordingly called
pergula, taberna, or *porticus.*"[1] The stone seats so often to
be seen in the porches of churches may have been the benches
on which children or catechumens once sat whilst they were
under the instruction of the " usher," and before their admission to the full privileges of the church. Evelyn, in his
Memoirs, says " that one Frier taught us in the church porch
at Wotton."[2] A tradition exists amongst some of the villages
in the High Peak of Derbyshire, such as Hope and Tideswell,
that school was held in the church porch. Some church
porches have rooms over them, others have inner galleries
approached by inner staircases.[3] At Hornsea, in East Yorkshire, school was held in the south aisle of the nave down to
about 1850.

The ancient Welsh laws declare that " if a town have leave
from the lord of the country to build a church and to bury
the dead in its cemetery, then that town becomes free, and
all its inhabitants (*homines*) are thereafter free."[4] To build
a church for the first time in a town was to create a new
" liberty." In England there are many ancient divisions
known as liberties, and at Ripon invasion of the liberty was a
complaint frequently brought before the ecclesiastical court.[5]
A new church, then, was the nucleus of a new liberty or free
community. " One of the first glimpses that we have of
Cambridge after that given by Domesday Book shows us a
gild building a church."[6] Such a church was the " house "
or public hall of a new lord, who presided over that community. It was the " house " of the village chief, or, to
adopt the modern term, of the lord of the manor. Now the
word " church," according to the best modern scholars, is

[1] SMITH's *Dictionary of Greek and Roman Antiq.,* ii. 97a, and
the authorities there cited.

[2] *Memoirs,* 2nd ed., 1819, vol. i. p. 3.

[3] See description in *Notes and Queries,* 8th S., x. 396, xi. 9.

[4] " Si villa habeat a domino patrie licentiam ecclesiam edificare,
et in cimeterio ejus corpora sepelire, tunc villa libera fit, et omnes
homines postea sunt liberi."—*Welsh Laws,* ii. 873.

[5] *Ripon Chapter Acts* (Surtees Soc.), *passim.*

[6] MAITLAND, *Township and Borough,* p. 175.

derived from κυριακόν, the lord's house. The Latin word *dominicum* and the Irish *domhnach* are used in the same sense. In the same way basilica is βασιλική, the king's house, lord's house,[1] so that church and basilica are virtually identical terms. Judging from the Spanish evidence the court held in the church seems to have been originally analogous to the old Greek *ecclesia*, the assembly of citizens summoned by the crier, as in Western Europe it was summoned by the church bell or by the " moot horn." " The bells of Totnes parish church are rung for council meetings, magistrates' meetings, and on Saturdays for the market as well as the curfew and day bells."[2]

The district attached to the new " liberty " was the parish, παροικία, a word which in the later civil law was applied to a rural commune, or community of peasant farmers.[3] The word was sometimes used in the sense of a judge's district.[4] " Domesday Book shows us many of the churches as the lords of wide and continuous tracts of land."[5] The English parish had some resemblance to the Old Norse *hreppr*, or poor-law district. " It is ordained in our laws," says the compiler of Grágás, " that we have lawful villages (*hreppar*) in our country. That is a lawful village in which twenty or more husbandmen (*böndr*) dwell. It is lawful for them to divide the village into five or four divisions for distributing food, and for apportioning the tithe."[6] Such divisions seem to be identical with the districts known in some parts of England as byrlaws. At Ecclesfield, in Yorkshire, the four byrlaws into which the parish was divided made separate contributions to the church. Each byrlaw had its own collectors.[7] The rector of a parish was formerly known as the

---

[1] Lange shows that in Plato's time the Athenian " king's hall " was called βασιλική.—*Haus und Halle*, 97, 153.

[2] See *Notes and Queries*, 9th S., iii. 151.

[3] SMITH's *Dict. of Christian Antiq.*, ii. 1554b.

[4] See *parochia* in Maigne D'Arnis. In Iceland, during the heathen times, a new temple became the nucleus of a new community or goðorð.

[5] MAITLAND, *Domesday Book and Beyond*, p. 226.

[6] *Grágás*, i. 443.

[7] GATTY's *Ecclesfield Registers*, 153 *et seq.*

" town reeve " or " person."[1] Whether we call him villicus, agent (*actor*), curator, procurator, rector, town-reeve, parson, or bailiff, he was still the fiscal officer of his district, and as such responsible only to his master the bishop.[2] He was entitled to the chief seat in the chancel.[3] In 1525 the Vicar of Penistone in Yorkshire was called the Proctor, and there is a Proctor's Pew at Silkstone in the same district. The rector was a man of dignity, " the person," or, as we should say, " your Honour," or " your Reverence."[4] A curious proof of the way in which the rector was regarded as the owner of the chancel may be seen in an order of council of the year 1307 when rectors of churches were ordered not to presume to cut trees down in churchyards, except when the chancel required repair.[5] In a recent case, where the Duke of Norfolk claimed the ownership of the chancel of the parish church at Arundel, it was held that the evidence showed that the chancel " had always been the property of the Duke and his predecessors in title."[6]

The chancel was the tribunal ($\beta\hat{\eta}\mu\alpha$),[7] and was the platform from which the speaking was done. The chancel screen was the lattice of open-work behind which sat the lord and his assessors. It was the presbytery or seat of the elders, and it does not appear to have been known in

---

[1] " *Uillicus, uel actor, uel curator, uel procurator, uel rector, tungerefa.*"—WRIGHT-WÜLCKER, *Vocab.*, 111, 13. " *Hic rector*, a person."—*Ibid.*, 680, 38. " Túngeréfa, rector pagi vel pagelli."— GRIMM'S *Rechtsalterthümer*, 757. In 1279 the *procurator* of St. Mary's Church at Scarborough is mentioned.—*Rot. Hundr.*, i. 131b. In CHAUCER'S *Reve's Tale* the miller is described as having married a wife " y-comen of noble kin : The person of the town hir fader was."

[2] LAPPENBERG, *England under the Anglo-Saxon Kings*, ii. 328.

[3] PHILLIMORE'S *Eccl. Law*, 1873, p. 1807.

[4] " Laicus quidam magnæ personæ ad nos veniens dicebat," etc.—MAIGNE D'ARNIS, s.v. *persona*.

[5] RASTELL'S *Statutes*, 1557, f. 56. It seems that the *culacium* or *colacium* of an ox-house was sometimes built by the lord, whilst the tenants built the ox-house itself. See *Domesday of St. Paul's* (Camden Soc.), p. 48.

[6] 49 *Law Journal Reports*, C.P., 782.

[7] PHILLIMORE'S *Eccl. Law*, p. 1777.

England as the "choir" till the end of the thirteenth century.[1]

One of the strongest proofs that the oldest English churches were true basilicas is to be found in certain crypts which still exist under the floors of churches. These crypts have such a striking resemblance to the subterranean chamber beneath the tribunal of the basilica at Pompeii, that they must all have been intended for the same purpose.

"At the west end," says Dr. Lange, "of the great hall"

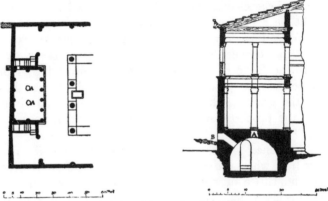

Plan and section of the tribune in the Basilica at Pompeii, showing Crypt.

of the Pompeian basilica, "are three rooms. The middle-most of these is the tribunal, which is raised 5½ ft. above the floor of the great hall, and is 32 ft. broad and 18 ft. 2 in. deep. On the sides of the tribunal are two side rooms about 18 ft. broad, such rooms being separated from the tribunal by two small staircases, and their floors being on a level with the side aisles. Their back walls are in a straight line with the back walls of the tribunal. The anterior enclosing walls of the staircases end towards the side rooms in three-quarter pillars. From the side rooms small doors lead into the stair-

[1] The earliest quot. in the *Hist. Eng. Dict.* is of the year 1297. The word πρεσβύτερος was sometimes applied to the "headman" of a village. See authorities in SMITH's *Dict. of Christian Antiq.*, ii. 1699*a*.

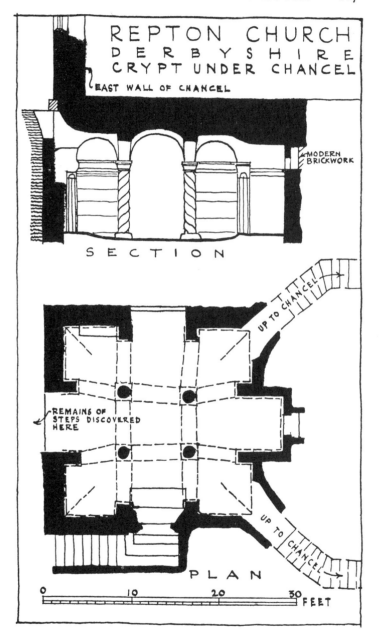

REPTON CHURCH
DERBYSHIRE
CRYPT UNDER CHANCEL
EAST WALL OF CHANCEL

MODERN
BRICKWORK

SECTION

UP TO CHANCEL

REMAINS OF
STEPS DISCOVERED
HERE

UP TO CHANCEL

PLAN

0   10   20   30 FEET

cases in which stairs, divided into two, four, and again two steps, lead into a subterranean chamber lying 11 ft. beneath the tribunal. This chamber, lighted up on its hind wall by two small cellar windows,[1] is connected with the floor above by two irregular holes (A A) whose ancient origin is probable, but not certain. As the doors of the subterranean chamber could not be locked, the hitherto prevailing opinion that it was a prison or treasure-room is untenable. Probably it served for depositing objects which were required in proceedings at law."[2] The basilica was built about 93 B.C.

Let us put the plan of this subterranean chamber and that of the crypt at Repton in Derbyshire side by side. The Derbyshire example dates probably from the seventh century A.D. The only material difference between the two crypts lies in the fact that at Repton the back walls of the " side rooms," otherwise the aisles, are not, as in the Pompeian basilica, flush with the east wall of the chancel. In some churches, however, e.g. at Sheffield, where there is a crypt,[3] the back or east walls of the aisles of the chancel are flush with the back or east wall of the chancel. " In the western angles [of the crypt at Repton] are two passages communicating by flights of steps with the church above."[4] This crypt was discovered in the last century by an accident. A workman preparing a grave in 1779 for Dr. Prior, the deceased headmaster of the school, was suddenly precipitated into it.[5] " In the south-west division is the repair of a hole broken through the vault."[6] Similar holes are found in other

[1] Beneath the present east window of Middleham Church, in Yorkshire, " are two low plain square windows (now blocked up), which have been considered by some to have been the windows of a former crypt."—ATTHILL's *Church of Middleham*, p. xvii.

[2] LANGE, *Haus und Halle*, p. 352.

[3] In this crypt there was a staircase on each side of the tribunal, that on the south side being now covered over, but used for gaining access to a vault. There is also a " cellar window " in the east wall as at Repton.

[4] Cox, *Churches of Derbyshire*, iii. 434.

[5] Cox, *ut supra*.

[6] *Derb. Arch. Journal*, v. p. 170. The opening at Ripon is covered by a stone slab. It resembles a " manhole."

crypts.   At Hexham,[1] " nearly in the centre of the vault, which shows some traces of the characteristic Saxon dressing, are traces of a small rectangular opening, like one in a similar position in the crypt at Ripon ; but for what purpose it has been used (the coincidence inclining me to think it is not merely accidental) it is not easy to conjecture."[2]   " The area of the crypt [at Repton] is nearly 17 feet square. The roof, of vaulted stone, is supported by four spirally-wreathed columns, with plain square capitals, and by eight fluted responds against the walls."[3]   In the east wall, under the chancel window, is a window for admitting light to the crypt. The entrance on the north side is of later date than the rest of the building.   It is not, therefore, an original entrance, and it is in the position occupied by the fire-place of the crypt at Hornsea to be presently described. The roof is plastered, and there are remains of coloured decoration on the capitals of the pillars.   The stones are smooth, as though they had been polished with sand.   The architecture is Roman, or Romanesque.   Brixworth Church, Northamptonshire, built chiefly of Roman bricks, has an apse surrounded by a corridor or crypt entered by steps from the chancel.[4]

A crypt under the east end of the chancel of Hornsea Church in East Yorkshire differs from that at Repton in having a fire-place, 6 ft. 2 in. wide and 3 ft. 2 in. high, on its north side,[5] and only one staircase, viz. in the north-west corner.   It is probable, however, that there was a corresponding staircase in the south-west corner.   The tomb of Anthony St. Quentin, the last rector, who died in 1430, stands above that corner, so that the entrance to the staircase may have been built up.   In shape the crypt approaches to a square measuring 15 ft. 5 in. from north to south, and, in the north

[1] There are five known Saxon crypts in England, namely, Ripon, Hexham, Brixworth, Wing, and Repton.   For drawings of the crypts at Hexham and Ripon see *The Builder*, vol. 76, pp. 323 *et seq.* and 349.

[2] RAINE'S *Hexham Priory*, ii. p. xxxix.

[3] Cox, *ut supra*.

[4] SMITH'S *Dict. of Christian Antiq.*, i. 386, where see a plan. There appears to be a staircase on each side.

[5] For a fire-place in the crypt at Bradfield see A. GATTY, *Life at One Living*, p. 221.

compartment, 14 ft. 2 in. from east to west. In the south
compartment the measurement from east to west is about a
foot less. In the east wall is a window splayed inwardly to a
width of nearly four feet, and diminishing to 1 ft. 8 in. in
the narrowest part. The crypt is at present approached by
a ladder under a trap-door over the staircase in the north-
west corner, and near the modern altar steps. In 1840 we
are told that " there is a vaulted crypt beneath the chancel ;

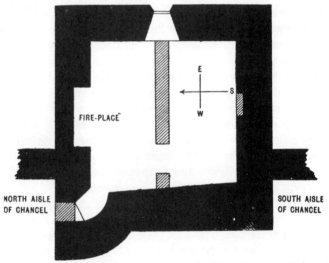

Plan of the crypt under the chancel at Hornsea, East Yorks.

the entrance is by a flight of steps under the farthest arch."[1]
The width of the staircase so far as it can now be traced is
2 ft. 7 in., and the lowest of the old stone steps is yet in its
place. The steps led into the north " side room," or aisle,
of the chancel, the approach being now closed by a modern
wall. The chancel has aisles, in three small bays, on the
north and south sides. There are holes in the jambs of the
fire-place, as if for the insertion of iron bars, and both the
jambs and the mantel-piece are rebated on the inner edge
to the depth of an inch and a half, either for ornament or
to hold a chimney-board when the fire-place was not in use.

[1] POULSON's *Holderness*, i. 330

The tapering flue of the chimney goes up the wall to the height of 6 ft. above the level of the ground outside, when it is turned out by a neat curve, the aperture being a horizontal hole, like a small loop-hole laid on its side, immediately under the sill of the large north window above. The hole measures 10 in. horizontally, and 3½ in. vertically, and its edges, as well as the adjoining sill of the window, are much blackened by smoke. Besides the great east window of the chancel there are two side windows adjoining, one in the north and the other in the south, all three being supported by the walls of the crypt, and the space included by them forming a kind of apse. The walls of the crypt, as inferred from their thickness in the small east window, are 3 ft. thick. They are built of sea cobbles, and the crypt seems to have been plastered within. The little window is protected by iron bars. There seems to have been a niche or cupboard in the south wall. It is now built up, and only the topstone or head-piece remains. The outside walls above the crypt are built of excellent masonry. The roof of the crypt is unhappily of modern brick, and has been raised about a foot to give height to modern altar steps. This is much to be regretted, as the old church floor was flat. A brick wall, with a foundation of sea cobbles, now divides the crypt into two parts, and excludes much of the light which once shone through the window. From the top of this wall two modern brick barrel arches spring, their opposite sides resting on the north and south walls of the crypt. The extreme height of the arches is 6 ft. 10 in. There is a legend in the village that, once upon a time, the crypt was inhabited by a being called Nanny Cankerneedle. Possibly " cankerneedle " refers to the hot iron rod which caused a " canker " in the hands of the guilty after the ordeal by fire. The name will remind the reader of St. Wilfrid's needle in the crypt at Ripon. There was a church at Hornsea in 1086,[1] but the present building does not seem older than the fourteenth century. The crypt, however, may have been built before the Conquest.

Under the east end of a Coptic church at Cairo is a crypt

[1] *Domesday Book.*

eight or nine feet below the surface of the church. It measures about seventeen by twenty feet, and is approached by
two flights of steps. In the north wall is a recess corresponding in position to the fire-place at Hornsea. In the opposite
or south wall is a corresponding recess, as at Hornsea. There
is also a recess in the middle of the east wall where the window should be, and where an altar now stands.[1]

In the old English church the altar did not stand at the
east end of the chancel, but the apse, anciently known as
the " shot," was behind the altar.[2] Such, probably, was the
case at Repton and Hornsea. Amongst its other names the
English chancel was known in mediæval Latin as *secretarium.*
Now " from the fifth century causes were exclusively heard
in the *secretarium* or *secretum.* The public was shut off by
cancelli and curtains (*vela*), which in exceptional cases were
drawn aside."[3] The " side rooms " or aisles of numerous
chancels resemble those at Hornsea, and these " side rooms "
were commonly divided from the central room of the chancel
by lattices or open wooden screens, many of which still
remain. Elyot, in his Latin Dictionary, 1542, says that " *cin-
clidæ*[4] are bayes or parclosis made about the places of judgment, where men not being sutars may stand, beholde, and
here what is done amonge the juges and pledours. Such a
lyke thing is at Westminster Hall about the common place,
and is called the bekens."

We have just seen that pleading was done on the Mootstow-hill at Stoneleigh. Some of these open-air courts still
remain in a more or less complete form, and they are often
near old churches. In such an open-air court the judge sat
on a round mound. Below on the left-hand of the judge sat
the plaintiff ; on his right hand sat the defendant. According

---

[1] MICKLETHWAITE in *Archæologia*, xlviii. 405, where plans, etc.,
are given.

[2] A vocabulary of the tenth or eleventh century has : " *Pro-
pitiatorium, uel sanctum sanctorum, uel secretarium, uel pastoforum,*
gesceot bæftan þæm heahweofode."—WRIGHT-WÜLCKER, *Vocab.*,
186, 20. " Chamber wherin a sexten of a churche or like churche
keper doth lye—*Pastophorium.*"—HULOET'S *Abcedarium*, 1552.

[3] SMITH's *Dict. of Greek and Roman Antiq.*, i. 248.

[4] That is κιγκλίδες.

THE CHURCH OR LORD'S HOUSE   193

to the ancient Welsh laws " the lord is to sit with his back to the sun or wind, lest he be incommoded by the sun, if powerful, or by the wind, if high. And the judge is to sit before the lord, so that he may hear and see each of the two parties to the suit. And the defending party is to sit on the lord's right hand, and the claiming party on the left ; because the right is to support, and the left to claim."[1]

This description can only apply to an open-air court, and, as the court was held in the morning, the lord must have sat in the east, with his face to the west. In this respect the indoor court was a copy of the outdoor court.

---

[1] *Welsh Laws*, ii. 203. The Continental practice, as in the Pompeian basilica, was for the judge to sit in the west. On this point see the quotation in GRIMM's *Rechtsalterthümer*, p. 807. Italian churches are not oriented.

CHAPTER XI[1]

THE HOUSE AS THE BASIS OF THE ENGLISH COINAGE

The ratio between house and land—A table defining this ratio—Standardisation of the bay—The bay corresponds to the shilling—A passage in Saxo Grammaticus—The etymology of " shilling "—Normal size of the bay—Bays computed and subdivided as shillings and as ounces—The house with an aisle perhaps reckoned in ounces and the house without aisle in shillings—Subdivision of the bay into pennies—" Penny " and " pane "—Penny-weights and a nursery rhyme—A table based on the house with larger bays.

IT can be shown beyond dispute that a relationship, or ratio, once existed between the size of a peasant's dwelling-house and the quantity of arable land, or arable land and meadow, which he held.[2]

As we have seen, houses were erected in bays of 16 ft. in length and were estimated or valued by the number of bays which they contained. They were measured by a perch, or rod, of 16 ft. in length, and this was a unit of measurement.

This length of bay was not an arbitrary quantity. It arose from the fact that the normal yoke of oxen required 16 ft. for their standing-room, and this length, having been fixed by the yoke, was adopted not only in ox-houses, but in every kind of rural building.

Now from an examination of numerous documents relating to the apportioning of land and houses, it appears that there once existed a rule by which six acres of land were apportioned to each bay of a peasant's dwelling-house—or, in other words, a rule that the length of his house must be exactly proportioned to the size of his holding. Thus a virgate of

---

[1] The material in this and the following chapter was first published in *Notes and Queries*, beginning in Series 9, vol. iv. p. 431.

[2] This fact was first pointed out by the author in a letter to *The Athenæum*, April 15, 1899.

thirty acres[1] was held with a house of five bays, which together measured 80 ft. in length.

Since this rule seems to have been at one time almost universally recognized in this country it is not unreasonable to
suppose that the monetary unit of pounds, shillings, and
pence were related to the bays. As oxen once counted for
money, it would be likewise convenient to estimate a man's
wealth by the space required for their accommodation, and
finally by the whole contents of his house-room. It would
be easier, moreover, to tax a man, or to estimate his wealth,
by the number of his bays, or by the whole contents of his
house-room, than by the actual number of his oxen, for the
bays were a fixed quantity, whilst the number of oxen may
have varied from time to time. It would be more reasonable
to tax a man in this way than to tax him, as was once the
case, by the number of windows in his house. Further, as
the bays and acres were accurately correlated, the bays
would form an accurate basis of assessment, and would
be more easily estimated than the numerous scattered
strips in the open fields of which the holdings were
composed.

Instead of saying that the length of a peasant's house was
exactly proportioned to the size of his holding, it would probably be more correct to say that the *superficial measurement*
of his house was exactly proportioned to the size of his
holding. And if we assume the accuracy of this last-
mentioned similitude of ratios—or, in other words, if
we assume that the bay had a normal breadth as well
as a normal length—some remarkable consequences
follow.

But before going further let us examine a table,
founded on evidence collected by the author,[2] which
will exhibit the relationship of the acres to the bays, as
well as the relationship of the bays to the monetary
units :

[1] It must be remembered that the size of the virgate, etc., was
not the same in all places. But the variations are nearly always
multiples of 6—as 18, 24. The normal virgate, as found in the
south of England, was thirty acres.

[2] Set forth in *The Athenæum, ut supra.*

Holding	Acres	Bays	s.	d.	Length of house in feet
Hide . .	120	20	20	0	320
Half hide .	60	10	10	0	160
Virgate . .	30	5	5	0	80
Bovate . .	15	$2\frac{1}{2}$	2	6	40
Half-bovate[1] .	$7\frac{1}{2}$	$1\frac{1}{4}$	1	3	20
	6	1	1	0	16

If the breadth, as well as the length, of a large number of bays in old farm-houses and farm-buildings were measured it would probably be found that in early times the breadth, as well as the length, of a bay was, to some extent, standardized. It appears from an entry in *Boldon Buke*[2] that the houses which villeins were accustomed to build in the twelfth century were 15 ft. in breadth. Some years ago the author measured the fork-built bays in the farm-buildings adjoining Offerton Hall, near Hathersage, built in 1658, and found them 15 ft. in length and 16 ft. in breadth, giving the superficial area of each bay as 240 ft. And as the houses mentioned in *Boldon Buke* were 40 ft. in length, corresponding to a bovate, we know that they consisted of two and a half bays, each entire bay being 16 ft. in length. Each of these bays, therefore, like those at Offerton, contained a superficial area of 240 ft.

If we refer to the table given above we shall see that the bay corresponds to the shilling. As there are 240 square feet in a bay, and as in the table a bay corresponds to a shilling, we get the following result :

1. 20 square feet of a bay correspond to a penny.
2. 12 by 20, or 240 square feet, correspond to a shilling.
3. 20 by 240, or 4800 square feet, correspond to a pound.

Therefore :

1. The twelfth part of a bay, or 20 square feet, corresponds to a penny.

[1] Quarters of bays, though occurring in estimates, were not actually erected. Thus, if a man held a half bovate, the distance between the forks of which his cottage was built was 20 ft. This is found both in surveys and actual examples.
[2] Pub. SURTEES SOCIETY, p. 4. And see p. 33.

2. The bay (=twelve pence) corresponds to a shilling.
3. Twenty bays correspond to a pound.

As, therefore, the bay corresponds to six acres as well as to a shilling, it follows that the acre corresponds to two pence, and that the hide corresponds to a pound. Hence the expression *liberata terræ*.

The Anglo-Saxons had a monetary unit of thirty pence, called *mancus*. It will be seen on reference to the table that this corresponds to a bovate of fifteen acres, and also to a house of two and a half bays.

At this point we may examine a passage in Saxo Grammaticus in which bays and payments in money are associated in a very remarkable way. In relating, about the end of the twelfth century, how a king called Godricus imposed an unusual tax on the Frisians, the author says :

" Primum itaque ducentorum quadraginta pedum longitudinem habentis ædificii structura disponitur, bis senis distincta spatiis, quorum quodlibet vicenorum pedum intercapedine tenderetur, praedictae quantitatis summam totalis spatii dispendio reddente."[1]

A building 240 ft. long was erected in twelve bays of 20 ft. each in length. At one end sat the receiver or tax-collector ; at the other end stood a brazen vessel into which every Frisian had to throw a penny with such force that the receiver could hear it ring when it fell into the vessel.

The meaning of the words following " tenderetur " is not very clear, but they probably imply that the bays of this building were 20 ft. square. If that is the meaning, then the bay contained 400 square feet, and the whole building contained 4800 square feet, or exactly the same quantity as that contained in the 20 bays which, according to the table, were associated with the English hide and pound.

But whether this interpretation of the concluding words of the passage is right or not, one cannot fail to notice the numbers 12, 20, 240, for they remind us at once of the

---

[1] Lib. viii. p. 167, quoted from JACOB GRIMM'S *Rechtsalterthümer*, 1854, p. 77. See also RICHTHOFEN, *Friesische Rechtsquellen*, xv. 42.

number of pence in a shilling, of shillings in a pound, and of pence in a pound.

If Saxo's house, as here interpreted, had consisted, like the hypothetical English hidal house given in the table, of twenty bays containing 240 square feet each, the resemblance in form would have been exact. As it is, though the shapes are different, both houses contain precisely the same number of superficial square feet.

It is possible that Saxo's account contains a legendary element, and he may have mixed up the figures. At all events, the old Frisian laws mention this tax, which they call *klip-schild*, and say that the penny must be so big that it will resound through nine bays, instead of twelve bays as in Saxo's account.

In a little book by Otto Lasius[1] a plan, drawn to scale, of a Frisian farm-house, built in 1551, is given. The large building which contains the threshing-floor and the cattle-stalls, consists of thirteen bays, the whole length of the building being a little more than 203 ft. This would give the length of each bay as about 15 ft. $7\frac{1}{2}$ in. Substantially, therefore, the bays of this Frisian building correspond in length to the bays of English rural buildings. The breadth of the bay is twice as much, and, in addition, the building contains aisles.

Perhaps the most striking feature of our table is the correspondence of the bay to the shilling. That the bay was a unit of measurement we have proved elsewhere. It was also a unit of value, for houses were sold, let, and apportioned by the bay. Is it not, therefore, likely that a monetary unit may have been invented to represent the bay as a unit of value? And may not the word " shilling " itself mean " bay ? "

According to Kluge,[2] the word is derived from the Old Germanic *skellan*, to ring or resound. In England, however, the shilling does not appear to have been known as a piece of coined money till the reign of Henry VII, though it was known as a monetary unit in Anglo-Saxon times. Prof. Skeat

[1] *Das friesische Bauernhaus*, Strassburg, 1885, p. 9.
[2] *Etymologisches Wörterbuch der deutschen Sprache*, 1883.

connects it with Icel. *skilja*, to divide, and says : " The reason for the name is not certain. In Icelandic the form of the word is *skillingr*, and the Icel. *skilning*, in modern usage *skilningr*, means separation, division. Now a bay is a division or partition of a building ; it is the space extended between any two pairs of pillars, " forks," or " crutches," which normally stand 16 ft. apart. In Yorkshire the partition which divides the bays of ox-houses into two equal parts is known as the " *skell-boost.*" More significant is the fact that in Wiltshire a *skilling* or *skillen* is an open cowshed. Ogilvie's *Imperial Dictionary* defines *skilling* as " a bay of a barn ; also a slight addition to a cottage."

Six acres to a bay may have been the rule in France, for a reference to Guérard's *Polyptique de l'Abbé Irminon*, i. 595, reveals that among the revenues of the abbey of St. Germain des Prés, in the reign of Charlemagne, there were sixteen hearths to six manses. Now, if we take the *mansus* as equivalent to the hide of 120 acres, this would give an average of 45 acres, or a virgate and a half, to each holding, and by the table on page 196, seven and a half bays to each hearth or house, for the house would have only one fire.

Prof. Maitland has made calculations which show that " some force, conscious or unconscious, has made for ' one pound, one hide,' "[1] It will hardly be doubted that the force was conscious, or that the correlation of houses, acres, and monetary units was the result of design.

It has been seen that in the table on page 196 the pound corresponds to the hide of 120 acres. In the *Domesday of St. Paul's*, compiled in the year 1222, the sums paid by the various tenants exactly correspond, in many cases, to the sums given in the table. Thus on page 4 a list of the *libere tenentes* and the sums paid by each is given :

	s.	d.
The first tenant holds half a hide, and pays . . .	10	0
The second tenant holds two out of three parts of a virgate, and pays	3	4
The third tenant holds a virgate and a half, and pays .	7	6
The fourth and fifth tenants hold a quarter of a virgate each, and pay respectively	1	3

[1] *Domesday Book and Beyond*, p. 465.

Then some variations follow, and afterwards the same scale of payment begins again. Such payments are sufficiently numerous to deserve notice.

For fiscal or other purposes land with its appurtenances is regarded as worth so much a year. Thus we find such expressions as *solidata terræ*,[1] a shillingsworth of land, or *deneriata terræ*, a pennyworth of land.

" There seems no room for doubt," says Prof. Maitland, " that *hiwisc* and the more abstract *hiwscipe* mean a household, and very little room for doubt that *hid* springs from a root that is common to it and them and has the same primary meaning."[2] Again, relying on Mr. Stevenson, he says, " The little evidence that we have seems to point to the greater antiquity in England of a reckoning which takes the ' house land ' rather than the ' plough land ' as its unit."[3] The hide is sometimes described as " terra unius casati," a *casatus* being a person to whom a *casa*, or house of some kind, has been allotted.

Let us now refer to evidence which helps to fix the normal size of the bay.

The size of the Roman bay, as we have seen, is given by Palladius, whose work on husbandry is ascribed to about A.D. 210. This author, in giving directions about the building of ox-houses, says :

" Octo pedes ad spatium standi singulis boum paribus abundant, et in porrectione xv."[4]

Each pair of oxen should have a length of 8 ft. for standing room ; that is, the bay should be 16 ft. long, and the breadth should be 15 ft. Here, therefore, we have a bay with a superficies of 240 (Roman) ft.

The English bay may now be compared to the Roman.

The size of the English bay in the twelfth century is given in *Boldon Buke* (Surtees Soc.), p. 33 :

" In Quykham sunt xxxv. villani, quorum unusquisque

---

[1] " *Solidatus*, a shyllyngworth."—WRIGHT-WÜLCKER, *Vocabularies*, 612, 37.

[2] *Op. cit.*, p. 359.

[3] *Ibid.*, p. 398.

[4] *De Re Rustica*, i. 21. Other measurements and further details are given in Chapter IV, *ante*.

tenet j bovatam de xv. acris, et solebant . . . in operatione sua facere unam domum longitudinis xl. pedum et latitudinis xv. pedum."

As English bays were 16 ft. long, this house contained 2½ bays, and accordingly each complete bay was 16 ft. long and 15 ft. broad. Each bay, therefore, contained 240 square feet.

In France, as in England, buildings were estimated by the bay. Thus in a document of the year 1548 we have " une grange contenant trois Espasses."[1] The usual French word was *travée*, which Cotgrave defines as " A Bay of building ; the space, and length, betweene two beames, or the two walls thereof ; in breadth about twelue foot, in length betweene nineteene and twentie."[2] A bay 20 ft. long by 12 broad would contain 240 square feet, like the Roman and English bay.

It will have been noticed that the building described by Saxo Grammaticus is 240 ft. long, and also that it is divided into 12 bays, each of which is 20 ft. square.[3] Each of these bays may accordingly be divided into 20 rectangular divisions, each measuring 4 ft. by 5 ft., and corresponding to the 20 pennyweights which make the ounce, and the whole building may be divided into 240 such divisions. It is obvious then that the whole building corresponds to a pound, and that the 12 bays represent the 12 ounces into which the pound was divided.

The Frisians had a land measure, or measure of surface, which they called *pundemeta*,[4] literally a pound measure. They had also a measure of land called *enze*, an ounce, which was the twelfth part of the *pundemeta*, and they spoke of so many " ounces of land." In Friesland therefore, as in England the monetary system flowed from the measures or values of houses and land.

The Gallic and the Welsh pound of silver, as well as the Frisian pound of silver, was divided into 12 ounces, each of

---

[1] Du Cange, s.v. *Spatium*.

[2] *A Dictionarie of the French and English Tongues*, 1632.

[3] Du Cange renders the mediæval *dispendium* by *detour*, and it seems impossible to interpret Saxo's words in any other way.

[4] Richthofen, *Altfriesisches Wörterbuch*, s.v.

a score pence, and there were 12 pence in the shilling. An ancient writer has the following definition :

" Juxta Gallos vigesima pars unciæ denarius est et duodecim denarii solidum reddunt. . . . Duodecim unciæ libram xx. solidos continentem efficiunt. Sed veteres solidum qui nunc aureus dicitur nuncupabant."[1]

We may infer that the bay had a fixed or definite area from the fact that hay and corn were estimated by the bay. In Derbyshire hay has been commonly sold by the bay in the present century, and may yet continue to be sold in that way. Palsgrave, in his *English-French Dictionary*, 1530, mentions a " goulfe of corne, so moche as may lye bytwene two postes, otherwyse a bay," but gives no French equivalent. The " two postes " are the pillars or " forks " which separate one bay from another. In Norfolk, according to Forby, every division of a barn is called a " goafe-stede." If the bay or " goulfe " had been of uncertain area, or even if the cubic contents of bays had varied materially, it would have been impossible to sell or appraise hay or corn in this manner. But if the bay had an ascertained area, such as 240 square feet, it would only have been necessary in such cases to take the height. During the sixteenth and seventeenth centuries there are so many instances, both in literature and unpublished documents, of the estimation of valuation of buildings by the bay, that one can hardly doubt the wide prevalence of a standard and well-understood size of bay during those periods.

A solicitor interested in antiquarian matters informed the author that bequests of bays are common in old wills.

If we compare the Frisian house, as described by Saxo Grammaticus, and its twelve bays, containing 4800 square feet, to the English house of twenty bays, we shall see that, whilst the pound was the highest unit of value in both cases, the Frisian bay, or segment of a house, represents twenty

---

[1] In *Pauca de Mensuris* (LACHMANN and RUDORF, *Gromatic Veteres*, p. 373), quoted by Mr. SEEBOHM in the *English Village Community*, p. 292. Mr. SEEBOHM, on the same page, says, " The division of the pound into 240 pence was very conveniently arranged for the division of a tax imposed upon holdings of 240 acres, or 120 acres, or 60 acres, or the 10 acres in each field."

pence and not a shilling. If the Frisian *pundemeta* of land had been equivalent to the English hide of 120 acres, the Frisian bay of 400 square feet would have corresponded to ten acres, that is, to the " ounce of land." The relationship of the house-room to the holding in arable land would have remained unaffected. The quantity of house-room attached to the *pundemeta* would have been the same as the quantity attached to the hide, and so on through the various divisions of these two land measures. In other words, the arithmetical relationship of acres to house-room would have been the same.

The substitution of the shilling for the ounce appears to me to point to a change in architecture. There were, as we have seen, two main kinds of houses—the winter house and the summer house—the winter house being the ordinary village house, and the summer house being the more slightly built summer residence on the hills, where the cattle went to pasture in summer. The winter house, like the summer house, was supported by forks or " gavels," each pair of forks supporting a room containing 240 square feet. But the winter house had an aisle. If we take the English bay of 16 ft. by 15, and put an aisle measuring 16 ft. by 10 on the long side, we shall have made an excellent ox-house for four oxen. The heads of the oxen would, of course, be turned inwards, and they would be fed from the main floor. Or if we take the French bay of 20 ft. by 12, and put an aisle measuring 20 ft. by 8 on the long side, we shall get a similar ox-house for five oxen. In both cases we shall have added 160 square feet to one of the sides, and thus made up the total area of 400 square feet.

It is true that the aisle or lateral cattle-stall annexed to a house or other building continued to be built down to a late period.[1] But it is also true that the introduction of separate cattle-stalls and other outbuildings began at an early date. As the monetary units followed the divisions of houses and land, the shilling took the place of the ounce of twenty pence when the ounce had ceased to represent the typical bay. The quantity of house-room remained unaffected, at all events for fiscal purposes. This is, of course, only a conjecture.

[1] See p. 88, *ante.*

Since the Frisian house described by Saxo Grammaticus was divided into 12 bays, representing the 12 ounces into which a pound of silver, or in older times a pound of copper, was divided, we may be led to suspect that the word " ounce " means " bay." The Latin *uncia*, Old Frisian *enze*, may be related to ἀγκών, a bend, bay, and to ἄγκος, a bend or hollow, a word which, according to Liddell and Scott, is akin to the Latin *uncus*. We have seen that the English bay, used as an architectural term, was otherwise known as a " goulfe." In Old Norse, too, this division of a building is called *gólf*.[1] Evidently the comparison of this section of a building to a gulf, bay, or recess was widely spread, and had taken deep root in the mind. There must have been some reason for the division of the *as*, *libra*, or pound into 12 ounces ; and if a certain number of bays, such as 12 or 20, were taken as the principal unit of value, the name of this regular and well-defined architectural division would naturally become the name of a lower unit of value.

This equation of ounce and bay is supported in another quarter. According to the *H.E.D.* the A.S. *gafol* means interest on money, as well as tribute. The *Epinal Glossary* of A.D. 700 has " *ære alieno*, gæbuli." And then we have *gaveller*, a usurer, and *gavelling*, usury. Amongst the Romans the law of the Twelve Tables in 451 B.C. established *unciarum fenus*, i.e. a twelfth part of the principal or $8\frac{1}{3}$ per cent, payable yearly, as the normal rate of interest.[2] If the Roman bay had a fixed size, and if the Romans, like ourselves, sold hay or corn by the bay, it would be easy to pay interest in hay, and by the " gavel," or by the bay. And we know that they often paid interest in corn. It is remarkable that *fenum* means hay, and *fenus* interest. Cotgrave gives a French proverb, " De mauvais payeurs foin, ou paille "—from a bad payer take hay or straw, i.e. get what you can. So English

---

[1] The word is usually rendered as " floor," " room," " apartment." But it clearly means a bay of building. Thor's hall in the Edda is said to have consisted of 540 *gólfa* and to have been the biggest house that had ever been made. Compare " In My Father's house are many mansions " (μοναι), John xiv. 2.

[2] One ounce in twenty, or one bay of hay in twenty, would have been 5 per cent.

lawyers speak of a poor man as a man of straw. These sayings are reminiscences of a time when debts were paid in cattle and the produce of the field.

Since the pound corresponds to the hide of land and its associated house of 20 bays, and since the shilling corresponds to the bay of 240 square feet, or the twentieth part of that house plus six acres, it follows that the penny corresponds to the twelfth part of such a bay plus half an acre.

Though a house could be built in bays of uniform size, and therefore be valued, taxed, or alienated by the bay, we cannot divide the bay itself in this manner. We can divide a bay of 240 square feet into halves by a " brattice," or partition, and we can divide it into quarters ; but it would be impracticable to divide it into twelve actual portions. We can so divide the acres, but not the bay.

In such a case it would be convenient to make use of a diagram to represent the indivisible floor of a single bay.

Now if we take a sheet of architects' " sectional lines," in which, say, the eighth of a square inch represents a square foot, we can readily divide a surface representing 240 square feet into 12 rectangular divisions. Each division will be 5 ft. long and 4 ft. broad, and will contain 20 square feet. And then if we colour every alternate division black we shall have a representation of an incomplete chess-board.

An actual bay could be marked out in this way, or the divisions on its floor could be represented by alternate pieces of black and white marble.

But a simpler plan would be to paint or draw the twelve divisions in miniature on a board or stone.

However absurd or childish the actual division of the bay by means of a diagram may at first sight appear to us, we must bear in mind that in no other way could the relationship between the quantity of house-room and the quantity of land, or between both these quantities and the monetary units, have been demonstrated. If a law of proportion between house and land be applied to the greater quantities it must also be applied to the lesser. Further, we must remember that in days when arithmetic was either not popularly understood or was of the rudest kind, this marking out of the floor of the bay into portions resembling the " squares " of a chess-board may have been of real service in making calculations. To enable people to understand such a coin as the penny, which did not, like the shilling, represent the annual rent arising from an undivided corporeal thing,[1] it may have been necessary, in the first instance at any rate, to use actual demonstration, in order that they might see, with their very eyes, that the coin represented an aliquot part of the rent arising from an undivided share of real property.

Now the " squares " drawn on the floor of the bay, or on the substituted diagram or reckoning-board, might very well have been called *panes*, or, in Latin, *abaci*. Skeat says a penny is " a little pledge, a pawn," and he refers us to the word " Pawn " in his dictionary. Under that word he refers to the French *pan*, a pane, and says that the English *pane* is a doublet of *pawn*. He might also have referred to the mediæval Latin *pannus*, a portion. The *Prompt. Parv.* has " pane, or parte of the thynge," and Way, in a note on the word, says that, according to Forby, " in Norfolk a regular division of some sorts of husbandry work, as digging or sowing, is called a *pane*." The word *penny*, according to Kluge, may be derived from *pan*, a broad, shallow vessel, or it may be associated with *pawn*, and a hypothetical base *pand*.

If then the A.S. *penning*—a word which is common to the Teutonic languages—is the name of one of the portions of an undivided bay of 240 square feet, or, as the case may have been, of 400 square feet, we may reasonably believe that it is compounded of a Teutonic prefix *penn*, or *pann*, and a termination -*ing*, as in shilling or farthing.

These divisions of the bay seem to be connected with the reckoning-board or calculating-table.

One of the commonest signs of an old English inn was " The Chequers." This sign, according to Larwood and

---

[1] It may be remarked that *solidus*, the Latin word for " shilling," means " undivided," and is usually regarded as equivalent to " solidus nummus." The Gothic *saliþwos* in John xiv. 2 means " bays," and is akin to O.H.G. *selida* (with open *e*), a dwelling, and possibly to A.S. *selde*, as in *sumorselde*, a summer-house. The summer-house was a booth of one bay.

Hotten's *History of Signboards*, p. 488, is "perhaps the most patriarchal of all signs," and may be seen "even on houses in exhumed Pompeii." These authors quote an explanation of the sign given by Dr. Lardner :

"During the Middle Ages, it was usual for merchants, accountants, and judges, who arranged matters of revenue, to appear on a covered banc, so called from an old Saxon word meaning a seat (hence our bank). Before them was placed a flat surface, divided by parallel white lines into perpendicular columns ; these again were divided transversely by lines crossing the former, so as to separate each column into squares. This table was called an Exchequer, from its resemblance to a chess-board, and the calculations were made by counters placed on its several divisions (something after the manner of the Roman abacus). A money-changer's office was generally indicated by a sign of the chequered board suspended. This sign afterwards came to indicate an inn or house of entertainment, probably from the circumstance of the innkeeper also following the trade of money-changer— a coincidence still very common in seaport towns."— *Arithmetic*, p. 44.

There is a nursery jingle, common everywhere in England, but now in a corrupt state, which relates to counting up to twenty. Some years ago the Rev. Carus Collier sent the author the following version from Bridlington in East Yorkshire :

> One, two, come buckle my shoe ;
> Three, four, knock him o'er ;
> Five, six, chop sticks ;
> Seven, eight, *a pennyweight ;*
> Nine, ten, a good fat hen ;
> Eleven, twelve, dig and delve ;
> Thirteen, fourteen, here we've brought him ;
> Fifteen, sixteen, here we fix him ;
> Seventeen, eighteen, here we hoist him ;
> Nineteen, twenty, we've done him plenty.

The most usual version of the jingle begins :

> One, two, come buckle my shoe ;
> Three, four, knock at the door ;
> Five, six, chop sticks ;
> Seven, eight, lay them straight.

In the *Dialogus de Scaccario* of the year 1178 the chequered table in the Court of Exchequer is thus described :

" Scaccarium tabula est quadrangula. Superponitur autem scaccario superiori pannus niger virgis distinctus, distantibus a se virgis vel pedis vel palmæ extentæ spacio. In spaciis autem calculi sunt."

In another passage the *Dialogue* shows that in the twelfth century the origin of the Exchequer table was unknown. But these lines, which have probably been repeated in some form by every English child in every English village, tell us of pennyweights, of counting up to twenty, and of laying out the *virgæ* or " sticks " by which, as it seems, the black cloth of the reckoning-table was divided into " squares " or " panes," and they seem to tell us of " fixing " the " sticks."

It will be seen that the lines refer, not to the twelve pence which make the shilling, but to the twenty pennyweights which make the ounce. Accordingly they may refer to the 20 portions of 20 square feet each into which, as we have seen, a bay of 400 square feet could be divided.

If we adapt bays containing 400 square feet each to the hide of 120 acres and the various divisions of the hide, we shall get the following table of acres, bays, and annual rents :

Holding	Acres	Bays	Length of house in feet	Square feet in bays	Rent s.	d.
Hide . . .	120	12	240	4800	20	0
Half-hide . .	60	6	120	2400	10	0
Virgate . .	30	3	60	1200	5	0
Bovate , .	15	$1\frac{1}{2}$	30	600	2	6
Half-bovate . .	$7\frac{1}{2}$	$\frac{3}{4}$	15	300	1	3
	10	1	20	400	1	8

As the bay of 240 square feet corresponds to 6 acres, so the bay of 400 square feet corresponds to 10 acres. In both cases the penny represents a " square " or " pane " of 20 square feet, together with the corresponding half-acre.

In assigning 10 acres to a bay of 400 square feet, instead of 6 acres to a bay of 240 square feet, we shall only have altered the shape of the house. We shall not have changed the proportion between the house-room and the monetary units or between the house-room and the land. The bovate, for instance, will still consist of 15 acres, and its proper house-room will still be an area of 600 square feet. If the area of the bay be 240 square feet the house attached to the bovate will be 40 ft. long and 15 ft. broad. If the area be 400 square feet it will be 30 ft. long and 20 ft. broad.

Obviously the large bay of 400 square feet will be more suitable for the open, basilical form of house, whilst the small bay of 240 square feet will be more suitable for the enclosed, quadrangular form of house, for 20 bays of 240 square feet each will make a better quadrangle than 12 bays of 400 square feet each.

The fork-built bays of an old barn at Barlow-Woodseats, near Dronfield, were measured some time ago, and the sides found to be 19½ ft. by 19½ ft. This was inside measurement.[1]

The pound, the shilling, the penny, the halfpenny, the farthing, and possibly also other monetary units, were originally the expression, in weights or pieces of silver, of the values of annual chief rents charged on defined and graduated areas of house-room or house-space and on areas of arable land proportioned or correlated to the size of every such area of house-room. These areas are the " squares " of the Roman *agrimensores*.

The term " chief rent " is here used in the sense of " land tax " or *rente censive*, and the words " arable land " include the common rights appurtenant thereto. This " chief rent " was sometimes called *redditus albus*, or white rent, because it was paid in silver.

The nominal measure of value was a real or imaginary house containing an area of 4800 square feet, divided into 20 bays of 240 square feet each, or 240 spaces of 20 square feet each. The whole house corresponded to a pound of silver, every bay corresponded to a *solidus*, or shilling, and every space of 20 square feet corresponded to a penny. Or, to express the same thing in terms of ounces instead of shillings, the nominal measure of value was a real or imaginary house containing an area of 4800 square feet, divided into 12 bays of 400 square feet each, or 240 spaces of 20 square

---

[1] Information by Mr. WIGFULL of Sheffield, architect.

o

feet each, the whole house corresponding to a pound, every bay corresponding to an ounce of 20 pennyweights, or pennies, and every space of 20 square feet corresponding to a penny. A farthing corresponded to a space of 5 square feet, plus half a rood. Whether we reckon in ounces or shillings, the area of house-room was to the area of arable land as 1 to 1089.

We have been trying to put together the scattered parts of an old economic machine. In doing this we have kept in view the sporadic occurrence in England of the rule or law of gavelkind, and have seen how well these regular and minute divisions of houses and land were adapted, not only for the purpose of apportioning chief rents on partition, but also for the purposes of division and subdivision amongst heirs ; for real property in the ancient world was divided specifically, or in kind, and not, as with us, by a distribution of the net proceeds of sale.

CHAPTER XII

IN the last chapter we considered the peasant's house
as a measure of value, and incidentally as a measure
of quantity. But value depends on quantity, and we
will now treat value as a sequel or corollary to the main
thesis, and exhibit the peasant's house as the measure of
the agrarian units. It is true that the English imperial acre
is not a multiple of the bay of 240 square feet ; but two
acres, and all even numbers of acres, are multiples, and
originally all the English, as well as all the Roman, land
measures were multiples of the bay of 240 square feet.[1]

When we find a house described in an old document as
a *mensura* or *mansura* we may be sure that it was the measure
of something. It was the measure of the acres held there-
with because its area was exactly proportioned in size to
them. This equality or similarity of ratios may be seen even
more clearly in the French *masure*, or exact area or spot on
which the bays stood, and with which their foundations
coincided. Again and again we read in English documents
of the *toftum ædificatum* and the *toftum vastum*.[2] In the
former case the toft or area had received its superstructure
of timber-work, of moss, and clay. In the latter the structure had perished, and only the toft remained as evidence

---

[1] The relation of English and Roman land measures was pro-
pounded by the Author in *Notes and Queries*, 9th S., vi. pp. 303,
381.

[2] Compare the *vacua mensura*, *i.e.* toft, of French records, and
the mediæval Latin *metatus* or *metatum*, meaning " house."

of the amount of arable land, with other appurtenances, assigned to its late tenant.

The owners of ancient messuages or dwelling-houses in the village of Royston, near Barnsley, were lately known as "metestead owners," and such owners were alone entitled to common rights in the wastes and unenclosed lands of their township. At a court held 22 September, 32 Eliz., Elizabeth Speight surrendered "a messuage or tenement called a *meestead* or the Newe Walles." At another court, held a few months later, the same house is described as "a messuage called *meastead* or the new wales."[1] The place-name Medstead, near Alton, in Hampshire, may be identical with this word. One can hardly doubt that "metestead" means "measuring-place," and, in a derived sense, "taxing-place." The form "meestead" seems to be owing to assimilation with the Anglo-French "messuage," and "mes-place," or "mese-place."[2] It is probable that "messuage" also means "measuring-place," and is not connected with the verb *manere*. Jamieson, in his *Scottish Dictionary*, which I quote from the small edition, defines "mete hamys" as manors, and "methowss" as "a house for measuring." The same meaning must be given to the Yorkshire place-name and surname Metham or Mettam. These words are connected with the Icelandic *meta*, to tax, value, and with *met-orð*, a valuation. If "messuage" means "measuring-place" or "taxing-place," the term "capital messuage" must orginally have meant "principal measuring-place." That is to say, it must have meant a house of twenty bays containing 240 square feet each, corresponding to a hide, or, as the case might have been, of twelve bays containing 400 square feet each. The house-space attached to the hide might have been covered by one large building, or it might have been distributed rateably amongst the several agrarian divisions of which any hide was, for fiscal purposes, made up, and such a distribution was, no doubt, the general practice. Clear evidence of the apportionment of house-room amongst the various tenants of a hide appears in the *Domesday of*

[1] Court Rolls of the Manor of Dewsbury.
[2] The word sometimes occurs as simply " mese " or " meese."

St. Paul's (pp. 43–47), which mentions " *quælibet* domus de hida " and " *unaquæque* domus hidæ."

Since the quantity of a man's agrarian rights depended on the size of his house we may be sure that he would do nothing that would be likely to diminish those rights. If his house fell into ruin he would rebuild it as soon as possible on the old site and in the same form, and equality and regularity in the size of tofts would favour the transportation of wooden houses from one site to another. If he could not immediately rebuild, he would at least preserve the territorial evidence of his title. He would keep the stones on which his decayed forks or pillars stood *in situ*, or the bare forks themselves would remain on their stone bases as dumb, but visible witnesses. On the other hand, he would do nothing that would be likely to increase his obligations.

If he had a single bay of 240 square feet, on which he paid a shilling for chief rent or royal tribute, he would not build another bay to his house, and so incur the danger of paying twice as much chief rent. Or, to put it in another way, if he was taxed by the number of forks which supported his house, i.e. at the rate of one fork to a bay, he would not add another fork, and so possibly become liable to pay twice as much *gafol*.[1]

What, then, was the poor man to do as his family grew larger, and wanted bedrooms or other decencies of life ? He could get over the difficulty in two ways : he could make a little chamber in the roof, or he could affix " outshots " to the ends of his one bay, or even on its sides. In earlier chapters we have given plans of old Lancashire houses in which there was no upper story, and in which the central and fork-built living-room had received these lateral additions. The " outshots " were not fork-built ; they were smaller than the living-room or single bay which formed the central or original dwelling. This living-room was there called the " house-part," and elsewhere the same room is known as the " house-place " or " house." We took this " house " to be an abbreviated expression for " fire-house," or room containing the fire, but it may also

---

[1] For the meaning of *gafol* see p. 221 *post*.

be that the " house-part " was the only part of the building
which was fiscally recognized. It is not ascertainable
whether the window tax imposed by the statute 7 Will. III,
c. 18, immediately followed an older tax on the bays of the
houses, though the window tax itself has been aptly compared to the Roman *ostiarium* or tax on the doors of houses.
What is certain is that people did their best to escape the
window tax by building up windows, and, in farm-houses,
by painting " cheese-room " or " dairy " over the sills, so
as to come within the authorized exemptions. And this
having been the case, we may be sure that the same thing
was done in an earlier time when people were taxed, not
by the window, but by the fork or bay. This is not to say
that the Lancashire cottages which we have described were
old enough to have been once subject to *gafol* or bay tax.
They may, or may not, have been so subject, but, at any
rate, the form in which they were built seems to be a record
or survival of attempts to escape taxation, if not of the due
maintenance of an equality of ratios between house and land.

To meet the possible objection that we are here relying
too much on recent evidence, and, moreover, that this
evidence is drawn from one English county, we will " put
in " a German builder's plan[1] of the year 820. Amongst
other things it describes a gardener's cottage, consisting
of a single room with narrow " outshots," which Prof.
Henning calls *Verschläge*, or partitions, on three sides. The
" outshot " or partitioned space on the long side has an
entrance passage in the middle, and the remaining parts of
the partitioned space contain the *cubilia famulorum*, or
servants' beds. One of the " outshots " at the ends is the
gardener's private chamber, warmed by a small stove
in the corner, the " outshot " at the opposite end being
the storeroom where his tools and seeds are kept. The
resemblance between the plan of this house and the
plans of the Lancashire houses which we have described is
most striking ; even the very storeroom and chamber at

[1] HENNING, *ut supra*, p. 143. The plan was printed in facsimile
by Ferdinand Keller at Zürich in 1884, and relates to the monastery
of St. Gall.

the ends are reproduced. But the important point to notice is that the single room round which the little " out-shots " are grouped is described on the plan as *ipsa domus*, i.e. the house itself, or " house-part." Those who believe in the abiding force of custom will see nothing strange in these parallels. Irregular " outshots " or appentices could not have been measures of land.

The rule was : no house, no gavel. In his *Glossarium*, *s.v. Gabella*, Spelman quotes the laws of Ina thus :

" Si quis componat de virgata terræ vel amplius ad gablum et araverit, si dominus velit terram illam tenere ad gablum, vel opus : non necesse est hoc excipi si nulla domus commissa sit."

A man might take a farm of thirty acres or more ; he might plough it and reap his crops ; and yet if he had no house, no gavel or property tax was payable. The house alone was the measure of his fiscal obligations, as it was the measure and the source of all his agrarian rights. He was assessed in the rate-book by the number of forks, or, which was the same thing, by the number of bays which his house contained.

At what period the house became a measure of the land it is hard to determine. The works of the Roman *gromatici* in Lachmann's edition reveal no trace of the custom. But neither are houses nor building-plots mentioned by these authors. The adjustment of taxation was not a thing which concerned them or their art. The rule which we have dis-covered seems to have been of wide application, for even the old Swedish laws declare that " tompt är ackers mod-hir," the toft is the mother of the land. Ihre, who quotes these words, with the reference, says : " Pro area villæ est etiam mensura areæ in agro." This is a good definition, and we may well adopt it. As the area of a man's house was, so was the measure of his land.

But not only was the house a measure of land ; it was also a measure of communal rights and liabilities. Before discussing this new proposition, however, it will be necessary to say something more about the word *messuage*, which obviously means measure. In mediæval records the commonest form of the word is *mesagium,* and in Yorkshire a messuage is still called a " message." *Mesagium,* according to Du Cange, means a house, and he quotes this passage, in which it plainly means a measure[1] ; " Singulis diebus liberatur cuilibet canonico Mesagium panis, id est, quinque panis libræ." Every canon was to have a measure of bread weighed out to him, that is, he was to have five pounds of bread daily. Surely he was not to have a " mansion " or " dwelling-house " of bread ! The English word, borrowed from the French, was *mese, mes, mease,* or *meese.* So in Blount's *Glossographia,* 1674, we have " *Mease,* a measure of Herrings containing 500. Also taken for a Messuage or House." Again, in Huloet's *Abecedarium,* 1552, we have " mease of herynge," " mease of meate," and " mease of pottage." In Cotgrave the French *mets* is said to stand for *més,* " a messe, course, or seruice of meat ; also a house or tenement." And in Yorkshire they still speak of a *meeas* of porridge. A " mess of pottage " is therefore a measure of pottage, and the common derivation of E. *mess* from Lat. *missus* is wrong.

Having ascertained that " messuage " means measure, we are led to inquire whether other old names of building sites and peasants' houses may not have been connected with mensuration. One of these is the Late L. *mansus.* Jacob Grimm says that this word may, with the greatest probability, be derived from *manere,* to dwell, just as F. *meson, maison,* have been derived from L. *mansio,* and this seems to be the opinion of all subsequent etymologists. Grimm, however, refers to Huydecoper, who, he says, wasted his ingenuity in trying to prove that *mansus* was formed not from the participle of *manere,* but from the participle of *metiri,* to measure, so that *mansus* stands for *mensus,* a measure. It is by no means clear that Huydecoper was wrong. Grimm says himself that the *mansus,* like the O.H.G. *huopa,* was a piece of hedged and measured land. and that in German documents it is often equivalent to *area,*

[1] For further quotations from DU CANGE and an important extract from the Black Book of Peterborough, see a letter by the author in *Notes and Queries,* 9th S., v. 521.

curtis,[1] and, as if he were helping Huydecoper to prove his case, he thinks that *huopa* may be connected with O.N. *hōf*, moderation, measure, though Schrader connects it with Greek κῆπος, a garden. It may be worth while to mention the Greek στάθμη, a rule, measure, and σταθμός, a dwelling, abode, though I am not aware that the Greek peasant's house was ever regarded as a measure.

The word *mensio*, "measure," would as easily turn into *mansio* as *mensura* would turn into *mansura*; and when we read in Domesday Book of *minutæ mansiones* at York, fifty feet wide, it is difficult to believe, after all the evidence which I have produced, that these words mean anything else but "small measures," like *mansiunculæ*, or like the "half-tofts" of later records. We may compare the Danish *maal*, "measure," which has also the meaning of home, house, and the obsolete *maalsjord*, land for a town which is measured or allotted to the inhabitants. Of the Swedish *maal*, "measure," Ihre says : " Prius notat locum qui usui esse potest, atque adeo in partitione areæ in censum venit, posterius id, quod inutile est, atque mensuratæ terræ summam non auget."

The *area* in this passage must be the area of the house, on which ground rent or land tax was imposed in the name of the entire holding. On partition of the house and holding the land tax was originally apportioned by the bay, but afterwards—when the practice of apportioning holdings by the bay fell into disuse, and when the possession of a house had ceased to imply the possession of an aliquot part of arable land and communal rights, and therefore ceased to be of use in measuring acres or apportioning land tax—the word came to mean simply a house or measure, without reference to the thing measured.

Not only was a man's house the measure of his arable land; it was the source of all his communal rights. His house became the visible symbol or certificate which proved him to be a shareholder in a company of landowners, and a participator in the advantages arising from the possession of land, and it was as much the measure of the quantum of

---

[1] *Rechtsalterthümer*, p. 535.

interest which he held in that company as the share certificates of a modern investor are measures of the quantum of interest which he holds in any undertaking. In both cases the valuable interest consists, or consisted, of shares, not stock. The man whose name was on the register, so to speak, of the ancient landowning company must either hold a unit or some multiple of that unit. If the capital of the company was divided into shares of six acres each, he must not hold less than that quantity, and those six acres must be measured by a house consisting of one bay of 240 square feet, which formed, as it were, his share certificate; and so in a modern company limited by shares of £100 each, a shareholder must not hold less than one share, and if he holds more, his quantum of interest must consist of a multiple of that one share. You can divide the capital of the modern company by that one share of £100, as you can divide the hide of 120 acres and any number of hides by six. If again the capital of the ancient company was divided into shares of ten acres each, a shareholder must hold not less than that quantity, and those ten acres must be measured by a house consisting of one bay of 400 square feet. And you can divide the hide by ten as well as by six.

But the ownership of a house conferred obligations on a man as well as rights. On the one hand it gave him, in addition to a share in the arable land of the community, a right to participate in common advantages, such as rights of pasturage and water, and rights to cut wood for building purposes. On the other hand it subjected him to an amount of land tax, which was fixed by the number of his bays, and also to public duties.

In a valuable essay[1] on " Communal House Demolition " Mr. Round has discussed a remarkable custom found in " the ancient community of the Cinque Ports." It seems that the governing bodies of those towns consisted of a mayor and twelve jurats, and every person who might be elected a member of one of such bodies was bound to take office on pain of having his messuage demolished. Mr.

[1] *Feudal England*, p. 552.

Round quotes the Custumal of Sandwich from Boys's *Sandwich*, p. 431 :

" Si maior sic electus officium suum recipere noluit, primo et secundo et tercio monitus, tota communitas ibit ad capitale messuagium suum, si habuerit proprium, et illud cum armis omnimodo quo poterit prosternat usque ad terram. . . . Similiter quicunque juratus fuerit electus et jurare noluerit, simile judicium."

Mr. Round says that this custom has not, so far as he knows, been found elsewhere in England, but observes that it was of widespread occurrence abroad, particularly in Flanders and Northern France. A similar custom prevailed, however, at Scarborough in the time of Henry III, when the burgesses of that town complained to the king against the Sheriff of Yorkshire. They said :

" The Sheriff in person has come into harbour and wished to take all the herring from the fishermen of Scarborough and others without market : and, if anyone says to the contrary, he is threatened with imprisonment and to have his house burnt."[1]

In a Derbyshire village where the author spent some years of his boyhood a man who had beaten his wife, or had committed some other grave offence, was taken round the town in a cart, and finally soused in a horsepond. The culprit was followed by a crowd of men and boys, who made an excruciating din by rattling tin cans, and singing some lines beginning :

Ran, dan, dan,[2]
With an old tin can.

It seems possible that the first word of this doggerel may be *ran*, a house, as in *ransack*. In modern times the townsmen dare not demolish a man's house or burn it, so they seem to have given the rascal who had offended them a dose of water instead of fire.

On the Continent the demolition of a house was a public ceremony. The church bell tolled, and the offender was " rung out of his freedom " amidst the crash of his

[1] *Yorkshire Inquisitions*, ed. by W. Browne, i. 122.
[2] I am told that at Whitwell, in Derbyshire, they say " ran, *tan*."

falling house. Now what is the meaning of this ceremony? Was it not intended to deprive the offender of his status in the community, to excommunicate him, and make him an outlaw? And does it not mean that as the offender's house was the measure of his communal rights, so the demolition of that house deprived him of his share in those rights? "So essential," says Mr. Round, "was the power of distraint, as we might term it, given to the community over its members, by the possession of a house, that it was sometimes made compulsory on a new member to become possessed of a house within a year of his joining." And in proof of this statement he quotes a charter of Louis VI, dated 1128 :

"Quicunque autem in Pace ista recipiatur, infra anni spatium aut domum sibi edificet, aut vineas emet . . . per que justiciari possit, si quid forte in eum querele evenerit."

To use the technical word of this document, a man was "justified" by the possession of a house, and, in some cases as it seems, by the possession of vines. A new member of the community had to "qualify," to use the modern term, by showing that he was possessed of so much property, or to "justify," as sureties to the court sometimes do now, by swearing that they are worth so much money.

We come now to the question of taxation based on house property.

It appears from the *Ancient Laws and Institutes of Wales* that houses were estimated by the "fork," in Anglo-Saxon called *gafol*. Thus in the Dimetian Code we are told that "the worth of a winter-house, for every fork which supports the ridge-beam [is] twenty pence." And again, in the *Leges Wallice* the following statements occur in the section "De fractione domus et combustione" :

"I. Precium hyemalis domus est xxti denarii de unaquaque furca que sustinet laquear, et de laqueari xla denarii.

"II. Si denudetur, tertia pars totius precii redatur.

"III. Domus estiualis, xii. denarii."

Estimation by the " fork " or *gafol* is equivalent to estimation by the bay, for the surveyor would not count both
ends, so that in counting " forks " he would really be
counting bays.   Thus a house of six bays would contain
seven " forks," and the surveyor would leave out the first,
just as in framing a scale or foot-rule a man would begin with
zero.

It appears that the Anglo-Saxon *gafol*, fork, or " crutch,"
as it is sometimes called in Yorkshire, and *gafol*, tribute, are
identical.   It further appears that the word *gavelkind* implies
a division of the house and its appurtenances among the
heirs by the " gavel," which was equivalent to division by
the bay.   It implies the actual or physical partition of houses
and land.   " Gavelage " is the payment or estimation of
tribute by the " gavel."

In the year 1200 King John granted a charter to the burgesses of Scarborough declaring that they should have all
the customs and liberties which the citizens of York had.
The charter further declares that

" for every house in Scarborough whose gable is turned
towards the street they shall pay to us 4*d*. yearly, and as
regards the houses whose sides face the street, 6*d*. yearly."[1]

Here then we have a tax imposed on town houses whose
gables (*gabula*) faced the street, with a proviso that the tax
should be higher if the gable did not face the street.

In the year 1250 an inquisition was made at Scarborough
" concerning eight messuages with the appurtenances
claimed by the King as his demesne from the Abbot of
Cîteaux."   A jury was impanelled, and they on their oaths
said

" that the Abbot holds eight messuages with the appurtenances which the King claims against him as his demesne,
where the capital messuage of the Abbot is situate, and he
renders to the King yearly in the name of gabelage 6*d*.

---

[1] " Et ipsi de unaquaque domo de Escardeburg cujus gabulum
est tornatum adversus viam nobis reddent singulis annis quatuor
denarios, et de illis domibus quarum latera versa sunt versus viam
sex denarios per annum."—HARDY, *Rotuli Chartarum*, part i. p. 40.

222 EVOLUTION OF THE ENGLISH HOUSE

The said eight messuages, while they were separate, yielded to the King in gabelage by the year 3s. 10d. ; but now, as they are included in one messuage, they ought, according to the custom of the borough, to yield in the name of one gabelage (*nomine unius Gabulagii*) 6d. ; for the custom of the borough is such, that if any burgess inclose in one eight messuages or more yielding gablage [*sic*] severally, he shall yield one gablage only, that is 6d."[1]

Let it be noted that the tax is here called *gabulagium*, being with great probability derived from *gabulum*, the gable or forked end of a house. We may infer from the charter of 1200 how the sum of 3s. 10d. charged on the eight messuages was made up. The houses on seven of the messuages had their sides, and not their gables, turned to the street, and so rendered 6d. each. The remaining house had its gable turned to the street, and therefore rendered 4d.

It is obvious that the abbot had been trying to evade the tax, or to pay less than his just share of it. He was doing what people did a long time afterwards, when they built up windows in their houses to evade the window tax. There was no legal reason why a man should not have had only one window in his house, in order to pay tax on that window and no more. And there was no legal reason why the Abbot of Cîteaux should not have turned his eight messuages into one, and by doing so have defeated the collectors of the revenue. Of course we are not concerned here with the morality of the thing. As regards the charter of King John, it looks as if, some time before the year 1200, the burgesses of Scarborough had been trying to evade the payment of gavelage by making it appear that if they built their houses contiguously, or turned the sides of the houses to the street, they would not be liable to pay this tax. One of the objects of the charter seems, therefore, to have been to defeat this attempt, and to assess at a higher rate the persons who had thus been trying to evade payment.

Now, if it can be proved that the gables of houses invari-

[1] *Yorkshire Inq.*, Record Series (Yorkshire Arch., etc., Association), vol. i. p. 21.

ably, or even usually, faced the street, we shall know for certain that *gabulagium* was a tax on gables. Any book on English domestic architecture will produce evidence that in old towns or cities the gables faced the street. The document known as *Fitz-Alwyne's Assize*, dated 1189, shows that the gables of London houses faced the street.[1] Du Cange defines *gabulum* as (1) " frons ædificii " and (2) " census, tributum." In the fifteenth century the *Catholicon Anglicum* explains " gavelle of a howse " by the word *frontispicium*—i.e. front view. And the *Ramsey Chartulary* of the thirteenth century shows that to speak of houses which had doors opening on the street was tantamount to speaking of dwelling-houses.[2] As the doors were in the gable ends, it is easy to see that taxing doors was virtually the same thing as taxing gables. The difference therefore between the Roman *ostiarium*, or door tax, and the later *gabulagium*, or gable tax, is only nominal.

Gavelage appears to have been payable in Scarborough as late as 1697, for in that year De la Pryme thus describes a ceremony which was performed there :

" The town is a corporation town, and tho' it is very poor now to what it was formerly, yet it has a......who is commonly some poor man, they haveing no rich ones amongst them. About two days before Michilmass day the sayd......being arrayed in his gown of state, he mounts upon horseback, and has his attendants with him, and the macebear[er] carrying the mace before him, with two fidlers and a base viol. Thus marching in state (as bigg as the lord mare of London), all along the shore side, they make many halts, and the cryer crys thus with a strang sort of a singing voyce, high and low :

> Whay ! Whay ! Whay !
> Pay your gavelage, ha !
> Between this and Michaelmas day,
> Or you'll be fined, I say !

[1] RILEY, *Munimenta Gildhallæ Lond.*, p. xxx.
[2] " Item quælibet domus, habens ostium apertum versus vicum, tam de malmannis, quam de cotmannis, et operariis, inveniret unum hominem ad lovebone, sine cibo domini, præter Ricardum Pemdome," etc. Cited by Vinogradoff, *Villainage*, p. 460.

Then the fiddlers begins to dance, and caper, and plays, fit to make one burst with laughter that sees and hears them. Then they go on again, and crys as before, with the greatest majesty and gravity immaginable, none of this comical crew being seen as much as to smile all the time, when as spectators are almost bursten with laughing.

" This is the true origin of the proverb, for this custom of *gavelage* is a certain tribute that every house pays to the ......when he is pleased to call for it, and he gives not above one day warning, and may call for it when he pleases."[1]

We must not lose sight of the fact that the houses in Scarborough which paid gavelage were town houses, belonging to burgesses and fishermen. We do not know their sizes, but it would have been manifestly unjust to tax a small house at the same rate as a large house, and we have shown that in ancient Wales houses were valued by the number of " forks " which they contained.[2] But we are not concerned with the sizes of houses now. We are merely proving that gavelage was a tax imposed on " gables."

The evidence which we have produced is of the very best kind, and on considering that evidence it is scarcely possible to maintain that the A.S. *gafol*, tribute, is a derivative of the verb *to give*. Some of the best dictionaries, however, have so derived it, without hesitation. Kluge and Lutz appear to be the only modern etymologists who have escaped this pitfall. In their *English Etymology* (Strassburg, 1898) they content themselves with mentioning the Late Latin, Italian, French, and Spanish forms of the word, and refer it to a Teutonic substantive *gabula*. The Latin *gabalus*, a fork or gibbet, is of course a cognate form.

Jacob Grimm, in his book on the antiquities of German law,[3] quotes a document, made in the year 889 and confirmed in 993, relating to the *decima tributi*,

" quæ de partibus orientalium Francorum ad fiscum domini-

---

[1] *Diary of Abraham de la Pryme* (Surtees Soc.), p. 126. The proverb to which he refers is the " Scarburg Warning."

[2] See p. 85 *ante*.

[3] *Deutsche Rechtsalterthümer*, 1854, p. 298. Late Latin forms of *stiura* are *steura* and *steyra* (DU CANGE).

cum annuatim persolvi solebat, quæ secundum illorum linguam *steora* vel *osterstuopha* vocantur."

He does not know what *osterstuopha* means, but says that if *stauf*, a stoup, a cup, be meant, we ought to read *stoupha* instead of *stuopha*. He thinks that the word refers to a tax paid at Easter. As regards *steora*, Kluge has suggested a connexion between the modern German *Steur*, tax, and O.H.G. *stiura*, a post, pillar ; and *stuopha* in *osterstuopha* appears to have the same derived meaning, so that, to put the combined word into an English form, we might call it Easterstoop, i.e. Easter tax (or taxes). The Late Latin *stopharius*, which Du Cange quotes from an old glossary,[1] appears to mean a man who was taxed by the stoops or posts of his house, as the *gabularius* was a man who was taxed by the gables of his house.

Not only do English mediæval records tell us of *gafol* and *gabulagium*, but on the Continent we meet with *forcagium*, which also seems to mean fork-tax.[2] In addition to *forcagium*, Du Cange gives *forchagium*, *forciagium*, etc. He says that *forchagium* is a tribute exacted from every *furcia*, or house, and that it means the same as *foagium*, hearth-tax. He also mentions *forcia*, which, perhaps mistakenly, he regards as a tax extorted by violence ; and he defines *forcatica* as a tribute which, in his opinion, was paid on booths (*stationes*) at fairs, such booths having been supported by " forks."[3]

---

[1] The words quoted are, " Tributarius Romanus et Stopharius nominatur qui censum Regi solvit." From what source does the Late Latin *stuiva*, tribute, come ? And what is the origin of the English verb *to stump up*, to pay cash ? The word " stoop " is common enough in the Midland counties. When I was a boy there was an inn in Dronfield called " The Blue Stoops." Posts of wood painted blue, stood in front of the principal entrance. WACKERNAGEL has *stûpe*, *staupe*, a post.

[2] " Dedi Majori-Monasterio . . . decimas omnium meorum reddituum . . . præter talliam meam et Forcagium." " Forchagium. Census qui a singulis furciis seu domibus exigitur, idem quod Foagium."—DU CANGE.

[3] " Tributum, ut opinor, quod pro statione in nundinis, quæ furcis fulciebatur habenda, pensitabitur." *Cf.* " Et faciunt in nundinis Sancti Cuthberti singuli ij villani unam botham."—*Boldon Book* (Surtees Soc.), p. 4. " Boothage," of which an example is given in the *N.E.D.*, may be also compared.

P

That peasants' houses were supported by " forks," even in classical times, may be seen from passages in several authors. In particular one might refer to the description of a cottage in Seneca, *Epist.*, 90, of which a translation is given on p. 50.

Here we have a small cottage supported by a "fork" at either end, and apparently consisting, like an ordinary booth, of one bay. Such a cottage may have been strange to the eyes of the philosopher, and he drew from it a lesson in morals by comparing the slaves who dwelt beneath marble and gold to the free men whose bodies were sheltered by a roof of thatch held up by wooden " forks."[1]

If in our day it seems difficult to understand that men should have been taxed by their pillars or " forks," we must remember that these wooden posts were the most striking, as well as the most costly, parts of peasants' houses, the walls being composed of sticks and mud, which could be removed from time to time, like a worn-out coat, and renewed.

It might be suggested that the Latin *stips*, genitive *stipis*, a contribution in small coin—a word which is only found in the oblique cases—may be connected with *stipes*, *stipitis*, a post. It is a curious fact that the Late Latin *stips* and *stipes* both mean a fork or gibbet. For the former word Du Cange quotes a document of the year 627, and for the latter a document of the year 863. There seems to be an unmistakable connection between the Roman *columnarium* and *ostiarium* and these later taxes. Moreover, it is at least possible that pillar tax and door tax are older than the time of Cicero. The suggestion about *stips*, however, is advanced with hesitation, because there seem to be philological objections to it, and because the opinion of an ancient writer is against it.

In Smith's *Dictionary of Greek and Roman Antiquities*, it is said that *columnarium*, mentioned by Cicero, " was probably imposed by the *lex sumptuaria* of Julius Cæsar, and was intended to check the passion for the building of

---

[1] I quote the passage in Seneca from FACCIOLATI's *Lexicon* (English edition, 1828), s.v. *casa*, and do not know to what part of the world, or to what time, it refers.

palaces, which then prevailed at Rome." No authority, however, is cited in support of this opinion, nor is any proof given that the pillar tax mentioned by Cicero differed in any respect from the *columnarium* levied by Metellus Scipio in Syria, in 49–48 B.C.

At first sight gavelage seems to have been imposed on the houses of the Scarborough burgesses without regard to size. But it is possible that only a *selda*,[1] or booth fronting the street, was intended to be taxed. In the borough of Whitby, in the same neighbourhood, we read of a man granting an annual rent of 3s. out of the *selda* and the *solarium* (upper room) of his house towards the street, with power to distrain on the whole of his house (" per totam domum meam ") in case the distraint on the *selda* and *solarium* were not sufficient.[2] At Pontefract in 1258 there were 120 *seldæ*.[3] And the Hundreds Rolls of 1279 show that there were many *seldæ* in Oxford, with or without *solaria*. Now if these *seldæ* were mere booths, consisting of a single bay each, one can understand how gavelage would fall on them with equal incidence. Equality of taxation at Scarborough may thus imply equality of size in the burgage tenements, but it must be admitted that the point remains obscure.

We can find no direct evidence, either English or Continental, showing that houses were taxed by the *number* of the " forks " or posts which they contained ; but it is improbable that such a cottage as the one described by Seneca would bear the same burden of taxation as a house supported by many " forks," or by many columns, either in town or country. In ancient Wales we have proof that houses were supported by rows of "*gavaels*, forks, or columns," and that such houses were valued by the number of *gavaels* which they contained.[4]

[1] A.S. *selde*, a porch. *Cf. winterselde* and *sumorselde* (Sweet). The mediæval *selda* usually meant a shop. *Cf.* also the Lucken Booths or shops, which formerly stood in Edinburgh.

[2] " In selda et solario domus meæ in Hakelsougate in Whiteby versus vicum."—ATKINSON, *Whitby Chartulary*, i. 20.

[3] *Yorkshire Inq.* (Yorkshire Arch. Society, Record Series), i. 50. For *seldæ* in Winchester, where linen-drapery was sold, see MORGAN's *England under the Norman Occupation*, p. 166.

[4] SEEBOHM's *English Village Community*, p. 239.

SUMMARY

THE main results attained in the foregoing pages may now be given in a brief summary.

The earliest remains of houses, properly so called, in Great Britain are of a round shape, with a central open hearth. They were built of wood or basket-work. Light was admitted by the door, or by the aperture in the roof which formed a vent for the smoke. Such houses were made wind-and-water tight by a plastering of mud-clay. They appear to have been thatched with reeds or heather. The so-called beehive houses are imitations in stone of these round houses. Many prehistoric round houses were probably built of mud.

Holes in the earth and cave-dwellings are older than the round houses just mentioned. They belong to a very remote antiquity, and can hardly be called houses at all. They are little better than the burrows of the rabbit or fox.

The beehive houses show a tendency towards a rectangular form. The rectangular house, however, was not evolved from the round house, but from the temporary booth or tent built by shepherds for their summer residences on the mountains or summer pastures. Such a booth was erected by placing two wooden " forks " or " crutches " at a convenient distance apart, and extending a ridge-tree from the apex of one " fork " to the apex of the other. The framework so made was covered with whatever material was most suitable for use.

The rectangular house was evolved from such a booth or tent. The way in which this was done can be well illustrated by noticing how children build houses with packs of cards. First they incline a pair of cards towards each other so as to make a kind of tent, and then they adjust the cards all round the tent in such a way as to make the outer walls upright and to leave the sloping tent within. In these toy houses the whole tent stands within ; in the rectangular house of real life only the triangular wooden framework of the tent stands within.

The booth which was supported by a couple of " forks " might be extended to any length by adding other pairs of " forks " at the ends. The space included between any two pairs of these " forks " was known as a " bay." As the " bays " were of uniform length, the practice arose of speaking of a building as containing so many " bays."

The normal length of the bay was 16 ft. Its length was therefore the same as that of the rod or perch in land measurement. Both buildings and acres were measured by the rod of 16 ft. The length of this rod was determined by the standing-room required by the " long yoke of oxen, whether standing in the stall or the plough-team.

Just as the booth or tent supported by a pair of " crutches " could be extended in the direction of its length, so it could be widened at its sides. This was done by affixing aisles, or, as they were called, " outshots " at the sides. A building so framed consisted of a nave with an aisle on one or both sides. These " outshots " were sometimes formed by a complex wooden framework affixed to the " crutches," as in the example from Bolsterstone (p. 94). Usually, however, upright pillars took the place of the " crutches," and then the form of the building was like that of the typical parish church in which the nave is separated from the aisles by two parallel rows of pillars.

The typical dwelling-house contained a hall and bower, and a buttery or store-room. The hall was the men's apartment, but, as it contained the fire, the food was cooked there. The men slept in the hall, and the bower was the women's apartment.

As was the case in other countries, it is probable that in the largest form of dwelling the cattle were housed in the aisles of the fire-house or hall, the men sleeping in a loft over the horses, and the women in a corresponding loft over the cows. In such cases there was an exedra at the end for the use of the master of the household and his family.

In form such a building resembled a church, with nave, aisles, and chancel.

The bower was sometimes called " the woman house." It corresponds to the *stofa* of the Norsemen and the *gynæconitis* of the Greeks.

In ancient cities the forms of the houses and the arrangement of the streets were modified by foreign influence. The space available for building purposes was limited by the walls or ramparts, and this limitation of space caused the houses to be built to a greater height than in the country. The chief apartment was on the upper floor, and the basements, and even the cellars, were occupied as shops. The upper stories projected over the basements. Most of the streets were too narrow to permit the use of carriages or vehicles in them. The two main streets, which intersected each other at right angles and passed through the four gates, were used for carriage traffic.

Usually the chimney or flue which carried the smoke was built of wood, plastered with mud-clay. The perishable nature of such a structure, together with the confusion which has arisen from the use of the word " chimney " in various senses, has led to the belief that chimneys were not in early use. It seems, however, that a " cover," or wood-and-plaster hood, stood over the hearth, whereas some authors understood a " chimney " to mean only a stone flue, built into, and forming part of, an outer wall.

In ancient buildings of every kind the frequent use of colour-wash, both on the inner and outer walls, has to be noticed. Wall-painting was much used. The interiors of houses, including churches, were whitewashed and decorated with mural paintings. Often their exteriors were covered with colour-wash.

In the great country house of the Middle Ages, or manor-house as it may be conveniently called, the chief rooms were the hall, or men's apartment, which corresponded to the Greek *andronitis*, and the bower or chamber, which corresponded to the *gynæconitis*. A chapel was frequently added. To these chief apartments other rooms, such as a kitchen, brewhouse, washhouse, stables, etc., were often annexed, and then the whole range of buildings were usually grouped round a quadrangular area. When the chapel, hall, or bower were on an upper floor, access to them was obtained by outside stairs. In many of these buildings distinct traces of Greek and Roman influence may be seen. The chief windows opened into the quadrangle.

The castle, properly so called, was a stronghold used for the defence of a particular district. It was supported by taxation, and its officers were appointed by the Crown. Frequently it occupied the site of a prehistoric fortified village, and the Old English *castel* meant " village." The most characteristic of its buildings was a watch-tower or keep, which often occupied the site of an earlier toot-hill or specular mount. From this keep watch was kept over the surrounding country, and signals of approaching danger given. Church towers, like the Irish and Scotch round towers, were often, perhaps generally, used as watch-towers. In many cases they belonged to the municipality, and in form and construction resembled the watch-towers found in castle yards.

Modern scholars have shown that the word " church " means " lord's house," and the evidence which we have given proves that this " house " was the public hall, town hall, or basilica of a district or community. It was used both as a temple and a court of justice. It was also the place where the local council met. The forms of these buildings are identical with the forms of the heathen basilica. This identity is especially apparent in the striking correspondence between the crypts found in some English churches and the crypt of the basilica at Pompeii. The double staircases, the holes in the roof, and the small " cellar-windows " are found as well in the Pompeian crypt as in crypts of English churches. There are, besides, other points of resemblance.

In early times a relationship existed between the size of a peasant's house and the quantity of land which he held. There appears to have existed a rule by which six acres of land were apportioned to each bay of a house. If we construct a table showing the correspondence of bays to acreage we shall find that 20 bays go with 120 acres, i.e. one *hide*. Now the hide is closely associated with the pound and if we divide the pound into twenty shillings, we find, according to our table, that one shilling corresponds to one bay. The association of bay and shilling can be supported etymologically; for instance, by the existence of the word "skilling" which, in some parts of the country, has the meaning of bay. This theory postulates the standardization of the bay both as regards length and breadth. The standard length we have seen to be 16 ft.; the standard breadth was probably 15 ft., so that we get a superficial area of 240 ft. in each bay and a total area of 4800 square feet in the real or hypothetical hidal house of 20 bays.

A passage in Saxo Grammaticus, a twelfth-century writer, describes a building in twelve bays, each 20 ft. square. The total area of this building is the same as that of the English hidal house, but the subdivision seems to indicate a scale of 12 ounces to the pound, each "ounce" or bay of 400 square feet being easily divided into 20 "penny-weights" of 20 square feet each. It seems possible that subdivision into ounces and pennyweights was at one time the universal method, and was based on the winter house with an aisle. When separate cattle-stalls began to be built the aisle was dropped and the narrower breadth of bay (i.e. the fork-breadth without aisle) became the unit and the new computation of shilling and pence was adopted.

The house was the measure of a man's holding of land. We find such a word as *metestead*, meaning "measuring place," and it is almost certain that *messuage* is connected with *metiri*, to measure, and not, as many have supposed, with *manere*, to remain. It was clearly not in the interests of a householder to diminish his agrarian rights by letting his house fall to ruin, nor to increase his liabilities by building more bays than his holding of land warranted. There was, however, a way in which he could increase his house-room without increasing the taxation on his property. He could build "outshots." These were not built on "crucks," did not form part of the "house-place," and were not fiscally recognized.

From being an accurate measure of a man's territorial possessions, the house became, in a wider sense, a measure of communal rights and responsibilities. House-destruction was a not uncommon means of punishment for social delinquencies. Taxation was regulated by the number of " crucks " in a man's house, and it appears that the Anglo-Saxon *gafol*, " gable " or " cruck," and *gafol*, " tribute," are, in spite of a difference of gender, identical. Besides *gavelage* or *gabulagium*, i.e. tax by the gable, we find also in mediæval times, mention of *forcagium* or tax by the " cruck," otherwise known as pillar tax.

The progress of man in the arts can be measured by the difference between the cave-dwelling and the cathedral. The first links of the long chain of evolution which extends between the lowest and the highest forms of human dwellings were forged by the men who tilled the land and watched the flocks. It was they who fashioned and maintained the shapes which for so many ages prevailed both in the cottage and the palace.

EXCURSUS I

On the removal and re-erection of houses in ancient times.

NUMEROUS documents bear witness to the comparatively common practice of transporting houses from one site to another. Henning[1] describes how the primitive Germans would not abandon the houses where their gods dwelt, but carried them wherever they went; he also quotes[2] one of the Vedic songs in which the dismantling of a house for transport is described. Sullivan, in his introduction to O'Curry's *Manners and Customs of the Ancient Irish*,[3] says that buildings erected during a tenancy became the property of the owner at the end of the lease, at a valuation; but that if the tenant was evicted before the term's expiration, he was entitled to take with him his buildings " which, as in Germany, in mediæval times, were considered as movable chattels."

Domesday Book[4] has the following entry: " Ipse quoque transportavit hallam et alias domos et pecuniam in alio manerio." The Welsh laws[5] have: " Let the posts and spars be cut even with the ground and let him depart with his house . . . for the land is no worse for transporting the house across it, so that corn or hay, or like be not damaged."

In the Assize of Clarendon,[6] dated 1166, it was enacted that if anybody received the heretics who had been excommunicated at Oxford into his house, the house should be taken outside the town and burnt.

The Hundreds Rolls[7] describe the removal of a house in these terms: " Eradicavit domum super illam terram fundatam precii xv solidorum."

[1] *Op. cit.*, p. 163.
[2] *Ibid.*, pp. 112, 113.
[3] p. cxc.
[4] i, 63.
[5] See Lewis, *Ancient Welsh Laws*, p. 20.
[6] See Stubbs, *Select Charters*, 9th ed., p. 173.
[7] *Rot. Hundr.* ii, 174 b.

In the *Feodarium Prioratus Dunelmensis*[1] we read of a property transaction in which the Prior undertook either to move certain buildings to a new site or to pay for them at a valuation indicated by assessors ; he also undertook either to move a water-mill to another place on the same river or to build a wind-mill.

The *Durham Halmote Rolls*[2] record that a certain person " illud mesuagium vastavit et meremium [= timber] asportavit et aedificavit in libero tenemento suo apud Scotteshouses."

In Kerry's *Municipal Church of St. Lawrence, Reading*, 1883, p. 44, it is stated that " In the fine collection of MSS. at Losely House, near Guildford, belonging to Wm. More Molyneux, Esq., there is an account of the removal of certain tents or wooden lodgings from Oatlands to be re-erected at Chobham anno 38 Hen. viii by Henri Harthorn."

A further example is given by Stow,[3] who describes how Thomas Cromwell annexed the gardens of his neighbours in Throgmorton Street ; finding a house in the way, it was " loosed from the ground " and born " upon Rowlers into my Fathers Garden 22. foot, ere my Father heard thereof."

Finally, we may quote in full a contract, dated 1321, for removing and refixing a hall and chamber. The document is in the British Museum, Add. MS. 6670, p. 293. It is entitled, " A Copie of the Byll for the removinge the Hall Rogeri Columbell de Darley arm." The copy contains some misreadings, but it is here faithfully reprinted as it stands in the MS.

" Ista indentura testatur quod die sabbati proxima ante festum invencionis scẽ Crucis Anno Dñi 1321 Ita convenit inter Joħem de Derlegh ex una parte et Wiħm de Keylstedis cementarium ex altera vidz̧. quod dictus Wiħmus concessit et fide mediante fideliter manucepit se removendam Aulam et Cameram Joħis de Derlegh et illas reparandas in quodam loco qui vocatur Robardyerd : Aulam vidz̧ de eadem mensura sicut steterat in antiquo loco et duas fenestras in

---

[1] Ed. SURTEES Soc., p. 189.
[2] *Ibid.*, i, 15.
[3] *Survey of London*, 1633 edition, p. 187 a.

Aula quaque fenestra de duobus luminaribus et duas gabeles tabulatas sep Aulam longitudo Camẽ. vidƺ. quadraginta pedum inter parietes. latitudo. vidƺ. Sicut meremiũ antiq̃ Camẽ dcc̃ postulat cum tribus fenestris   quaque fenes̃t de duobus luminaribus et una fenestra de uno luminare et uno Chimino de meremio usque le baas cum ij gabelis tabulat^s. cum uno Warderobe et uno oriell predicte [camer]e pertinente cum novem hostiis de petris aule et camere pertinente et predict^s Wiłłm^s debet ponere . . . . singultum sup Cameram quod fuit sup Aulam. Ad quā quid Convencoẽ fidelit^r. faciend dictus Wiłłm^s. . . . . . s^e heredes ex executõr suos et oı̃a bona sua ad districtione cujusq̃ Judic̃ Ecc̃astia vełt . . . . Et dict^s. Joħes concessit pro se et hered suis dare dc̃o Wyłło pro dc̃a op̃acõe octo marcas . . . pro vicus Sicut opus suũ opav̓it et unam robam svient̃ . . . . ip̃ius usuał. In cujus . . . . datum apud Derl . . . . (cetera des^t.)."

EXCURSUS II

Extracts from " A Survey of Lands belonging to the Mannor of Sheffield, 1611."

From the MS. collections of John Wilson, Esq., of Broomhead Hall, now in the possession of his great-grandson, Charles Macro Wilson, Esq.

" Tennamentts and Landes surveyed by Mr. Will'm Leighe, Baylyffe of Sheffeld.

" SHEFFELD TOWNE.

" *Gilbert hauldsworthe.* One dwellinge house 2 baies, 2 chambers, one parler, one kitchen, one stable 2 baies, one hey house 2 baies, one beast house 2 baies, one barne 2 baies, one swinehouse.

" *James hill.* One dwellinge house 2 baies, 2 chambers, one barne 2 baies, one parler with a chimney, one kytchen, one warehouse.

" *Franncis horner.* One dwelling house 2 baies, one

parler, one kitchen 2 baies, one chamber, 2 stables, one slaughter house 2 baies.

" *haulecar farme.* One dwelling house 4 baies, one corne barne 4 baies *et di.*, one hey barne 2 baies, beast houses 3 baies, 2 outshutts.

" *R. Hadfeild farme.* One dwelling howse   baies, one kitchen   baies, two corne barnes   baies, one hey barne   baies, one kilne house with mault chambers, two stables, two beast houses   baies, one shepe house   baies, one cottage, one wainehouse.

" *Simon heathcote farme.* One house 2 baies, one parler, one chamber, one houell to set beast in corne barne made of poules very badd.

" *Vid. Sikes farme.* One house 2 baies, one beast house one bay, one cottage one bay, one parler, one litle house of the comen.

" *Laurence Eyre farme.* One house j bay slated, j part couered with thack 2 baies ; j barne couered with thacke one bay, one fald.

" *Christopher Limer farme.* One house 4 baies, one parler, one chamber, one beast house with a chamber ouer yt, one smethey, j bay, one barne 3 baies, one outshutt at the end.

" *Edw. Hill.* One house j bay, one chamber, one beast howse 2 baies.

" *Robert Taylior.* One house 2 baies, one parler, one barne 2 baies.

" *Christopher Hawksworthe.* One house 4 baies, one parler, one beast house one bay, one chamber, one outshutt, one barne 3 baies.

" *Steel farme.* One house j bay, one chamber, one parler, one chamber ouer the kytchen, one barne 2 baies, one outshutt, one wainehouse one bay, one beast house 2 baies, with a chamber ouer yt.

" *John Lansdale.* One house 3 baies, one parler, on chamber.

" *John Smithe farme.* One house 2 baies, one barne 2 baies, one outshut.

" *Robert Hauksworthe farme.* One house 3 baies, one

parler, one barne 2 litle baies, one other barne j bay, one beast house j baye, one kilne in the well close, one ould house to sett beast in 3 baies, 2 other ould howses to put fuell in.

" *Vid. Hoyland farme.* One house 4 baies, one turfe house j bay, two parlers, one barne 4 baies, one beast house 2 baies, one beast house j bay, one swine coate.

" *Geo. Morrey farme.* One house 3 baies, one parler, 2 chambers, one beast house, one barne slated 3 baies, one beast house 2 baies, one kilne house.

" *Thom. Unwin farme.* One house 3 baies, 2 parlers, one chamber, one cowe house 2 baies, one barne 2 baies, one outshutt, one turffe house 2 baies.

" *John Fearneley farme.* One house one bay, one chamber, one kitchen one bay, one parler, one parler with a chimney, one chamber ouer the same, one beast house 2 baies, one hey house 2 baies, one barne 2 baies, one waine house, one tann house.

" *Vid. Moore farme.* One house 3 baies, one chamber, one parler, one barne of one of the 3 baies, one outshut at the end of the said house for catle.

" *Nich. Sampson farme.* One house one bay, one parler aboue the house, 2 baies beneath the house for beast howses, 2 parlers newly builded, 2 chambers ouer the parler, one barne, 4 baies, 2 outshutts, one beast [house] 2 baies, j hay house 2 baies.

" *James heaton.* One house j bay, j barne one bay.

" *Will'm Brodhead farme.* One house j bay, 2 parlers 2 baies, beast houses 2 baies, one hey barne one bay, one corne barne 4 baies, one ouen house j bay, beast houses 3 baies.

" *Richard Wilson farme.* One house 7 baies, one corne barne 3 baies, one hey barne 2 baies, beast houses 4 baies, a swinehull, one kilne house j bay, one wainehouse 2 baies.

" *Robert Beard farme.* One dwelling house ij baies, one parler, one ouen house j bay, one smythey j bay, one barne 2 baies & 2 outshutts for cattle, one swinehull.

" *Robert Carr farme, Butterthwayte.* One house 3 baies, one parler with a chimney, 3 chambers, 2 chambers with chimnies, one kitchen one bay, one cowe house 2 baies, one hey howse, one stable one bay, one barne 3 baies, one outshutt for beasts, one oxehouse j bay, one hey barne 2 baies, one bay of hey couered with brome, one backe house 2 baies.

" *John Wilson farme.* One house 2 baies, 2 chambers, j parler, 2 cott. 2 baies, 2 chambers 4 baies, one barne 2 baies, one stable.

" *Christopher Wilson farme,* vocat. Pogges. One house 3 baies, 2 parlers, j chamber, one barne 3 baies in decay, one hay house j bay in decay, and other house fallen downe."

SOME BOOKS CITED

THE chief literary sources of information about the early English house are old surveys, deeds, court rolls, building accounts, and building contracts, monastic inventories and cartularies, chronicles, old dictionaries, and ancient laws, together with numerous public records, printed or unprinted. To these may be added occasional references or descriptions in old poems, such as *Beowulf*, *Piers Plowman*, and the *Canterbury Tales*. The Icelandic Sagas are also useful, but this source of information must be treated with caution. The number of books and journals relating to architecture, topography, and British antiquities, is very great, and it need hardly be said that many valuable facts are scattered about in them.

The following is a list of the principal works referred to in the course of this work. It is, of course, not intended as a complete bibliography of the subject.

Anderson, Joseph. *Scotland in Early Christian Times.* Edinburgh, 1881.

Andrews, W. *The Church Treasury of History, Custom, Folk-lore, etc.* London, 1898.

Blight, J. T. *Churches of West Cornwall.* London, 1865.

Clark, G. T. *Mediæval Military Architecture in England.* 2 vols. London, 1884.

Fergusson, James. *A History of Architecture in all Countries.* 4 vols. London, 1874–76.

Guest, Edwin. *Origines Celticae, and other Contributions to the History of Britain.* 2 vols. London, 1883.

Hale, William H. *The Domesday of St. Paul's of the year MCCXXII.* Camden Society. London, 1858.

The leases of manors during the twelfth century printed at the end of this volume, some of which contain descriptions and measurements of buildings, are very useful.

Henning, R. *Das deutsche Haus in seiner historischen Entwickelung.* 1882.

Kluge, F. *Etymologisches Wörterbuch der deutsche Sprache.* 7th ed., Strassburg, 1910.

Lange, Konrad. *Haus und Halle : Studien zur Geschichte des antiken Wohnhauses und der Basilika.* Leipzig, 1885.

Maitland, F. W. *Domesday Book and Beyond.* Cambridge, 1897.

Maitland, F. W. *Township and Borough.* Cambridge, 1898.

Meitzen, August. *Das deutsche Haus in seinen volksthümlichen Formen. Seperat-abdruck aus den Verhandlungen des deutschen Geographen-tages.* Berlin, 1882.

Meitzen, August. *Wanderungen, Anbau, und Agrarrecht der Völker Europas nördlich der Alpen.* Berlin, 1895.

This work contains, amongst other valuable matter, an essay on " Das nordische und das altgriechische Haus."

O'Curry, Eugene. *On the Manners and Customs of the Ancient Irish.* Edited by W. K. Sullivan. 3 vols. London, 1873.

Record Office Publications :

  Ancient Laws and Institutes of Wales. 2 vols. 1841.

  Chronica Monasterii S. Albani (ed. H. T. Riley). 1863.

  Diplomatarium Anglicum Aevi Saxonici (ed. Thorpe).

  Munimenta Gildhallæ Londoniensis (ed. H. T. Riley). 1859–62.

  Rotuli Hundredorum. 2 vols. 1812.

Seebohm, Frederic. *The English Village Community.* London, 1883.

See pp. 187, 194, and 239 of Mr. Seebohm's book.

Surtees Society Publications :

  Bishop Hatfield's Survey, 1857. (Vol. 32.)

  Boldon Buke, 1852. (Vol. 25.)

Q

Cartularium Abbathiae de Whiteby, etc., 1879.
(Vols. 69 and 72.)

Depositions and other ecclesiastical proceedings from the courts of Durham, 1845. (Vol. 21.)

Feodarium Prioratus Dunelmensis, 1872. (Vol. 58.)

Halmota Prioratus Dunelmensis, 1889, etc. (Vol. 82.)

Rural Economy in Yorkshire, 1857. (Vol. 33.)

Testamenta Eboracensia, 1836–1902.
(Vols. 4, 30, 45, 53, 79 and 106.)

Turner, T. Hudson. *Some Account of Domestic Architecture in England from the Conquest to the end of the Thirteenth Century.* With numerous illustrations of existing remains from original drawings. Oxford, 1851.

This was followed by three more volumes, edited by J. H. Parker, and bringing the subject down to the reign of Henry VIII. It is an excellent work.

Viollet-le-Duc, M. *Dictionnaire Raisonné de l'Architecture Française du XIe au XVIIe Siècle.* 10 vols.
Paris, 1858.

Withals, J. *A dictionarie in English and Latine.* 1616.

Wright, Thomas. *The Homes of Other Days : A History of Domestic Manners and Sentiments in England from the earliest known period to modern times.*
London, 1871.

Wuelcker, R. P. (ed. T. Wright). *Anglo-Saxon and Old English Vocabularies.* 2nd ed. London, 1884.

INDEX OF SUBJECTS

Lantern, where placed, 104
" Lanterns " in church towers, 169, 170
Leaves and flowers, decoration by, 134, 135
Lesche, 137
" Little bay," 55, 93 *n.*
Locker or ambry in wall, 144, 150
Loop-hole, meaning of, 132
Louvre, 30, 126, 128, 132
" Low side windows," 181
Lucken Booths, 116

Manor house, 138 *et seq.*
  rooms in, 138
  halls in, dimensions of, 152
Manor house, pigeon-cotes in, 149
  hall and bower the essential parts of a, 153
Mansus = measure, 216
Mantellum camini, 127
Mantel-tree, 62, 69, 72, 128 (*see* " Aitch ")
Mapalia, 47, 50
Megaron, the Greek, 75, 80, 131, 135
Mensura, 211
Meremium, timber for building, 121 *n.*
Messuage = " measuring - place," 212, 215, 216, 232
" Mess of pottage," meaning of, 216
" Metestead," 212
Mossing of houses, 123, 136
Moot hills, 156, 175, 176, 192
Mud house in East Yorkshire described, 61 *et seq.*
Mud houses, 61-5, 124
  walls, method of building, 63
" Municipal buildings," absence of early, 174
" Municipal buildings," in church-yards, 175

Narrow streets, preference for, 113
" Nave," in architecture, 50, 66 (*see* " Ship-shaped House ")
" Nave," without aisles, 90
Nave and aisles in domestic buildings, 90, 92, 105, 106
Noggin houses, 136
Norse house, typical, 82, 83, 84
Norwegian summer huts, 59, 60
Nubilaria, 141

Open fire, the, 102
Oriel, 236
Orientation, 30

Orientation of stables, 103
Ostiarius, 182
" Outshuts," " outshots," 41, 66, 67, 213, 229 (*see* " Little Bay ")
" Outshuts " described, 66 *et seq.*
Oval houses, 30, 38
  difficult to build, 30, 38
Oven house, 238
Ox-house, 81, 83, 86, 93, 99, 139
  English and Roman, 86
Ox-house, loft above, 93, 101
  in barns, 93
  living in, 99
Ownership, divided, of the same house, 118

Pairs of principals, late introduction of, 53
" Pan," or " pon," 28, 52
Parclose, 69, 120, 192
" Parging," or " sparging," 124
Parish, what it was, 184
" Parpoint " walls, 125
Party-walls of freestone, 119
Passages connecting adjoining huts or cells, 32
Peasant's house as a measure of value, 194 *et seq.*
" Pennpits," 36
Penny, derivation of the word, 206
Perch as unit of measurement, the, 87, 88
Pergula, 110, 112
Pigeon-houses, 149
Pillar tax, 226
Piscina, 148, 150
Pit dwellings, 32
Porch, teaching in the Church, 182, 183
" Pot moul," 134-5
Projecting stories, object of, 117, 118
Prospects from houses, disregarded, 151, 152
Pundemeta, 201, 203
Putlock holes, 149

Quadrangles, building in, 144, 145, 152

Raths and duns, in Ireland, 33, 36 *n.*
Ratio between house and land, 194, 195, 203, 215
" Reared house," 122
Rearing a house, what it was, 122, 123
Rectangular house, origin of its form, 30 *et seq.*, 228

Table, uses of, 79
forms for, 151
precedence at, 79
round, place of honour, 79, 102
with trestles, 151
Table dormant, 77 *n.*
Tacitus, his description of German
houses, 106, 107, 134 *n.*, 136
" Taverns," underground shops,
110 *n.*, 111, 116, 123
" Tavern stairs," 111
obstructions caused by, 112, 113
Taxation based on house pro-
perty, 220 *et seq.*
Thatch of rye straw, 70
heather, 99, 136
rushes, 136
" Thief and reever " bell, 170
Three-naved buildings, 96
Threshold = threshing-floor, 81
none where no barn, 81
buildings divided transversely
by, 82
Threshold, serpentine marks on,
135
" Threskeld," 81 *n.*
Tie-beam and king-post, gradual
introduction of, 53
Tiles, the old name for bricks,
125
" Timber " = to build, 121, 122
Timber buildings, town, 119, 122
Timber foundations, 27
Toft and croft, 107, 211
Toot hills, 156
Town house, description of one,
119
Town houses, 109 *et seq.*
height of, 118, 119
Trades, in different quarters of
towns, 115, 116
" Trance " = entrance, described,
145
" Trap hetch," or " throp hetch "
(trap door), 63, 78
Trisantia, 145
Trollies, 114
" Tunc " or " dung," a winter-
room or underground room,
35, 36
Turf house, 238
Turf nook, 101
Turnpikes, 115

Underground dwellings, 32–5
warmth obtained in, 35, 36
Underground passages, 33
Upper rooms, absence of, in old
houses, 152

Virgate, 194, 195, 196, 208

" Waldlure," 153 *n.*
Wall-plate, 28, 58
Walls, outer, built after the hou s
had been set up, 52
Walls, decoration of, 133 *et seq.*,
230
materials for, 52
party, of freestone, 119
surrounding manor house, 149
Walls of concrete, 160
thick, in castles, 160
Warderobe, 236 (*see* " Gardrobe ")
Ward-penny, 154
Washing room, 101, 138
Watch-towers (see " Church
Towers ")
cardinal points in, 160, 172, 173
Watch-towers, rooms in, 160
concealed roof of, 161
Watch-towers, beacon fires on,
161
Watch-towers, raised doorways in,
161
Watch-towers, living room in, 161
rooms in walls of, 161, 168
Watch-towers, watchmen for, 164
circular, 167, 168, 172
compared to Sardinian núraghs,
167
fire-place for, 164, 165
Watch-towers, position of outer
door of, 167
Watch-towers, attached to
churches, 168
Watch-towers ascended by lad-
ders, 169
Watch-towers, Irish and Scotch,
called " round towers," 172,
173
Watch-towers, watch-room in, 173
Water, supplied from reservoir,
150
Wattles, or rods, building with,
26, 32, 40, 46, 50, 67, 124
Wattles, substitutions for, 52, 69,
72, 74
Weaving room, 78, 101 (*see*
" Spinning House ")
Wells, in and near houses, 64, 98
White dwellings, 133 *n.*
Whitewash, early use of, 135
a protection against fire, 135
Whitewash, applied to church
walls, 135–6
Whitewash, of chimneys, 127
Wicker house, 24, 133
Wind-braces, 39, 41

INDEX OF PLACES